THE INDUSTRIAL DEVELOPMENT OF BENGAL, 1900-1939

The Industrial Development of Bengal
1900-1939

A Z M Iftikhar-ul-Awwal

VIKAS PUBLISHING HOUSE PVT LTD

VIKAS PUBLISHING HOUSE PVT LTD
Regd. Office: 5 Ansari Road, New Delhi 110002
H.O. **Vikas House, 20/4 Industrial Area, Sahibabad 201010**
Distt. Ghaziabad, U.P. (India)

ISBN 0-7069-1579-8

1V2I0918

Printed at The Central Electric Press, 80-D, Kamla Nagar, Delhi-110007 (India)

Preface

The present work examines the industrial experience of Bengal during the period 1900 to 1939 with particular emphasis on the role of the government as the main instrument for growth. For this work, available statistical material has been utilized for the sake of precision as well as to strengthen the qualitative evidence.

The book contains eight chapters. While Chapter I builds up the case for industrial development, Chapter II examines in detail the industrial policy of the Bengal government in the light of its own limitations as a subordinate authority to the Government of India and that of Whitehall. Chapter III is an investigation of the labour market in Bengal with emphasis on the supply of labour to jute, tea and coal industries in relation to wages and conditions of work. In Chapter IV, I have examined the rates of profitability and security of industrial investments. In this chapter, I have also examined the financial institutions of the time and their role in the industrial development of the province. Chapter V points to some of the difficulties experienced by Indian entrepreneurs, and in the above light looks at their contribution to the larger industrial establishments of Bengal. The next two Chapters VI and VII examine the growth and development of the two biggest manufacturing industries of our period—jute and handloom cotton weaving industries. The concluding chapter, is an estimate of the industrial progress made in the province during the period under review.

This book is a slightly revised version of my Ph.D. thesis submitted to the University of London in 1978. In the preparation of this thesis, I have accumulated an enormous debt of gratitude to my Supervisor, Dr. K. N. Chaudhuri whose careful vigilance and timely intervention saved me from many factual errors and infelicities of style. My thanks are also due to Mr. J. B. Harrison, who went through some of my preliminary chapters during the absence of Dr Chaudhuri in 1975-76 and made many useful observations. I am also indebted to Dr. Serajul Islam of Dacca University for helping me with some necessary corrections.

Here I take this opportunity also to express my deep gratitude to the UK Commonwealth Commission which offered me a scholarship for three years which enabled me to undertake this research work. Needless to say without their financial help it would have been virtually impossible to pursue this course of studies. I also wish to thank the University of Dacca for granting me the necessary study leave.

There remains also a special group of people—without whose cooperation, patience and tolerance, this work would not have seen the light of day. In this group belong the library staff of the British Library (including the Newspaper Section at Colindale), Senate House Library, the library of the School of Oriental and African Studies, and particularly, the India Office Library and Records (including their Newspaper Section at the Bush House). I take this opportunity to thank Mr. J. Sims of the India Office Library and Records for being so helpful in tracking down apparently untractable official documents. I wish to thank the staff of the Bangladesh Secretariat Record Room and of the Secretariat Library, Dacca for extending me all possible facilities in carrying out my research work. Finally, I owe a special debt of gratitude to my wife, Lilly whose support and constant encouragement over these years was invaluable in completing this work.

A.Z.M.I.A.

Contents

List of Tables

Abbreviations

AFR	Annual Factory Report, Bengal
AMR	Report of the inspection of mines in India; Report of the Chief Inspector of Mines in India
BFP	Bengal Financial Proceedings
BGP	Bengal General Proceedings
BISC	Report of the Bengal Industrial Survey Committee, 1948
BLCP	Bengal Legislative Council Proceedings
BPBEC	Bengal Provincial Banking Enquiry Committee, 1929-30
BRP	Bengal Revenue Proceedings
BSR	Bangladesh Secretariat Records, Dacca
DOIB	Department of Industries, Bengal
ICBEC	Indian Central Banking Enquiry Committee, 1931
IIC	Indian Industrial Commission, 1916-18
IIYB	Investor's India Year-Book
IJMA	Indian Jute Mills Association
IOR	India Office Records
IPG	Indian Planters' Gazette and Sporting News
PAI	Proceedings of the Department of Agriculture and Industries, Bengal
PP	U.K. Parliamentary Papers
RAB	Report on the Administration of Bengal

1 Introduction

In the last quarter of the nineteenth century, an intensive debate began on the relative economic conditions of the Indian people prior to and during the British rule. There were two schools of thought—one always referred to the increasing prosperity of the country and people, showering unstinted praise on England as the creator of this prosperity while the other incessantly dilated upon the rapidly-growing and alarming impoverishment of both the country and the people.[1] Due to lack of statistical data a satisfactory answer to this vexed question could not be found. However, it became obvious from various estimates, that India still remained one of the poorest countries of the world. The gross annual income per head as calculated by Dadabhai Naoroji was Rs 20.[2] The official figure calculated by Sir E. Baring was Rs 27.[3] These figures when compared with other countries were found to be the lowest in the scale. If India's per capita income was low, that of Bengal was lower. Compared to just over Rs 30 in the case of Central Provinces and Bombay, Bengal's estimate was only Rs 22-28.[4] If the unequal distribution of wealth among different sections of the community was taken into account, it needs but little imagination to comprehend the miserable existence of the great mass of people. At a meeting of the Indian Section of Arts in London, O' Connor described the economic condition thus:[5]

> ... India remains in a very elementary condition compared with the poorest of European countries .... The great mass of people are occupiers of extremely small holdings, imperfectly

[1]William Digby, '*Prosperous*' *British India* (London, 1901), p. XIX.
[2]C.S. Deole, *The State in relation to Indian Industries* (Bombay, 1916), p. 2.
[3]*Ibid.*, pp. 2-3.
[4]*The Statesman and Friend of India* (Weekly edition), 28 March 1891, p. 1.
[5]*Industrial India*, Vol. I, No. 6 (June, 1904), pp. 155-56. See also, pp. 123-24 for an introductory note on O' Connor and his paper.

cultivated by reason of their poverty, and landless labourers, living in conditions so far below the standard of this country (England) that it is difficult to make you realize the difference . . . men whose garments are limited to an unclean rag round their loins and another round their heads, whose miserable huts possess not even the rough rope-strung frame which in India does duty for a bedstead, who eat an insufficient meal from an earthenware platter or a large dry leaf, who are unconscious of luxuries, and happy if they can get a full meal of the coarse, inferior grains which are their staple food.

It was this destitution of the people which first turned the attention of the thinking people towards industrialization.[6] They saw before them countries like Japan and Germany being industrialized

TABLE 1.1

GROSS EARNINGS PER HEAD OF CERTAIN SELECTED COUNTRIES, c. 1916

Country	*Average per capita income (in £)*	*Country*	*Average per capita income (in £)*
Scotland	45	Norway	20
Australia	40	Switzerland	19
United States	39	Spain	16
Belgium	28	Austria	15
France	27	Italy	12
Canada	26	Russia	11
Germany	22	Turkey	4
Holland	22	India	2

SOURCE: C. S. Deole, *The State in relation to Indian Industries* (Bombay, 1916), p. 3.

in a matter of few decades and improve the material conditions of the people immeasurably. Moreover, when they looked back they found most of the ingredients necessary for successful industrialization

[6]See, for further illumination on this point, Bipan Chandra, *The Rise and Growth of Economic Nationalism in India* (New Delhi, 1966), Chapter II.

in the economy. Raw materials required for almost every industry were available in India. The idea that the country ought to be able to produce most of the manufactured articles which it required was not one which its natural resources rendered utopian. "People argue—and argue rightly that these resources should be utilised for the benefit of India itself and not for that of other countries".[7] Similarly, India possessed vast sources of potential labour-force. So far as rural industrialization was concerned there were excellent artisans ready at hand. This wealth and treasure in the shape of trained labour was lying idle and a vast quantity of national prosperity was being wasted. Millions of skilled labourers were starving instead of being prosperous. It was asserted that there was no dearth of capital. "There is capital ready to hand awaiting secure investment".[8] What was really needed, as believed by Hon'ble Rao Bahadur M.G. Ranade, was the task of reorganizing credit, both real and personal, on a sound and progressive basis which had already been undertaken by Continental statesmen and thinkers in the last fifty years. By doing so, they had succeeded in bridging the gulf which separated the saving few from the producing many in a way which commanded attention. If this task of reorganising credit facilities was undertaken in the same spirit in India, Ranade felt, the nation would soon start upon a new phase of life with its power invigorated, and its energies awakened in a way no other single agency could accomplish.[9] Thus the country had all the requisites of an industrial power—raw materials, labour and capital; and yet it remained one of the least industrialized nations of the world. The Swadeshi movement which originated in Bengal towards the beginning of this century thus sought to call into existence the directing capacity, the technical skill and the requisite capital "so that our own labour and money may convert our raw materials

[7]Hon'ble Mr. Hewett, Member for Commerce and Industry, at the Indian Legislative Council on 28 March, 1906. See, *Report of the Second Indian Industrial Conference* held at Culcutta, December 1906 (Calcutta, 1907), Part II, 'Brief Account of Industrial Activity in India in 1906 January to October', pp. XX-XXI.

[8]Hon'ble Rao Bahadur M.G. Ranade, 'The Reorganization of real credit in India,' *Report of the First Industrial Conference held at Poona*, August 1891 (Poona, 1891), p. 61.

[9]*Ibid.*, pp. 61-62.

into the commodities which we now import".[10] This they thought would substantially add to the wages of the workmen and the profits of the capitalists, depressing to an appreciable degree, the misery of the lower orders.

But what was it that restrained the country from being industrialized in the nineteenth century in spite of its potentiality? The answer does not lie so much on whether India could industrialize or not but on the political and economic thinking of the period. This revolved round the classical theory of free trade and the Adam Smithian doctrine of international trade as a dynamic force generating a great upward surge in the general level of productivity of the trading countries. According to this theory each country need only concentrate its productive effort along lines of greatest comparative advantage, and participate freely in the trading pattern that evolved of necessity. This would maximise total world income, and the income of each participating country would also be maximised. As regards which goods a country should import and what it would export, the classical theory gives the following answer. Each country will produce those goods for which it is especially suited on account of its climate, qualities of soil, other natural resources, and the innate and acquired capacities of its people. The real capital which it possessed as a heritage from its past, such as buildings, plant and equipment, and means of transport should be particularly helpful.[11] Accordingly, India was chosen to be a raw material producer in view of her bountiful soil, and her climate, ordinarily propitious to agriculture. The role of the state came to be concentrated on the improvement of communications and facilitating the flow of trade and not unnaturally on the development of agriculture. Trade continued under the above conditions consisting mainly of exports of raw material and imports of foreign manufactured products. Any departure whereby the state was called upon to expend money

[10]Presidential address of Dewan Bahadur Ambalal Sakerlal at the Third Indian Industrial Conference held at Surat on 30 December 1907. See *Report of the Third Indian Industrial Conference* (Madras, 1908), p. 27.

[11]Gottfried Von Haberler, *The Theory of International Trade, with its Application to Commercial Policy* (translated by A. Stonier and F. Benham and printed in Great Britain by William Hodge and Company, Ltd, Eighth impression, 1961), p. 125.

on development of industries was considered unnatural. In the words of the Hon'ble Sir C.E. Trevelyan, Financial Member of the Council of the Governor General:[12]

> It is a misdirection of the resources of India to enter into competition with England in this branch of industry. On the other hand, India has, on the cultivation of the rich products of her prolific soil and climate, resources of her own, the development of which is limited only by the insufficiency of labour and capital. To divert these elements of production from a profitable to an unprofitable employment, is surely a mistake. Our true course is to adhere to the great division of labour which nature herself has established.... If the Burwai or any other Iron Works in India are profitable, there is no want of private enterprise and unemployed capital to undertake them.

But private enterprise as Sir E. C. Buck later pointed out was always more or less checked by dread of the cost of initial experiment. Having no other object in view but quick dividends (the advantage of the country being no consideration), holders of capital preferred to put their money into assured business and held back from new undertakings to which the government gave no direct or indirect support.[13] Under the above circumstances, industrial development of the country was minimal, rather as S. S. Thorburn in his lecture to the Fabian Society in London pointed out "our commercial policy from first to last has been to destroy her few industries and prevent the establishment of new manufactures, which may interfere with our trade".[14]

Nor did agricultural specialization in India fulfill the expectations of the political and economic thinkers of the nineteenth

[12]IOR : MSS. Eur. F. 78, File No. 59/8B, Sir Charles Wood Collection. See, Minute by the Hon'ble Sir C. E. Trevelyan, Financial Member of the Council of the Governor-General on the Burwai Iron Works, Calcutta, 13 June 1863.

[13]Sir E. C. Buck, *Report on Practical and Technical Education* (Calcutta, 1901), pp. 37-38.

[14]See *Indian Agriculturist*, 1 March 1902, p. 81.

TABLE 1.2

MEAN DENSITY OF POPULATION IN BENGAL, 1872 TO 1931 (PER SQUARE MILE)

Year	*No. of people per square mile*
1872	422
1881	450
1891	484
1901	521
1911	563
1921	578
1931	616

SOURCE: *Census of India*, 1931, Vol. V, Bengal and Sikkim, Part I, Report (Calcutta, 1933), p. 66.

century.[15] On the contrary, it has been the root of misfortune. This was basically due to certain peculiar circumstances of the country of which very little was previously thought of.[16] The population which was fairly dense at the time of the inauguration of this policy began to go up by leaps and bounds (see Table 1.2). Even after accounting for the recurrent losses from scarcity and famine, an increase of one per cent per annum was being admitted by optimists.[17] This population increase exerted tremendous pressure on the limited natural resources of the province particu-

[15]However, at the initial stages of the establishment of wider commercial contacts with the West, the propulsive effects of international trade possibly led to an increase in the per capita national income in different proportions among the different sections of the community. See, M.M. Islam, Agricultural Development of Bengal: a quantitative study, 1920-1946 (unpublished Ph.D. thesis, London University, 1972), pp. 24-25.

[16]One of the very few exceptions who predicted and pointed out the severe effects of such economic laws, if applied to India, was Nassau Lees. See, W. Nassau Lees, *The Land and Labour of India. A Review* (London, 1867), pp. 6-10.

[17]*The Statesman and Friend of India* (Weekly edition), 4 February, 1893, p. 8.

larly on land. It was now only by buying out other tenants, or in some other way acquiring the right of cultivating previously occupied land, or occasionally, by bringing inferior land under cultivation, that the tenant could add to his holding. As a matter of fact, a more than ordinarily prosperous tenant might have done this but the tendency, in most parts of the country, owing to the ever-increasing pressure on land, had long been towards a progressive diminution, of the average area of individual holdings.[18] Since there was no alternative to agriculture, the increasing population progressively fell back on the limited land. The result was that the part of the population which was in excess of the requirements of agriculture ate up the profits that would otherwise spring from the industry. "It is not suprprising", observed the Famine Commission (1880) "that in a country thus situated material progress is slow".[19] Moreover, the rapid increase in population was gradually absorbing the surplus raw materials which once formed the bulk of outward trade. Thus in his Narrative of the Famine of 1896-97, Holderness pointed out that seventeen years ago the total food production in the country was 51,530,000 tons, as compared with requirements of 47,165,000 tons; so that there was a surplus of 5,165,000 tons available for export and storage. However, this surplus had by then dwindled down to 1,700,000 tons, barely sufficient to provide for the exports alone.[20]

There were other considerations as well which made development of agriculture difficult. Apart from the personal skill of the farmer, agriculture was dependent on the conjunction of meteorological conditions and natural fertility. Thus the years 1891-92, 1896-97, 1899-1900 and 1907-08 were unfavourable due to unseasonable and deficient rainfall.[21] The cumulative effect of such unfavourable years coming one after another not only dislocated agricultural production but also caused severe strain on the resources of the provincial government. The Bihar famine of 1873-74 (so called

[18] *The Indian Agriculturist*, August 1, 1898, p. 232. The average area actually cultivated by a cultivator and his family did not even reach 3 acres in 1921. IOR: Vol. 10971, BFP (Commerce) April 1921, No. 29, p. 103.

[19] *Report of the Indian Famine Commission*, Part I, Para 103 (PP LII of 1980), p. 442.

[20] *The Indian Agriculturist*, 1 August, 1898, p. 232.

[21] K. L. Datta, *Report on the Enquiry into the Rise of Prices in India*, Vol. I (Calcutta, 1914), p. 127.

from the part of Bengal province which was worst affected) alone cost the State £6,000,000; while at the height of 1897 famine, no less than 0.75 million persons were on relief in the permanently settled districts of Bengal, costing the Bengal Administration Rs 10,804,000 or £720,266.[22] Moreover, famines also had a deplorable effect on cattle, which brought misery and ruin upon classes who were not usually compelled to seek relief.

Agricultural specialization with a view to exports also created a certain element of instability in the economic life of the provide. This arose due to extreme sensitivity of raw materials to external occurrences beyond its control. The violent fluctuations in the prices of raw jute in Bengal compared to manufactured jute is a case in point.[23] The effect of such fluctuations on exports not only caused hardships to individual ryots but also adversely affected nation building activities of the government as imports essentially depended upon the quantum of exports. Furthermore, there was the overriding question of the freedom of the seas from molestation. A war in which England failed to hold command of the seas for six months would plunge India into grave distress. The cotton, opium, jute, seeds and wheat industries would be disorganized for years, while a prolongation of the blockade would mean financial ruin to the Empire.

When agriculture failed to improve the economic condition of the people and created an element of uncertainty in the economy, the demand for industrialization was intensified. It was considered a mistake to treat the two apart and the argument was that "the only way to add to the material well-being of the mass of mankind is by increasing the production of wealth . . . in a word, how to make two blades of grass grow where but one grew before" and to "secure a really satisfactory result it is necessary that Indian industries as well as Indian agriculture should be developed".[24] By diversifying the economy thus, industrialization was expected to create new sources of wealth side by side with agriculture. As mentioned earlier,

[22]See, Resolution of the Government of India on "Certain recent criticisms of the Land Revenue Policy of the Indian Government", the *Indian Agriculturist*, 1 February, 1902, pp. 45-46.

[23]Commercial Intelligence and Statistics Department : *Index Numbers of Indian Prices, 1861-1931* (Delhi, 1933), Graph V.

[24]*The Friend of India and Statesman* (Weekly edition), 22 February, 1900, p. 5.

Bengal did not lack in raw materials. Raw jute produced in Bengal was mostly exported to other parts of the world to be made into gunny bags and sacks, so that the profit of capital and labour went abroad. Likewise, hides and skins worth millions of rupees (the value of exports amounted to over Rs 56 million in 1900-01 alone) were annually exported from Bengal.[25] Export of other raw materials like paddy, tobacco, raw silk, etc., also could have been increased. Nor did Bengal lack in mineral resources like coal and iron and hence there was the opportunity of establishing engineering industries as well.

There was also the possibility of wealth creation through the revival and regeneration of cottage industries. The opportunity arose as a result of a great reaction in India against foreign made materials, particularly cotton goods at the turn of the twentieth century. The market for such products within the province was also large. If properly organized there was thus a good possibility of subtituting imports in this direction. Nor could the possibility of overseas exports in such materials be overlooked. As Hon'ble F.A. Nicholson pointed out:[26]

> There is a vast market in Europe and America for Indian Art goods with which Irish and European Art goods are not in competition; and the demand can be increased almost indefinitely by a properly organized supply of tasteful goods . . . .

A secondary aspect, though very important result of the wealth created by industries would be its effect on the public revenues.[27] Moreover, the whole economy would be much more stable being less dependent on foreign markets.

Industrialization, including the revival and regeneration of cottage industries was also advocated to provide employment to hundreds and thousands of "idlers" who having nothing to do were seen

[25]*Statistics of British India for 1909-10 and preceding years, Part II, Commercial* (Calcutta, 1911), p. 21.

[26]*The Indian Agriculturist*, 2 December, 1901, p 371.

[27]*Report of the Indian Fiscal Commission*, 1921-22 (PP II of 1922, Second Session), p. 357.

moving freely during the hours of labour.[28] The establishment of manufacturing industries could at least afford avenues of employment to a portion of those engaged in agriculture. It was only by such divertion of a part of the population that one could hope for any substantial improvement in the material well-being and the standard of living of the masses.

Finally, as the Fiscal Commission so emphatically puts it:[29]

> One of the most important results that may be anticipated from a development of industries in India is one that cannot be measured in terms of money. A country industrially undeveloped tends to suffer from a certain intellectual deadness. The outlets for diversity of talents are few. Those who might have shone in a wider sphere have their energies and ambitions cramped in the mould of uniformity. It is hardly too much to say that a certain measure of industrial life and opportunity is an essential condition for building up a vigorous national character. And with regard to India the effect on the national character is likely to be particularly marked and particularly beneficial.

But the process of industrialization could hardly be undertaken without the active assistance of the state which the protagonists thought should create the essential pre-conditions for "take-off". They certainly recognized the importance of the extension of roads, railways and canals, improvement of seaports, placing of machinery on the free list of customs tariff, and the abolition of internal customs duty. But they also wanted a change in the government's

[28]Thus James Caird who by reason of his wide agricultural and economic knowledge was especially invited to tender advice to Her Majesty's Government on questions affecting the agricultural population of India had this to say on this point: "In no agricultural country that I know of are so many people to be seen stalking idly about during the hours of labour as in India. The streets and court-house and yards are full of idlers; the roads are never empty, and the railway stations and natives' railway carriages are crammed with people. Entering a village at any hour of the day you are surrounded by idlers. Much of this arises from the absence of other occuption than agriculture..." See, *Report on the Condition of India* (PP LIII of 1880), pp. 138-39.

[29]*Report of the Indian Fiscal Commission*, 1921-22 (PP II of 1922, Second Session), p. 358.

commercial policy which, as already mentioned, had a devastating effect on the indigenous industries of the province, and prevented others from being naturalized. "The commercial difficulties,... are the crux of the whole matter, and even a partial solution of them would probably lead to an industrial expansion in India which would materially contribute to establish her prosperity".[30] They also demanded a change in the Stores Rules which required virtually all goods for government consumption to be purchased by indent on the Secretary of State for India. Similarly, the demand for technical and industrial education arose which they thought will infuse new life into this grand old country, teeming with resources".[31] The state was also expected to provide information regarding markets and set up the necessary machinery for the collection and dissemination of commercial intelligence which it had sometimes opportunities of securing, not available to private persons. The state was urged to provide, or at any rate facilitate the provision of industrial finance; and to take steps to provide cheap transport for manufactures made under certain conditions, either for internal consumption or for export. It was also urged to introduce improved processes; to demonstrate the use of small engines for factories; and to improve the organization of home industries. In asking for such active co-operation of the government, it was pointed out, they were only following the proposition which had already been laid by some civilized countries like Germany and Japan. They hoped that "by the joint co-operation of the Government and the people, there appears to be no reason why India, with all its natural advantages, should not reach equal, if not a higher standard" among the manufacturing nations of the world.[32]

In this work an attempt has been made to study statistically, whenever possible, the growth and development of industries in Bengal over the period 1900 to 1939. Although such studies have been undertaken for most provinces of India and other regions on an all-India basis, it is surprising that no similar work on the in-

[30] *The Indian Agriculturist*, 1 May, 1901, p. 145. See, Memorandum on the industrial revival of the indigenous manual industries by Alfred Chatterton.

[31] *The Friend of India and Statesman* (Weekly edition), 2 January, 1985, p. 15. See, Letter to the Editor by J. Bowles Daly.

[32] Sir Ibrahim Rahimtoola in the Indian Legislative Council on 21 March, 1916. See, IOR. L/E/7/855.

dustrial development of Bengal has been carried out so far.[33] This study is, therefore, a pioneer work to fill in a major gap in the economic history of Bengal. However, since the scope of such work is virtually unlimited, the main focus has been directed towards the growth and development of the major manufacturing industries with special emphasis on the policies of the government, and the two major factors of production—labour and capital. It is only by such an unified approach that, full justice can be done to the subject.

Considerable difficulties had to be obviated in preparing this work on account of paucity of material and the lack of any recognized series for such a study. The Industries Department of Bengal was organized on a proper footing only after the First World War and was exclusively interested in the development of small and cottage industies. As a result virtually no material is available on the growth and development of large-scale industries as well as on matters relating to labour and industrial finance. Moreover, even the available material in the *Bengal Revenue Proceedings* (Industries) is not very encouraging as it provides no information about the structure, size, production and distribution of the various cottage and small-scale industries of the province. However, the proceedings of the Agriculture and Industries Department (Industries) available at the Bangladesh Secretarial Record Room Dacca contain some valuable records relating to the Industrial policy of the Government of Bengal during the period under review. We have also gone through the Bengal General Proceedings. Apart from one or two important documents normally not expected there, and a few papers on the stores policy of the Government of India, the records are none too encouraging. More useful are, however, the *Bengal Financial Proceedings* (Commerce)

[33]Similar works have been done on Madhya Pradesh, Mysore, Hyderabad, Rajasthan, Central Punjab, Vidarbha, Travancore-Cochin, Punjab, Madhya-Bharat and Kathiawar. All these original research works were carried out in various Indian Universities excepting one on Mysore by R. Balakrishna in 1939 from the University of London. See, A Preliminary Check List of Theses for a Comprehensive Annotated Bibliography on the Economic History of India (1500 A. D. to 1947 A. D.) in the Supplement to the *Indian Economic and Social History Review*, Vol. X, No. 1 (March, 1973). It appears, however, that the only published work among these is that of Balakrishna. See, R. Balakrishna, *Industrial Development of Mysore* (Bangalore City, India, 1940).

which in addition to providing valuable material on labour, also throw some light on the financial problems of the province aggravated by the depression in the 1920s and 1930s, and a few other useful documents on the existing industries of the province and their relationship with the government. Unfortunately, the financial proceedings prior to 1920 also lack in richness on industrial matters. Moreover, none of the proceedings mentioned cover the entire period of our study. For our purpose, we have also gone through relevent *Economic and Overseas Department Collections and Collections of Provincial Government Records.* While the former proved useful so far as the stores and tariff policy of the Government of India was concerned, the latter provided an insight into the financial condition of Bengal since "Meston Award" which as we shall see restricted the government from taking a more positive role in matters of industrial development.

Published works of the government likewise could not be said to have shed much light on various aspects of individual industries. Various annual reports, i.e., Industries Department reports, factory reports, mines reports are of limited use in view of the scope of such work. But it will be unfair to belittle the importance of such works as these at least provide a continuity and link to the gradual growth and development of industrial enterprises. Bulletins published by the Industries Department of Bengal and the Government of India are of limited use as these dealt mostly with the prospects of various industries rather than various aspect of existing industries. However, there are important exceptions which provide useful information which are unavailable elsewhere. The industrial surveys of Collin, Cumming and Gupta are of no great value except possibly in furnishing us with an over-all picture of the industrial panorama of the period[34] The importance of such documents simply lies in the fact that in the absence of relevant government documents for the period prior to First World War, they provide us with the vital link necessary to understand the subsequent era better. More important and throwing new light on such matters as labour and capital are the Indian Industrial Commission Report and the provincial and central banking enquiry committee reports with their evidence. Other government publications which we have used

[34]These Survey reports have been discussed in Chapter II, pp. 67-69.

are the various district gazetteers, census reports, Tariff Board reports, tea and coal statistics and various other statistical documents published by the Department of Commercial Intelligence and Statistics, Government of India. It may be noted that the statistics provided in these government publications suffer from serious defects, they do not always provide statistics in the same form as in previous years or sometimes they simply disappear or cease publication. Furthermore, the statistics provided are always deficient. Thus we do not have statistics on the investment of capital by banks on industries, the rate of profitability of various industries or the share of Indians in the invested capital in various industries or the particulars of share capital or statistics regarding the ownership of industrial enterprises. Likewise, we do not have much statistics on the wage structure in various industries or composition of workforce, figures on mortality, absenteeism, labour turnover, etc.

Since material from published and unpublished government sources are not always sufficient to throw light on all aspects of organized and unorganized industries nor did various industries necessarily publish their annual reports showing all aspects of their business organization and dealings, it has been necessary for us to look into contemporary newspapers, journals and periodicals. Among those consulted, the names of three stand out prominently. *Capital* (established 1988), a weekly journal published from Calcutta has been extremely useful in providing information about Calcutta share markets and their quotations and on all matters relating to capital and investment, and not the least on the jute manufacturing industry on which it had a particular interest. *The Friend of India and Statesman* (weekly overseas edition, title varies), also published from Calcutta, is important as it does contain substantial information on the jute, tea and coal industries of Bengal particularly as regards their supply of labour and capital and not the least on market conditions for those products. Of special value on the tea industry has been the *Indian Planter's Gazettee*, also published from Calcutta and without which no study on the tea industry of the period could be complete. All that material has been supplemented by private papers, parliamentary proceedings and debates, various non-official publications, pamphlets and contemporary works.

From these sources with their inherent limitations, we have tried in this book to evaluate the performance of the manufacturing industries of Bengal. We hope, in spite of our manifold difficulties, we have been able to contribute some knowledge on this hitherto unexplored aspect of Bengal's economic history for the period under review.

2 The Industrial Policy of the Government of Bengal

The industrial policy of the Government of Bengal during the period 1900-1939 has been examined in two parts. Part I, deals with certain limitations under which the provincial government had to function and analyses their implications on the industrial development of Bengal. Part II, is a general study of the industrial policy of the Government of Bengal, its achievements and failures.

In this chapter, we have tried to bring to the surface those limitations which to a great extent circumscribed the activities of the provincial government and hindered the optimum development of manufacturing industries. These limitations—both external and internal restrained the Government of Bengal from taking a "forward" and "bold" industrial policy and it was made to restrict its field of development to cottage and small industries. One such external limitation was the tariff policy of the Government of India, on which no provincial government had any say. The tariff policy, on the other hand, was dictated from Whitehall and free trade under which goods were imported free of duty (sometimes of course for revenue purposes minor duties were imposed on selected imports) was prescribed for India. In the year 1923, however, with the granting of fiscal autonomy, the Government of India adopted a policy of "Discriminatory Protection" whereby certain industries were protected by imposing suitable duties on foreign products. The second external limitation was on the purchase of stores. The rules framed by the Government of India allowed only certain products of local origin to be bought locally (if certain conditions well satisfied) and no preference whatsoever was extended to local manufactures. The third limitation was as regards the financial problems of the Government of Bengal, which was as much an external limitation as an internal one. It was an external limitation because the Central Government decided the level of provincial expenditures. It was done before the Reform Schemes by periodical "financial settlements" and later by the inequitable "Meston Award". In one sense it was also an internal limitation because after the settlements it was left to the provincial government to distribute the sum among different government departments. After examining these limitations of the provincial government, in Part II we have attempted to estimate the Bengal government's industrial policy carried out under the guidance of the Department of industries.

Part I

When the British Government decided to adopt free trade as its official policy, it gave considerable latitude to her Colonies to legislate their own tariff regulations. The British Colonies in Canada, for example, were permitted by an Imperial Act in 1846 to reduce or repeal by their own legislation, duties imposed by Imperial Acts on foreign goods imported into the Colonies. Canada took advantage of this when in 1849 the remaining navigation laws were repealed and the St. Lawrence was thrown open to vessels of all nations.[1] As regards Australasia, the colonies were empowered by an Imperial Act of 1852 to raise customs duties, subject to the proviso that they should not be contrary to the treaty, differential, or imposed on goods for the use of the Imperial forces in the colony.[2] In the South African colonies, no limitations were imposed on their powers with regard to customs duties when self-government was accorded. No restrictions were imposed on New Zealand under the Imperial Act of 1852.[3] There had been an exception only in the case of Ireland and India.[4]

The basis of tariff policy followed by Whitehall with regard to India was that of free trade and it remained in force till the origin of the fiscal autonomy "convention" in 1919. Under such a system of free trade between two unequal partners, India hardly got an opportunity to develop her manufacturing industries. Great Britain by virtue of her early industrialization and being the first industrial nation was in a preponderently superior position as

[1]Economic and Overseas Department Collections, IOR. See, 'Note on the Question of Fiscal Autonomy in the Dominions'.

[2]*Ibid.*

[3]*Ibid.*

[4]W. Cunningham, *The Case against Free Trade* (London, 1911), p. 86.

regards technical skill and experience. As a result she completely dominated the Indian market. Even infant Indian industries which possessed great natural advantages, like the cotton textile industry received no sympathy.[5] The policy of the British government at that time was concentrated towards the further development of commercial relations. The basis of this was the export of agricultural raw materials from India and the importation of finished products from England. This resulted in the insignificant development of large scale industries in India and the destruction of many old handicrafts, rendering the occupations of the people more predominantly agricultural than they were before.[6]

Among the large scale industries in Bengal before the First World War, jute and tea were the most important from the point of Bengal's export trade. Even these industries became heavily dependent upon foreign supplies. The dependence on foreign imports had been best described by J.C.K. Peterson, then Controller of Munitions, Bengal. He wrote in the *Englishman* in March 1918:[7]

> The two chief industries in Bengal for instance the jute and tea industries are almost entirely dependent on supplies from

[5]Even free traders were not unmindful of the special cases where manufacturing industries might be established by regulations, if such industries possessed great natural advantages. Adam Smith, for instance, was of the opinion that: "By means of such regulations, indeed, a particular manufacture may sometimes be acquired sooner than it could have been otherwise, and after a certain time may be made at home as cheap or cheaper than in the foreign country". See, Adam Smith, *An Inquiry into the Nature and Causes of the Wealth of Nations* (Edited by Edwin Cannan) (London, 1904), Vol. I, pp. 422-23. John Stuart Mill also felt that protective duties were sometimes justified if imposed temporarily especially in a young and rising nation, in the hopes of naturalizing a foreign industry. To him: "The superiority of one country over another in a branch of production, often arises only from having begun it sooner. There may be no inherent advantage on one part, or disadvantage on the other, but only a present superiority of required skill and experience. A country which has this skill and experience yet to acquire, may in other respects be better adapted to the production than those which were earlier in the field. . ." See, *Collected Works of John Stuart Mill* (University of Toronto Press, 1965), Vol. III, p. 918.

[6]*Minutes of the Evidence recorded by the Indian Fiscal Commission*, Vol. I (Calcutta, 1923), p. 280

[7]J. C. K. Peterson, 'Industrial Development in Bengal', *The Englishman* (Annual Financial Review), 4 March, 1918, p. 11.

> Europe. When war broke out if the supply of raw hide pickers from England had stopped most of the mills on the Hooghly would have had to shut down. . . .Most of the other leather stores used in the mills such as picker banes, roller skins, leather belting, etc., and all the machinery and machinery stores also come from Europe.
>
> Much of the Indian tea crop was, and still is, packed in boxes obtained from foreign countries. Patent chests are imported from Russia, Canada or Japan and the metal fittings required from England or America. Hoop iron, nails, clips for fastening the patent chests also come from foreign countries. Without these supplies it would be impossible to pack tea . . . : The prunning knives, hoes, forks, and kodallies used in the gardens and practically all the machinery required for the manufacture of tea are also imported. These instances show the danger to India of our dependence upon external supplies.

The above description of Peterson brings to light the state of Bengal's industrial development under free trade conditions. In fact, political pressure had long been focussed on this point, and in 1916, in the early days of the war, it had led to the appointment of the Indian Industrial Commission. The consideration of tariff policy was, however, expressly excluded from the terms of reference of the Commission by the proviso that their recommendations should not be incompatible with the fiscal policy of the Government of India. In spite of the Commission's recommendations including greater participation by the Government of India on matters of industrial development, the fiscal policy remained unchanged. How ever, in 1919 an important pronouncement came from the Joint Select Committee which was appointed to consider the Government of India Bill (1919). It carefully considered the relations between the Secretary of State and the Government of India and through it with the provincial governments. It was concluded that continued dictation of India's fiscal policy from Whitehall was likely to endanger the "good relations between India and Great Britain". Further, it recommended that the Secretary of State for India should "as far as possible avoid interference on this subject when the Government of India and its Legislature are in agreement. . . ."[8]

[8]*Report from the Joint Select Committee on the Government of India Bill*, Vol. I, Report and Proceedings (pp. IV of 1919), p. 11, Clause 33.

This was the origin of the famous Fiscal Autonomy "Convention" which was accepted subsequently by the Secretary of State in a despatch to the Government of India, dated the 30 June, 1921.[9] The Indian Government at once took the liberty of this declaration and on 7 October, 1921 appointed a Fiscal Commission "to examine with reference to all the interest concerned the Tariff Policy of the Government of India. . . ."[10]

The Indian Fiscal Commission came out in favour of discriminatory policy so as to make the inevitable burden on the community as light as was possible with due regard to the development of industries. In choosing the industries to be protected it laid down three fundamental conditions. Firstly, the industry must possess natural advantages, cheap power, sufficient supply of labour and a large home market. Secondly, the industry must be one which without the help of protection was not likely to develop at all or as rapidly as was desirable in the interests of the country. Thirdly, the industry must be one which would eventually be able to face world competition without protection.[11] The Government of India accepted the recommendations and in June, 1924 appointed a Tariff Board to give effect to the policy. Its main task was to study the applications for protection and refer its recommendations to the Government of India after it had made enquiries on the possibilities of granting protection.

The Tariff Board studied many applications and recommended the suitable ones to the Government of India which ultimately accepted or rejected the proposals. Many industries, which were granted protection showed excellent results. The cotton textile industry, for example, was granted protection in 1926-27 and the number of mills and their production increased greatly. In 1931 there were in Bengal 21 cotton mills[12] which increased to 46 in 1936.[13] As regards the production capacity, in 1926-27 Bengal

[9]See, Economic and Overseas Department Collections, IOR. L/E/9/1144. Note on the "Tariff Policy in India", No. 8322 of 1931.

[10]*Report of the Indian Fiscal Commission, 1921-22* (PP II of 1922), pp. 335-36.

[11]*Ibid.*, p. 384.

[12]Out of these 21 cotton mills, 4 were spinning mills, 4 weaving, 7 spinning and weaving, 4 in course of erection or recently registered, and 4 were idle. *Report of the Indian Tariff Board regarding the grant of protection to the Cotton Textile Industry* (Calcutta, 1932), pp. 9-10.

[13]Out of these 46, 24 mills were in course of erection or recently registered, 11 were spinning and weaving mills, 6 only weaving, 2 spinning and 3 were idle. DOIB: *Bulletin No. 75, Cotton Mill Industry in Bengal* (Alipore, 1973), p. 6.

cotton mills spun 31.54 million pounds of yarn and 31.8 million yards of piece-goods of various kinds which increased to 37.62 million pounds of yarn and 79.4 million yards of piece-goods by 1931-32.[14] The principal goods turned out were dhuties, the production of which had increased from 17.9 million yards in 1926-27 to 65.1 million yards in 1931-32, an increase of 47.2 million yards or 264 per cent; long-cloth and shirting; and coloured piece-goods the production of which had increased from 1 million yards to 3.9 million yards, an increase of 290 per cent.[15] The overall increase in the production of cloths of all sorts during the period 1926-27 to 1931-32 had been 149.69 per cent.[16] By 1936-37 the grand total of

TABLE 2.1

COTTON MILL PRODUCTION OF YARN AND WOVEN GOODS IN BENGAL, 1925-26 TO 1938-39

Year	*Yarn* (000 lbs)	*Woven goods* (000 lbs)
1925-26	24,123	8,708
1926-27	31,537	7,495
1927-28	34,347	8,307
1928-29	30,022	9,959
1929-30	37,053	14,357
1930-31	37,763	16,748
1931-32	37,620	17,204
1932-33	40,821	20,852
1933-34	39,912	23,642
1934-35	41,056	32,368
1935-36	40,991	32,601
1936-37	38,065	34,986
1937-38	38,303	36,855
1938-39	45,695	43,808

SOURCES : *Statistical Abstract for British India with statistics, where available, relating to certain Indian States from 1921-22 to 1930-31* (65th number) (London, 1933), pp.754-57; *Ibid., 1930-31 to 1939-40* (72nd number) (London, 1943), pp. 626-29.

[14]*Tariff Board Report on Cotton Textile*, 1932, pp. 13, 19.
[15]*Ibid.*, pp. 19-21.
[16]*Ibid.*, p. 21.

woven goods manufactured in the cotton mills of Bengal had increased to 156.2 million yards consisting of 153.2 million yards of grey and bleached piece-goods; 2.94 million yards of coloured piece-goods and small quantities of miscellaneous items like coloured goods, hosiery and mixed products.[17]

Similarly, due largely to foreign competition, not a single modern sugar factory existed in Bengal till 1932, the year the industry was granted protection. Yet by 1938-39 Bengal possessed 10 sugar mills having a total crushing capacity of 5,000 tons a day.[18] The number of sugar mills would probably have been much greater but for internal competition from sugarcane growing areas of the United Provinces and Bihar which had advantages in the cost of sugarcane cultivation and therefore gained greater benefit from protection.[19]

Iron and steel was another industry which really got a big boost, largely due to protection granted in 1924 that continued even after the partition in 1947. The Tata Iron and Steel Company was by far the greater beneficiary of this legislation. It increased its share of the available Indian market for rolled steel from 30 per cent in 1927-28 to 72 per cent in 1932-33.[20] In Bengal, Messrs. Sir Sarupchand Hukumchand & Company started Hukumchand Electric Steel Works at Ballygunge, a short distance from the railway station. The steel produced was of the highest quality and was expected to comply with grade "A" of the British Engineering Standard Specification.[21] Two other big iron and steel companies

[17]Grey and bleached piece-goods included chadars; dhuties; drills and jeans; cambrics and lawns; printers; shirtings and long-cloth; T-cloth, domestics and sheets; tent cloth; khadi, dungri or khaddar; and some other sorts. DOIB: *Bulletin No, 75, Cotton Mill Industry in Bengal*, p. 47.

[18]*Sugar Technologist's Association (of India) Year Book, 1939-40* (Cawnpur, n. d.), Appendices on the List of Sugar Factories and Refineries existing in India in the year 1938-39, List A, pp. 14-15.

[19]See, Chapter V of this thesis for further elucidation on this point.

[20]*The Indian Railway Gazette*, August 1934, p. 172.

[21]*Ibid.*, June 1925, pp. 212-13. The Hukumchand Electric Steel Works was established with a view to meeting the demand for steel castings which was mainly required by the great Indian Railways for their rolling-stock and also by the firms engaged in carriage and wagon building. Till then railways had to keep considerable capital idle in the form of stock of spares to replace breakages.

also benefitted in Bengal. The first was the Bengal Iron Company[22] which specialized in the production of pig iron, cast iron pipes, fencing posts and sockets, railway chairs and sleepers. In this section of trade, Bengal could hold its own against any country in the world.[23] The other was the Indian Iron and Steel Company which came into existence in March 1918 with an authorised capital of three crores of rupees.[24] The two were amalgamated in 1936 and the capacity of the company was 850,000 tons of pig iron and 100,000 tons of cast iron pipes, sleepers and general iron casting per annum.[25] In 1937 a new company called the Steel Corporation of Bengal was formed for the manufacture of steel from pig iron. The plant of the Steel Corporation was set up adjacent to the blast-furnace of the Indian Iron and Steel Company near Asansol, and the Corporation took hot metal from the latter under an agreement.[26] It produced structurals, heavy rails, sheets (black and galvanized), bars, spring and tool steel to certain specifications.[27] Due largely to the protection given to it, the iron and steel industry was able to stand firmly on its own feet "except against dumping".[28] Under its influence, the ship-building industry also prospered. The total number of joint-stock iron, steel and ship-building companies working in 1920-21 was 29. It rose to 39 in 1925-26, 59 in 1930-31 and in 1935-36 no less than 69 such companies existed in Bengal.[29]

[22]The Burrakpur Iron Works of Bengal Iron and Steel Company were originally established in 1875. But as this private enterprise was not a financial success, they were closed down in 1879. A few years later, the Government took up the venture, and carried it for 8½ years when the Bengal Iron and Steel Company took it up in 1889. See, *The Indian Railway Gazette*, March 1911, p. 84. The Bengal Iron and Steel Company was reconstituted in 1919 as the Bengal Iron Company with an authorised capital of £ 2,500,000. See, *RAB*, 1221-22, p. 41.

[23]*The Englishman* (Annual Financial Review), 4 March, 1918, p. 9.

[24]*RAB*, 1921-22, p. 41.

[25]*Report of the Indian Tariff Board on the continuance of protection to the Iron and Steel Industry* (Bombay, 1047), p. 9.

[26]*Report of the Indian Tariff Board on the continuance of protection to the Iron and Steel Industry* (Bombay 1947), p. 10.

[27]*Ibid.*

[28]*Ibid.*, p. 6.

[29]DOIB: *Bulletin No, 83, Report on the Growth of Joint-Stock Companies in Bengal* (Alipore, 1939), p. 11.

But in many cases the recommendations of the Tariff Board were not accepted or only partially accepted by the Government of India. One such case was the enquiry on the heavy chemical industry appointed in July 1928. The basis of the whole group of chemicals considered, was sulphuric acid. The Board found a high natural protection to the manufacture of sulphuric, hydrochloric and nitric acids in India due to the heavy sea freights on acids. Since the salts dependent upon the acids did not enjoy the same natural protection it proved difficult for the Indian manufacturers to compete against imports from other countries where the industry was highly developed.[30] Examination of the industry's claim to protection led the Board to recommend favoured duties at various rates on a number of heavy chemicals, with a bonus on super-phosphate fertilizer manufactured in India. It was hoped that this would lead to an increase in the output of this product and enable the sulphuric acid industry to be put on a paying scale. There were other miscellaneous recommendations such as a specially reduced railway freight rate for super-phosphates.[31]

The Government took a long time in considering the Report (it was submitted in May 1929 by the Tariff Board and government published it for general information in September 1931) and was ultimately unable to accept in full the recommendations of the Board. The government agreed to the duties recommended as a measure of protection to give the industry a chance to reorganize, but it was not satisfied with the scheme for the encouragement of super-phosphates which according to the government required further expert examination. Nor did the government accept subsidisation of chemical industries by means of freight reductions on the plea that railway rating policy did not fall within the scope of the Board's enquiry.[32] Moreover, the proposed protective duties were imposed for a period of two years until 31 March 1933. The Government of India, accordingly allowed the scheme to lapse after the expiry of the temporary duties.[33]

On the whole the Tariff Board had successfully carried out its reference terms. It had made realistic studies on the industries

[30]Economic and Overseas Department Collections, IOR. L/E/9/1027.
[31]*Ibid.*
[32]Economic and Overseas Department Collections, IOR. L/E/9/1027.
[33]*Ibid.*

under enquiry and recommended far reaching proposals for their development. It could probably have done more had it been an independent body without certain limitations on its path. These limitations seriously affected its working, and in the end brought the entire mechanism of granting protection under severe criticism. These limitations were four-fold. Though the Board had been in existence since its inception in 1924 (except for short periods in 1933 and 1934), it had never been a permanent body. Its continuation depended on the policy of the government which usually extended it from year to year or two years at a time.[34] The result was that the members suffered from periodical scrutiny and an apprehension that their services might be terminated if they failed to satisfy the government. This was a great hindrance to the successful working of the Board. Secondly, there was no machinery during the period the protective duties were in force. As a result the Tariff Board could not examine the progress of the industries and make further recommendations from time to time as to whether a revision of the policy of protection or the quantum of protection might or might not be needed with reference to the protected industries. However, the most important criticism was the manner in which the Government of India interpreted the laid down conditions. Sometimes the interpretations were harsh and rigid. The glass industry in India was deprived of protective duties simply because soda-ash, a raw material for its manufacture had to be imported.[35] The Government did not see the innumerable examples where one or more of the components of a particular industry had to be imported before the manufacturing processes could begin. Fourthly, the Government also unnecessarly delayed announcing whether a particular industry could get protection. The decision to refer the question of protection to the glass industry was taken by the Government of India in 1923. It took no less than eight years to request the Tariff Board to take up the enquiry, which it finished in one years. The Government took another three years before reaching its final decisions in 1935.[36] It was only in 1944 that the Government decided to liberalize the existing protective policy and eliminate some of the conditions

[34] *Ibid.*, IOR. L/E/9/994.
[35] *BLCP*, 27 February, 1939, Vol. I, p. 335.
[36] Economic and Overseas Department Collections, IOR. L/E/9/1030.

attached to the granting of protection to industries.[37]

The stores rules framed by the Government of India from time to time (with the sanction of the Secretary of State for India) for purchasing its requirements, viz., clothing for the army, machinery for the railways, stationery for offices, etc., was of vital importance to the development of industries. This was so in view of the fact that the government was the chief purchaser of manufactured goods in India.[38] A definite policy of systematic patronage as such could stimulate the local industries by injecting in them the element of demand. However, an examination of the official policy would show that there were gross anomalies both as regards the prescription of the policy and the manner in which it was administered.

Till 1908 only certain high officials of the Government of India and Local Governments were authorised to purchase stores of local origin not exceeding Rs 50 in value.[39] This rule was also applicable in the case of local boards of Bengal. They were required to obtain articles priced above this limit from England by indent upon the Secretary of State for India, even if such articles were available in India.[40] In 1908 the Governor-General in Council amended the earlier rule and revised the amount to Rs 250 for purchases of Civil Departments which could be procured in India by Heads of Departments, Commissioners of Divisions, and other officials of or above the rank of Collector whom the Local Government might select.[41]

Moreover, the rules themselves were far from being clear as regards its contents. In other words these were cast in a permissive form and did not give preference to locally produced

[37]Economic and Overseas Department Collections, IOR. L/E/9/994.

[38]The various goods purchased by the consuming departments of the Government of India were called "Stores" in the Accounts of the Home Treasury of the Government of India. Prior to 1876, stores rules did not permit local patronage and hence there was no question of purchasing any kind of Indian manufacture in the Indian market. Sunil K. Sen, 'Government Purchase of Stores for India (1958-1941)', *Bengal Past and Present*, Vol. LXXX (1961), pp. 47-48; and also Sunil Kumar Sen, *Studies in Industrial Policy and Development of India, 1858-1914* (Calcutta, 1914), p. 12.

[39]IOR: VOL. 7861, BGP (Misc.), November 1908, No. 79 p. 455.

[40]*BLCP*, 15 December, 1906, Vol. XXXVIII, p. 198.

[41]IOR: Vol. 7861, BGP (Misc.), November 1908, No 79, p. 455.

goods.[42] In addition, there were practical difficulties in implementing the rules which required a comparison to be made in respect of price and quality between the locally manufactured articles and those obtained from England.[43] No less was the complexity regarding the interpretation of the condition that an article manufactured in India from imported materials must not have been imported into India in a finished or partly finished state. The result was that the home indents of the railways, for example, prior to the First World War consisted only of articles such as earthenware, *sorais* for holding water, bricks and lime.[44]

During the First World War, Britain found it extremely difficult to keep up its export trade with India due to "paramount necessity of economising freight."[45] To reduce the load on the United Kingdom, stricter rules were framed for export from the United Kingdom into India of materials on the prohibited list. Goods could only be imported on Priority Certificates issued by the Government.[46] This was however, a blessing in disguise for India. It resulted in the temporary relaxation of the stores rules. Munitions Boards were set up at the Centre with Controller of Munitions in the different Circles for arranging supplies from India to the armies overseas. This led to the growth of some manufacturing industries. Their products were mainly required by various governments for their own use and for supplies overseas. In Bengal, the Munitions Board was itself purchasing two times as much as all other departments—municipal corporations and railway companies—put together.[47]

[42]This was the verdict of a Committee appointed in 1906 by the Government of India to enquire into the procedure prescribed for the purchase of stores for the use of Government Departments in India. It might be noted that the Committee's Report was not allowed to be published but a summary of the conclusion was given. See, IOR: Vol. 8139, BGP (Misc.), August 1909, Nos. 12-15, p. 187.

[43]IOR Vol. 8139, BGP (Misc.), August 1909, Nos. 12-15, p. 187.

[44]*Capital*, 29 October, 1930, p. 819.

[45]IOR: Vol. 10431, India Commerce and Industry Proceedings (Home Indents), March 1918, No.8. p. 37.

[46]Priority Committees were set up in this connection. Thus there were tea, jute, coal, general engineering and electrical priority committees. See, DOIB: *Annual Administration Report*, October 1917 to December 1919, pp. 2-3.

[47]J.C.K. Peterson, 'Industrial Development in Bengal', the *Englishman* (Annual Financial Review), 4 March, 1918, p. 11.

In following and implementing the rules, the officers also showed indifference and apathy. This indifference on their part to buy local products had been brought to their notice by the Secretary of State for India himself. In 1903 he wrote to the Governor-General of India in Council:[48]

> I am not satisfied that the general policy which has been recognised as applicable to the purchase of stores has been carried out as completely as is to be desired. That policy...is that, as far as possible, the purchase of stores of local manufacture should be encouraged....The information furnished in your letter under reply does not point to any progress in the desired direction.

The Secretary of State again drew their attention just prior to the First World War.[49] One probable reason for this indifference on the part of the bureaucracy to carry out the official policy could be the absence of suitable purchasing agencies in India prior to 1922. In its absence officers empowered to buy local products had to be on the look out for goods of suitable and reasonable price. Therefore, the officers found it more convenient to order stores from home. A centralized purchasing agency existed only in the case of medical stores and stationery, the purchase of which depended on the personal disposition of the purchasing officers. It was to a large extent due to the enthusiastic support of the Controller of Printing, Stationary and Stamps, Government of India that improvements in the manufacture of pencils, pens and pen-holders, leather goods, writing ink, carbonic paper, etc., were manifested during the Swadeshi movement.[50]

After the war, in pursuance of the recommendations of the Indian Industrial Commission, a Stores Purchase Committee was formed to enquire into the measures required to enable the departments of the Government of India and the Local Governments to obtain their requirements as far as possible in India; to study the relations between such agencies as might be formed for the purpose of purchase and inspection with one another and with the

[48]IOR: Vol. 6791, BGP (Misc.), July 1904, Nos. 7-8, pp. 11-12.

[49]IOR: Vol. 9370, BFP (Commerce), April 1914, No. 11, p. 11.

[50]IOR: Vol. 9033, India Commerce and Industry Proceedings (General), 1912, No. 37, pp. 69-70.

Stores Department of the India Office and to recommend the modifications of the stores rules necessary for the purpose.[51] The Committee (headed by F. D. Couchman, Member, Railway Board) recommended the setting up of the Indian Stores Department which would act on behalf of all Imperial departments of the Government of India and such as might desire to avail themselves of its assistance—provincial governments, company-worked railways, corporations, port trusts, municipalities, etc., so as to prevent the purchase of imported stores so long as goods of indigenous production of suitable quality and price were available.[52] In accordance with the recommendations of the Committee, the Government of India set up the Indian Stores Department in January 1922 for the purpose of purchasing various classes of stores required for the public service.[53] It consisted of four main branches at the headquarters (administration, inspection, purchase the intelligence sections), in addition to the Provincial Purchase Circles, the Provincial Inspection Circles, the Government Test Houses at Alipur and Bombay and the Metallurgical Inspectorate.[54] Each of these organizations rendered service of some sort or other directly or indirectly connected with the development of industries.[55] Though its services had been utilized by several Department of the Central Government as well as of Provincial Governments, Company Railways, Indian States and quasi-public bodies, in an appreciable and gradually increasing degree, recourse to the Department had been entirely optional.[56]

It was only in 1929 that the Government of India recommended that certain departments (i.e., the Indian Posts and Telegraphs Department; the Director, Geological Survey of India; the Chief Inspector of Mines, etc.) must purchase their stores through the Indian Stores Department, Delhi (henceforth called ISD, Delhi) if these were available in India and in conformity with the rules for the supply of articles for the public service.[57] However, the most

[51]IOR: Vol. 10749, BFP (Commerce), February 1920, No. 58, pp. 177-19.

[52]*Report of the Stores, Printing and Stationary Sub-Committee of the Retrenchment Advisory Committee, September, 1932* (Simla, 1932). p. 9.

[53]*Administration Report of the Indian Stores Department*, 1929-30, p. 1.

[54]Economic and Overseas Department Collections, IOR. L/E/9/939.

[55]*Ibid.*

[56]*Administration Report of the Indian Stores Department*, 1929-30, p. 1.

[57]*Ibid.*

important change of the stores rules came in December 1929 which revised all previous rules and adopted the Rupee Tender System (as the rules were popularly called) and which finally came into operation on 1 January 1931.[58] These rules were framed to give effect to the policy of the Government of India of making purchase of stores for the public service in such a way as to encourage the development of the industries of the country to the utmost possible extent consistent with economy and efficiency.[59] These rules prescribed that in purchasing stores preference should be given in the following order:

Firstly, to articles which were produced in India in the form of raw materials, or were manufactured in India from raw materials produced in India, provided that the quality was sufficiently good for the purpose;
Secondly, to articles wholly or partially manufactured in India from imported materials, provided that the quality was good for the purpose;
Thirdly, to articles of foreign manufacture held in stock in India, provided that they were of suitable type and requisite quality;
Fourthly, to articles manufactured abroad which needed to be specially imported.[60]

As a result of this new Rules purchase abroad had became an exception; whereas under all the rules in force previously purchase in India was the exception (see Table 2.2). After the formation of the ISD, Delhi; it even purchased such articles by Rupee Tender as wheels and axles, spare parts for motor vehicles, boiler tubes, transport flat and ferry staging, lighthouse equipment, and electrical equipment for Telegraph Department which were formerly purchased from abroad.[61] This process of buying local products kept on increasing and by the year 1938-39 goods worth almost nine crores of rupees were purchased annually by the ISD, Delhi and most of

[58]*Ibid., 1933-34*, p. 1.

[59]*Administration Report of the Indian Stores Department*, 1929-30, p. 2.

[60]See, Department of Industries and Labour Government of India), Resolution No. S. 217, dated 12 December 1929, in the Economic and Overseas Department Collections, IOR. L/E/9/939. Also, *Administration Report of the Indian Stores Department*, 1929-30, pp. 2-3.

[61]*Administration Report of the Indian Stores Department*, 1931-32, p. 2. The value of such articles purchased in India amounted to Rs. 4,844,400.

TABLE 2.2

VALUE OF STORES OBTAINED FROM INDIAN FIRMS, 1905-06 TO 1910-11 (FIGURES OF VALUE IN £)

Year	*Purchased from India* (*1*)	*Payment to the India Office* (*2*)	*Grand total* (*1*) + (*2*) (*3*)	*Precentage of* (*1*) *to* (*3*) (*4*)
1905-06	473,340	4,468,670	4,942,010	9.57
1906-07	498,342	5,020,443	5,518,785	9.02
1907-08	512,464	4,181,379	4,693,843	10.91
1908-09	477,534	5,013,618	5,491,152	8.69
1909-10	482,578	3,447,293	3,929,871	12.27
1910-11	461,350	3,072,565	3,533,915	13.05

SOURCE: IOR: Vol. 9370, BFR (commerce), April 1914, No.11, p. 12.
It may also be noted here that the stores purchased from Indian firms were not necessarily articles of purely Indian origin but were mainly articles manufactured abroad and held in stock in India. See, for example, the table showing the amount expended by the PWD, Bengal (Roads & Building & Irrigation Branches) on imported stores purchased in India and on Indian stores in IOR: Vol. 10749, BFP (Commerce), February 1929, No. 49, pp. 103-04.

these stores were purchased from Bengal (see Table 2.3), the products of which were mainly textile and leather goods, engineering, hardware and miscellaneous items.[62]

Though in the year 1926 the Secretary of State for India gave the Governor's provinces the right to frame their own stores rules, the Bengal government perferred to use the rules governing the purchase of stores for Central Departments promulgated by the Government of India subject to certain modifications necessary to meet the local requirements of this province. The underlying policy of the new rules published by the Government of Bengal in August 1926 was the encouragement of local industries. Simultaneously with the promulgation of the Stores Purchase Rules of 1926 the departments and officers of this government were instructed to utilize to the fullest extent the services of the Indian Stores Department, which was sanctioned that year on a permanent basis by the Secretary of State.[63] In the year 1933 the Government of Bengal

[62]*Administration Report of the India Stores Department*, 1931-32, pp. 63-64 Appendix VII.

[63]IOR: Vol. 12049, BRP (Industries), September 1935, No.22, p. 57.

TABLE 2.3

PURCHASE OF STORES THROUGH THE INDIAN STORES DEPARTMENT, DELHI, YEAR BY YEAR SINCE ITS CONSTITUTION AND THE VALUE OF STORES PURCHASED FROM BENGAL (Rs '00,000)

Year	*Total value of stores purchased through ISD, Delhi* (*1*)	*Value of stores purchased from Bengal* (2)
1922-23	1,65	N.A.*
1923-24	1,67	N.A.
1924-25	2,59	N.A.
1925-26	2,67	N.A.
1926-27	3,99	N.A.
1927-28	3,73	1,38
1928-29	3,60	1,35
1929-30	4,29	1,74
1930-31	3,77	1,28
1931-32	3,60	1,27
1932-33	3,31	1,38
1933-34	3,60	1,44
1934-35	4,76	2,09
1935-36	5,59	2,57
1936-37	6,49	3,37
1937-38	7,89	3,99
1938-39	8,77	5,66

SOURCE: *Administration Report of the Indian Stores Department*, 1938-39 (Delhi, 1909), Appendix XIX, p.132 for column (1); and *Ibid., 1926-27*, p.41; *Ibid., 1928-29*, p. 47; *Ibid., 1932-33*, p. 60; *Ibid., 1935-36*, p. 68; and *Ibid., 1938-39*, p. 82 for column (2).

* N.A. = Not available

revised its own rules to suit the Rupee Tender System, the main features of which were the removal of financial restrictions on local purchase and the allowance of a limited degree of preference in respect of price to articles produced or manufactured in Bengal.[64] Due largely to changes in the rules, the Bengal Government's own purchase on stores produced in India increased from Rs 3,17,838 in 1914-15[65] to Rs 23,81,000 in 1929-30.[66]

With the growth of the ISD, Delhi the fortunes of the India Stores Department, London underwent a tremendous change. The

[64]IOR: Vol. 12049, BRP (Industries), September 1935, No. 22 p. 57.

[65]IOR: Vol. 9882, BFP (Commerce), March 1916 No. 10, p. 8.

[66]IOR: Vol. 12049, BRP (Industries), September 1935, No. 22, p. 57.

first change was initiated with the introduction of the reformed constitution when the responsibility for controlling stores expenditure in England was devolved on the High Commissioner.[67] Previous to this, no effective control had been exercised in London and demands were generally complied with without question, provided that they were received from officers duly empowered to indent on the Department.[68] The India Stores Departments, London usually obtained the required goods by public advertisement in newspapers and technical journals (of U.K. only)[69] or in the case of specialised stores such as surgical instruments by invitation from manufacturers known by experience to be capable of supplying reliable stores of assured quality.[70]

However, the most important change was brought about by the Rupee Tender System. The India Store Department of London now became a subordinate body to the ISD, Delhi and on whose behalf it obtained tenders in London and transmitted those to India for final adjudication. On request from Delhi, it also inspected materials under manufacture in U.K. and in the continent.[71] Most of these manufactures consisted of equipment entirely of those categories of munitions of war which required close coordination with the Admiralty, the War Office and the Air Ministry.[72] The decline suffered by the India Store Department could be seen from Table 2.4. In about three years from 1929-30 to 1932-33 the purchases through London fell from over £ 5 million to nearly £ ½ a million a year. This also resulted in the reduction of the staff—84 in the year 1931-32 alone, consisting of 24 administrative and clerical officers, 11 technical officers and 49 members of the warehouse staff.[73]

Financial stringency was another limitation which restricted Bengal government's spending in nation-building activities of which

[67] *Report on the Work of the India Store Department, London*, 1924-25, p. 9.

[68] *Ibid.*

[69] *Ibid.*, p. 10.

[70] *Report on the Work of the India Store Department, London*, 1924-25, p. 2.

[71] *Ibid, 1932-33*, p. 1.

[72] *Ibid, 1934-35*, p. 3.

[73] *Ibid, 1931-32*, p. 3.

TABLE 2.4

VALUE OF STORES PURCHASED THROUGH THE INDIA STORE DEPARTMENT, LONDON, 1922-23 TO 1938-39 (FIGURES IN £)

Year	*Total value of stores*
1922-23	5,005,765
1923-24	3,205,360
1924-25	4,159,679
1925-26	5,178,908
1926-27	9,235,635
1927-28	4,879,018
1928-29	5,065,711
1929-30	5,013,957
1930-31	2,683,608
1931-32	1,328,261
1932-33	497,575
1933-34	417,947
1934-35	501,017
1935-36	978,243
1936-37	799,110
1937-38	1,112,543
1938-39	814,336

SOURCES: Compiled from *Report on the Work of the India Store Department London, 1924-25*; *1928-29*; *1932-33*; *1934-35*; *and 1938-39*. These figures do not include stores obtained through Departments of His Majesty's Government or small purchases by the Director of Inspection.

industrial development was one. Previous to the "Meston Award"[74] all revenues raised in any province from whatever sources belonged to the Government of India and the local governments got what they were allowed by the Supreme Government. This division of revenue was known as 'financial settlement', which in some provinces were settled for a period of five years and in others for lesser

[74]The Government of India by their Resolution No. 306-F, dated the 27 January, 1920 in the Financial Department set up a Committee "to advise on the financial relations between the Government of India and Local Governments under the Reforms scheme, and more particularly on the question of the contributions to be paid by the Local Governments in aid of the central exchequer". The Committee was set up under the presidentship of Lord Meston with two other members and a secretary. See. IOR: MSS. Eur. F. 136, File No. 30, Serial No. 25, Meston Collection. The Committee's recommendations have since been known as 'Meston Award'.

periods.[75] Under this system, some provinces actually had to pay much larger proportion of their income to the central exchequer than others. Bengal, for example, under financial settlements had to pay about 20 crores out of a total income of Rs. 27½ crores to the Imperial Government, while Madras paid Rs. 11½ crores out of Rs. 20 crores; Bombay Rs. 19½ crores out of Rs. 30 crores while the United Provinces paid about Rs. 5⅔ crores out of Rs. 13¾ crores.[76]

As a result some provinces were economically better off than others. Moreover, if we take into consideration the factor of population in each of the provinces, the unjust distribution of wealth becomes more clear. In the year 1917-18 the average per capita expenditure of the major administrative areas of British India could be seen in Table 2.5. Column (1) of the Table shows a glaring defect in the distribution of wealth among different Local Governments without sufficient justification to their reasons. Burma, Bombay and the Punjab were economically much better off than Bengal or the United Provinces. Due to this low grant to the Bengal government, its activities were also circumscribed. In January 1920, the Meston Committee was appointed (in accordance

TABLE 2.5

PER CAPITA EXPENDITURE OF CERTAIN INDIAN PROVINCES AND OF BURMA, 1917-18 AND 1931-32

Administrative Area	*Per capita expenditure in 1917-18 (1)*		*Per capita expenditure in 1931-32 (2)*	
	Rs.	Annas	Rs.	Annas
Burma	5	3	N.	A.
Bombay	5	0	6	12
Punjab	3	0	4	3
Madras	2	2	3	7
U.P.	1	15	2	5
Bengal	1	10	1	13

SOURCES: Column (1) from *BLCP*, 9 February, 1921, Vol. I, No. 2, pp. 142-43; and column (2) from IOR. L/F/9/22, Indian Financial Enquiry (Niemeyer), 1936, Vol. IV, Provincial Government Finances: Bengal and the United Provinces. See, "Note on Federal Finance" by B. Mukherjee, p. 2.

[75]*BLCP*, 9 February, 1921, Vol. I, No. 2, pp. 142-43.

[76]*Ibid.*, 1 July, 1920, Vol. LII, p. 700.

with the authors of the Montagu-Chelmsford report) to work out a system of financial relations between the Centre and the Local Governments. The Government of Bengal accordingly submitted its representations to the effect that the standard of expenditure laid down for Bengal by the Government of India was far too low and that Bengal with its population of over 45 millions should have a much higher level of expenditure.[77] The Meston Committee, far from listening to the arguments of Bengal, recommended a sliding scale of contributions, imposing a contribution of 6½ per cent in the first year and rising upto 19 per cent in the seventh year for the Bengal province as its direct contributions in view of Bengal's "size, intrinsic wealth and general economic possibilities".[78] On the other hand certain heads of expenditure, viz., customs, income tax, duties on salt were kept exclusively for the benefit of the Centre.[79]

The recommendations of the Committee generated tremendous heat in Bengal. The Bengal Legislative Council at once recorded "its deep sense of disappointment" and was of the view that this was "likely to jeopardise the successful working of the reforms in in the Presidency."[80] The Government of Bengal telegraphically protested against progressive increases of contribution[81] and the Committee fearing uproar objected to the publications of the evidence unless a note was forwarded with it.[82] However, with minor modifications by the Joint Select Committee of both Houses of Parliament, the report was accepted by the Government.[83]

[77]*BLCP*, 21 November, 1921, Vol. V, pp. 3-4.

[78]*Report of the Financial Relations Committee* (Delhi, 1920), pp- 9 & 12.

[79]*Ibid.*, p. 10.

[80]*BLCP*, 1 July, 1920, Vol. LII, p. 697.

[81]IOR : MSS. Eur. F. 136, File No. 32, Meston Collection. See, Copy of telegram from Viceroy to Secretary of State, dated 15 June 1920.

[82]The Secretary of State telegraphically communicated to the Viceroy on 29 April, 1920 that there were "grave objections" to publications of evidence unless accompanied by some such note:—"Owing to difficulty in obtaining competent stenographers the record of evidence is very incomplete and the Committee trust that it will not be read as more than a rough indication of the topics touched upon in the course of examining the witnesses," See, IOR : MSS Eur. F. 136, File No. 32, Meston Collection.

[83]The modifications were that in future some share in the growth of revenue from taxation on incomes be given to the provinces and that the Committee also took to note the peculiar financial difficulties of Bengal which they commended to the special consideration of the Government of India. *BLCP*,

The main criticisms against this Award so far as Bengal was concerned were as follows. Firstly, the central government had under its control by the division heads of taxation, the yields of which were constantly on the increase. These heads of taxation included customs, excise (other than alcohol and narcotics), income-tax and super-tax, salt and opium. In 1922 the contributions of the Government of Bengal to the central treasury amounted to Rs. 23 crores[84] which increased to nearly Rs. 27 crores by the year 1928-29, the highest paid by any single province in India (see Table 2.6). Secondly, the yield of revenue from the provincial heads, i.e., land revenue, excise of alcohol and narcotics, stamps, a share in the future of income-tax and registration fees were not the same in different provinces. The result was that some of the provinces had received proportionately more than others. As far as Bengal was concerned she had very little prospect of revenue expansion as her land revenue which was the mainstay of provincial finance under the settlement, was strictly circumscribed by the Permanent Settlement. Due to this the revenue earnings of Bengal was more or less

TABLE 2.6

PROVINCIAL REVENUES AND CENTRAL REVENUES COLLECTED IN THE PROVINCES, 1928-29 (FIGURES IN LAKHS OF Rs.)

Name of the province	*Provincial*	*Central (collected in the provinces)*
Madras	1,753	765
Bombay	1,522	2,484
Bengal	1,097	2,677
U.P.	1,145	422
Punjab	1,115	101
Burma	1,055	887
Bihar & Orissa	578	94
C.P.	536	36
Assam	274	39

SOURCE: Collections of Provincial Government Records transferred to London, IOR. R/3/2/69. See, Memorandum by the Government of Bengal on Federal Finance in its relation to Bengal, p. 3.

21 November, 1921, Vol. V, p. 4. Accordingly, Bengal's contributions to the Centre was remitted with effect from 1922-23, but the contributions payable by the other provinces were also remitted in 1926-27.

[84]*Capital*, 24 November, 1932, p. 775.

static over the years. In 1922-23 her revenue receipts amounted to 986 lakhs of rupees and ten years later in 1932-33 it totalled only 938 lakhs of rupees—a fall in the revenue.[85] Thirdly, the 'Meston Award' gave no power to the provinces to tax industrial activities and had therefore handicapped the industrial provinces as contrasted with the agricultural ones.[86]

The tale of financial bungling did not end there. Even jute from which Bengal earned considerable export duty was singled out for the benefit of the Centre, while at the same time leaving out wheat, salt, cotton-goods, sugar and so forth entirely for the benefit of the producing provinces. Anderson, the then Governor of Bengal thought this as "utterly anomalous"[87] and was of the opinion that the Centre could have no moral claim to any part of the jute tax except so far as there might be a disposable surplus after the legitimate requirements of the province had been met.[88] It was only after considerable exchange of personal and official correspondence that Anderson could procure for Bengal half of the proceeds of the jute tax in 1934.[89]

The new financial arrangement led to drastic retrenchment both at the initial stages of the Reformed scheme and during the early 30s. In spite of all these, the government found itself virtually impossible to carry on its functions. Its view was loud and clear:[90]

> It is impossible to balance the budget by retrenchment. To do so expenditure would have to be cut down by over 2 crores (about 20 per cent). This is an impossible task if Government is to continue to function. Retrenchment of this nature on the reserved side would produce chaos and on the transferred side would mean extinction. . . .

[85]Collection of Provincial Government Records transferred to London, IOR. R/3/2/71. See, Note regarding Bengal Finance, p. 1.

[86]*Capital*, 7 August, 1930, p. 270.

[87]Collections of Provincial Government Records transferred to London, IOR. R/3/2/71. See, Letter of Sir John Anderson to Rt. Hon. Lord Eustrace Percy, dated the 27 July 1933.

[88]*Ibid.*, IOR, R/3/2/70. Anderson to Grigg, dated 17th June 1934.

[89]*Ibid.*, IOR. R/3/2/71. See Letter No. F. 3(7)—B-34, dated Simla, the 30th June 1934. From the Hon'ble Sir Alan Parsons, Secretary to the Government of India, Finance Department to the Secretary to the Government of Bengal, Finance Department.

[90]*Ibid.* See, "Question of making an appropriate provision in the Constitution Act regarding Deficits on Revenue Account", p. 4.

In the Industries Department itself, which was made permanent in 1920 with ten gazetted officers, five had to be retrenched after preliminary training, viz., those of the Inspector of Technical Schools and the Industrial Engineer.[91] The post of the Assistant Inspector of Weaving Schools had to be abolished and local bodies had to be asked to increase their contributions towards the cost of peripatetic weaving parties.[92] Mining classes were done away with and the grant to Kanchrapara and the Calcutta Technical Schools had been reduced.[93] The financial stringency also led to the stoppage of the State Technical Scholarships since 1931-32.[94] In short, out of the scanty allocation of funds to the Industries Department (see Appendix I), a retrenchment of over seven lakhs of rupees had to be made.[95]

The financial condition of the province somewhat improved in 1936 when Sir Otto Niemyer in his report on the Indian Financial Enquiry, awarded Bengal 10 per cent of the entire income tax (including corporation tax) raised in India together with that of another 12½ per cent of the jute tax (which itself amounted to Rs. 42 lakhs annually).[96] About the same time the Government of India also came forward with grants-in-aid to the handloom industry, which became operative from 1 November, 1934 for a period of five years, i.e., till 31 October, 1939.[97]

[91]DOIB: *Annual Administration Report*, 1923, p. 1.

[92]Collection of Provincial Government Records transferred to London, IOR. R/3/2/71. See, the "Statement showing the savings effected by Government through retrenchment", p. 10.

[93]*Ibid.*

[94]*BLCP*, March 26, 1936, Vol. XLVIII, No. 2, p. 512.

[95]Collections of Provincial Government Records transferred to London, IOR. R/3/2/71. See, Council Question by Mr. Syamaprosad Mookerjee regarding reduction in provincial expenditure by Government since after the appointment of the Bengal Retrenchment Committee. Retrenchments in the Industries Department were made in the following years, the amount showing against it:

1921-22	Rs. 1,40,000
1922-23	Rs. 2,96,846
1924-25	Rs. 1,12,348
1930-31	Rs. 86,869
1931-32	Rs. 11,603
1932-33	Rs. 97,606

[96]IOR. L/F/9/20. See, Indian Financial Enquiry, Report by Sir Otto Niemeyer, pp. 14-15 and 19-20.

[97]IOR: Vol. 12049, BRP (Industries), November 1935, Nos. 5-6, p. 5.

PART II

Having considered the limitations of the Government of Bengal, we now venture to look at its industrial policy. Prior to the establishment of the Industries Department in 1917, there was no definite industrial policy of the Government. The development of indigenous products was left entirely to private enterprise in which the government took no particular interest. Its main emphasis was on the export trade to which the government devoted its entire energy.[98] However, during this period the Government of Bengal on its own initiative undertook large scale surveys of cottage industries and prepared several reports. The primary object of such reports were to ascertain the existing conditions of the indigenous industries with the object of enabling the government to determine what practical measures might be adopted to encourage and develop the most promising amongst such industries. But in most part, these reports remained only in paper and sometimes even remained confidential and hence unavailable to the public.[99] The main reasons for not implementing the recommendations appear to have been the unwillingness of the State to sanction any fund for creating new industries unless these were strictly limited to industrial instructions and avoided the semblance of a commercial venture.[100] The Government of India was only prepared to come forward in familiarizing the people with such improvements in the method of production as modern science and practice of European countries could suggest. Further than this the State would not go, and it was left to private enterprise to demonstrate that these improve-

[98]Although in 1905 the Government of India established its Industries Department, its object was not the promotion of industries development or to galvanize moribund industries but to do everything in its power to facilitate the transaction of business as between the Government and the commercial community, and to provide all facilities which it legitimately could for the more rapid, and cheaper, conduct of business. IOR: MSS. Eur. F. 111, No. 514, Summary of the Administration of Lord Curzon of Kedleston, in the Department of Commerce and Industry, March to November 1905, p. 4.

[99]As was E.W. Collin's Report on the Existing Arts and Industries in Bengal. See, J.G. Cumming, *Technical and Industrial Instruction in Bengal, 1888-1908*, Part I of Special Report (Calcutta, 1908), p. 2.

[100]See, A.G. Clow, *The State and Industry* (Calcutta, 1928), p. 4; and India Office Revenue Departmental Papers, L/E/7/855, No. 8417 of 1915.

ments could be adopted with commercial advantage.[101] This implied that the provincial governments could only go as far as technical education and industrial education was concerned and as far as its financial resources permitted.

However, it would be of interest to know what these reports were and what they recommended, not the least because those were the very first reports prepared by the government as regards the extent and value of indigenous industries in Bengal. The earliest report was prepared by E.W. Collin in 1890. The report investigated the principal arts and industries of the province and recommended suggestions for the improvements of these. The recommendations included the training of mechanical engineers in the workshops connected with State Railways, the institution of improved industrial schools and the encourgement of industrial classes, the stimulation of native industries by the purchase of materials for public works in India, etc.[102] But Collin ruled out the question of any large schemes for technical education on the ground that the native industries were scattered and unimportant and that it would be much easier to depute men to Europe to study the improvements which had been made in the system of manufacture.[103] By 1908 the Government of Bengal had adopted a system of apprenticeships in all the large Railway workshops, i.e., Kanchrapara, Jamalpur and Kharagpur but large scale training in the workshops belonging to the State had not yet started.[104] The Government had also started mining schools for mining students in connection with the coal mining industry.[105]

In 1908, two important reports were published. The first was the Special Report prepared by J.G. Cumming, officiating Commissioner of the Presidency Division and it contained two parts. Part I dealt with the progress of technical education in Bengal between 1888 and 1908 while the second brought upto date the industrial

[101]See, Despatch No. 51 of 1915, Government of India, Department of Commerce and Industry to the Right Hon'ble Austin Chamberlain, His Majesty's Secretary of State for India, India Office Revenue Departmental papers, L/E/7/855, No. 8417 of 1915.

[102]E.W. Collin, *Report on the Existing Arts and Industries in Bengal* (Calcutta, 1890), p. 31.

[103]Collin, *op. cit.*, p. 14.

[104]Cumming, *Technical and Industrial Instruction in Bengal*, p. 2.

[105]*Ibid.*

survey of the province carried out by Collin in 1890. His main recommendations were widely welcomed by all sections of the public and included such proposals as the appointment of an expert Superintendent of Industries or Director of Industrial Enquiries; the improvement of technical instruction by larger expenditure on central institutions; the subsidizing by government of the associations for the industrial or scientific education of Indians; the preparation or purchase, as far as possible, of materials for public works in India, and not in England; the giving of greater encouragement to district exhibitions of industries and industrial arts; and more dissemination among the public of information on industrial matters.[106]

The other important report was prepared by G.N. Gupta in 1907-08 for Eastern Bengal and Assam. This report for the first time suggested the creation of a new department of industries; the creation of a central Technological Institute (which was considered by Collin as useless); the opening of factories instead of schools with apprentice classes for imparting education regarding the process of manufacture and the idea of a direct state assistance by "pioneering" new industries and by rendering pecuniary assistance to firms or persons who were willing to engage in any profitable industry.[107]

Although very little of the recommendations of these reports were translated into practice, one of the steps that the Government of Bengal took was, however, the appointment of a Superintendent of Industries for Bengal in 1910. But due to the duality of his works not much was achieved.[108] In 1915, on the cessation of imports

[106] J.G. Cumming, *Review of the Industrial Position and Prospects in Bengal in 1908 with special reference to the Industrial Survey of 1890, Part II of Special Report (Calcutta, 1908), pp. 45-47.*

[107] G.N. Gupta, *A Survey of the Industries and Resources of Eastern Bengal and Assam for 1907-08* (Shillong, 1908), pp. 112-17.

[108] The post of a Superintendent of Industries and Inspector of Technical and Industrial Instructions in Bengal was sanctioned in April 1900, and one Dr. Denning was appointed to the post in June 1910 but in November 1911 he went on leave and retired in the following year. The next officer was W.H. Everett, who was a professor of Electrical and Mechanical Engineering at the Civil Engineering College, Sibpur. An arrangement was made with him to look after the department and for which he was paid an allowance of Rs. 200 a month. Due to this duality of his work development of local industries had been practically in abeyance. IOR: Vol. 9635, BFP (Commerce), June 1915, No. 4, p. 21.

from hostile countries (due to war) and on the recommendation earlier made by the District Administration Committee in 1913-14, the Government of Bengal thought it appropriate to appoint a Director of Industries. Accordingly, it wanted the sanction of the Government of India who refused it on grounds connected with financial considerations.[109] However, on being reprimanded by the Secretary of State for not sanctioning the post, the Governor-General gave approval[110] and accordingly a temporary Director of Industries was appointed in October 1917 with a temporary Department of Industries. But till the end of 1919 the post of the Director of Industries was held by the Controller of Munitions and the combined officer was known as Combined Controller of Munitions and Director of Industries.[111]

An indirect contribution of the Government of Bengal during this period (prior to First World War) were the publications of annual monographs so as to facilitate the private individuals interested in the industry to benefit by its study. These monographs[112] were written by qualified Indian (mostly) and British officers on the basis of reports submitted to them by various district and subdivisional authorities and by personal tours and research.

These monographs were of special interest as these were written to cover almost to the minute detail on the subjects under study. Thus, for example, in the case of iron and steel works, it studied the extent of the industry, the methods of production, the raw materials used, condition of labour and wages and the prospect of the industry. In this particular case, the reporter brought to the

[109]IOR: Vol, 10221, India Commerce and Industry Proceedings (Industries). 1917, No. 2, p. 133.

[110]*Ibid.*, Nos. 2-4, pp. 133-34. The Secretary of State had written that "...everything that makes for the development and diffusion of industry in Bengal appears to have urgent claims, alike for political and economic reasons, and I should not have regarded a definite recommendation as inopportune".

[111]DOIB: *Annual Administration Report*. October 1917 to December 1919, p 1.

[112]The monographs for the various years were as follows: Brass and Copperware (1893-94), Pottery and Glassware (1894-95), Dyes and Dyeing (1895-96), Cotton Fabrics (1896-97), Woolen Fabrics (1897-98), Silk Fabrics (1898-99), Ivory Carving (1899-1900), Wood Carving (1901-02), Tanning and Leatherwork (1902-03), Gold and Silverware (1903-04), Stone Carving (1904-05), Carpet Making (1905-06), Iron Work (1906-07), Paper Making (1907-08), and Ware and Tinsel Industry (1908-09). The publications of annual monographs seem to have stopped after this period.

notice of the prospective investors the benefit of the modern iron and steel industry in place of the primitive methods practised by the village blacksmiths.[113] However, it would have been much better had these monographs been written in vernacular rather than in English which was unintelligible to the vast majority of the people. Moreover, these reports were hardly available in the *mufassal* as there were no publicity or propaganda media.

As has been said the creation of the Department of Industries in 1917 was solely due to war conditions. During this time restrictions were placed on shipping space and on trade as a result of which goods needing immediate delivery had to be procured with Priority Certificates (issued first by the Secretary to the Government of Bengal, Financial and Commerce Departments till 1 April 1917 and later on by the provincial Director of Industries).[114] This shortage of goods on the one hand, and ready money price available on the other for a wide range of commodities, including a large variety new to the manufacturing economy of India focussed the attention of the people on the development of industries.[115] To guide such development on sound lines as was possible within the capacity and interest of Government, in other words it was to mobilize information regarding the availability of raw materials for industrial purposes, to institute special programmes of research and to give the required technical advice, and also to organise the training of personnel, both labour and executive; that the Department of Industries was established.[116]

After the war, new development took place. The question of the implementation of the report of the Indian Industrial Commission (also known as the Holland Commission) came to the forefront. The Commission, appointed in 1916 was instructed to ascertain the possibilities of further industrial development in India and to submit its recommendations as to :

"(*a*) whether new openings for the profitable employment of Indian capital in commerce and industry can be indicated;

[113] E.R. Watson. *A Monograph on Iron and Steel Work in the Province of Bengal* (Calcutta, 1907), p. 53.

[114] DOIB: *Annual Administration Report*, October 1917 to December 1919. pp. 2-3. From 1 April, 1917 to 28 October, of the same year, the duty was transferred to the Controller of Munitions.

[115] *Ibid., 1935-36*, p. 3.

[116] *Ibid.*

(*b*) whether and, if so, in what manner, Government can usefully give direct encouragement to industrial development. . ."[117]

The report of the Commission was submitted in 1918 and it made certain radical propositions "quite different from the laissez faire that had come before."[118] It proposed far-reaching state intervention compared with past policy. Its recommendations included, among other things, the constitution of permanent department of industries, direct state aid to industries, establishment of pioneer and demonstration factories, the creation of an Imperial Industrial Service and of an Imperial Chemical Service, the creation of a central organization for the purchase of stores under the Imperial Department of Industries and the local Department of Industries in each province.[119] In accordance with the recommendations of the Commission, the temporary Department of Industries which was set up in 1917 in Bengal was made permanent in 1920 with an Advisory Board of Industries to advise on the main questions of industrial development throughout the province. However, most other recommendations of the Commission fell through owing to the intervention of the Montagu-Chelmsford Reforms of 1919 which made the development of industries a provincial subject.

The Montagu-Chelmsford Reforms of 1919 also introduced the system of division of subjects into "reserved" and "transferred" in the provinces. The "reserved" departments were administered by the Members of the Governor's Exective Council who were not responsible for their actions to the Legislative council. On the other hand, the responsibility of working the "transferred" subjects were left to Indian ministers, who were to be responsible both to the legislature and to the Governor. Generally speaking, government

[117] *IIC* (PP XVII of 1919), p. 25.

[118] Clive Dewey, 'The Government of India's New Industrial Policy, 1905-25, a Study in Failure', a paper presented at the Institute of Commonwealth Studies (Postgraduate Seminar) on 10 July, 1975.

[119] By 'pioneering' the IIC meant the establishment of an industry on a small commercial scale in order to ascertain and overcome the initial difficulties and to discover if the industry could be worked at a profit. On the other hand 'demonstration factories' were those industries which would pass successfully through the pioneer stage and would prove a useful training ground. The object was to use those as schools for the training of men as operatives, foremen or manager under strictly commercial conditions. *IIC* (PP XVII of 1919), pp. 166-67.

departments which were considered not of sufficient importance and whose actions were not likely to jeopardise the peace and stability of the province were left to the Indians. As such, the nation-building departments like education, agricultural, irrigation, etc., were in Indian hands. 'Industries', however, was divided into two groups, namely, "reserved" subjects and "transferred" subjects. The "reserved" subjects, viz., Factory Inspection, Boiler Commission, Smoke Nuisances Commission, the Electrical Licences and Inspection, Stores Purchase, Industrial and Commercial Intelligence and Labour were administered by the Commerce Department.[120] On the other hand, the Department of industries dealt with two sectors only—the development of Industries and technical and industrial education.[121] While, no doubt, this led to a simplification of work of the Industries Department, it also resulted in the separation of subjects which were so intimately linked up with one another that from efficiency point of view it would have been better to retain them under one administrative authority.

However, it was not before 1 November, 1922 that the Department of Industries became entirely "transferred". [122] Prior to this, the Department also temporarily looked after the "reserved" subjects. In the 1930s, in addition to the development of industries, and technical and industrial education, the Department of Industries also administered the Bengal States Aid to Industries Act and the work relating to the Unemployment Relief Scheme. The first was to grant financial assistance to the industrialists introduced in 1931 and the object of the second was to give relief to the unemployed youths by teaching vocations along cottage industries lines.

But as development of Industries was a very large field and the Department had not the resources and manpower to tackle these, it had to limit its action to the field of small and cottage industries only. In making their decisions they thought that the cottage and small scale industries were the ones which needed most help in view of their highly disorganized state. On the other hand, the large-scale industries were in a better position to fully compre-

[120] DOIB: *Annual Administration Report*, 1922, p. 1, *Ibid., 1931-32*, p. 8.

[121] *Ibid., 1920*, p. 1; Department of Indian Industries and Labour: *Bulletin No. 57, State Action in respect of Industries, 1928-35* (Delhi, 1936), p. 2.

[122] DOIB: *Annual Administration Report*, 1922, p. 1.

hend and organize themselves corporately, and to provide for their economic and technical needs. Moreover, it was thought that, next to agriculture, the economic condition of the largest number of people in Bengal depended on these industries and therefore the cottage and small industries had a prior claim to demand attention than others. Hence, in the words of the officiating Director of Industries:[123]

> ... it was decided that, Bengal being primarily an agricultural province, the attention of the Department should, primarily, be devoted to the organization of such industries as are dependent on the products of the soil or for which raw material are naturally available.

Therefore, now onwards the accepted policy of the Bengal government became the encouragement of local industries with a view to improve the economic condition of the masses.[124] Having decided this, the government laid down the possible lines of action through which the objectives could be realized. These were the supplying of correct and up-to-date information on commercial and industrial matters; carrying on research for the most economic utilization of raw materials available within easy distance and demonstrating the results in localities where they were likely to strike root; finding markets for local industries whenever possible; and making provisions for technical education and training necessary to keep the industries well abreast of the times.[125]

Bengal government's most important work was in the field of textile industry and the tanning industry, and in this respect it claimed to have placed "these industries in a much stronger position than they would otherwise have been".[126] The government set up weaving demonstration parties, the main task of which was to demonstrate to the weavers the different methods of weaving.[127] In addition to this, the government had established peripatetic and

[123] *Journal of Indian Industries and Labaur*, Vol. I, Part 3, August 1921, p. 362.

[124] *Bengal Legislative Assembly Debates*, 13 March, 1940, Vol. LVI, No. 4, p. 16.

[125] *RAB*, 1925-26, p. 1v.

[126] IOR: Vol. 1 1988, BRP (Industries), March 1933, Nos. 1-2, p. 15.

[127] The improved processes demonstrated by the weaving demonstration parties enabled weavers to receive increased orders for their cloths. See, copy of letter dated the 26th February, 1936 from Babu Fakir Chandra Bhar of

Chart showing Staff of Department of Industries, Bengal

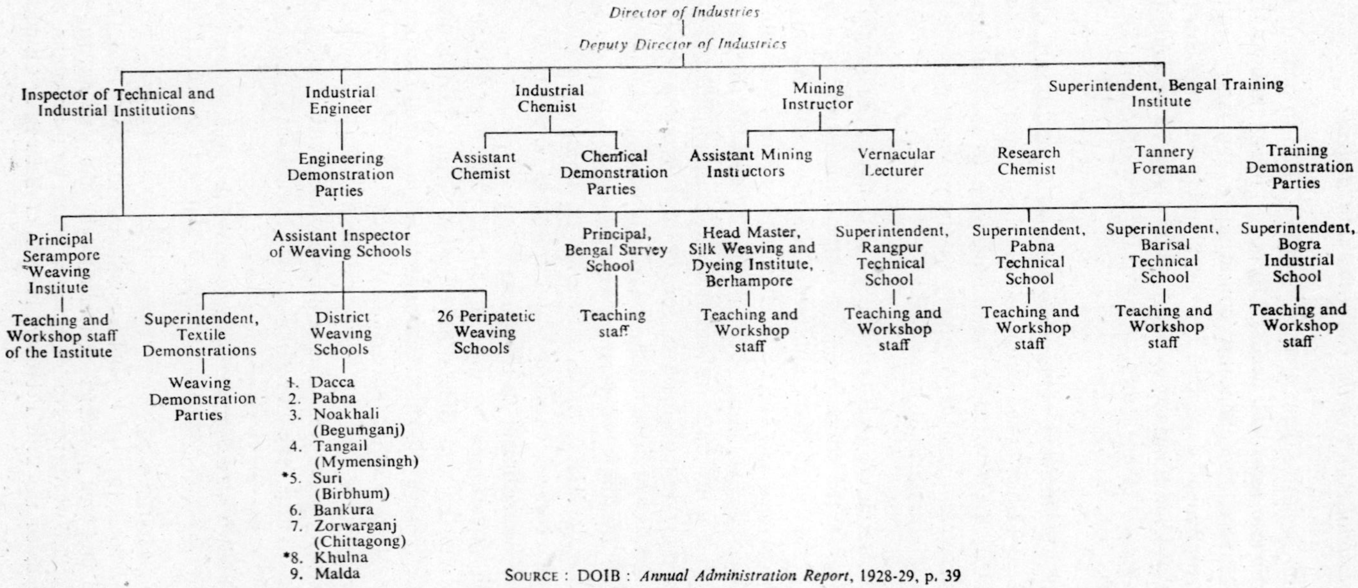

*Temporary.

SOURCE : DOIB : *Annual Administration Report*, 1928-29, p. 39

district weaving schools the purpose of which was to introduce up-to-date and economical methods of weaving with improved appliances for increasing the efficiency an earning capacity of the workers as well as for improving the quality and standard of the finished products.[128] These improved appliances included the introduction of fly-shuttle looms by which the shuttle was jerked backwards and forwards by a string and lever instead of being passed between the threads of the warp by hand as was done in the case of old throw shuttle looms; the supply of fly-shuttle sleys for pit looms; warping machines; the introduction of improved dobbies for ornamental work which enabled the weavers to weave simple and effective designs requiring a number of shifts; and even jacquard machines for weaving patterns. With a view to make available to the weavers yarn at reasonable price, the government also established co-operative methods of yarn sale in the towns and villages. But the attempt to solve the problem of yarn supply and distribution as well as of marketing the products was far from successful due to financial problems of the Bengal government itself.[129] Till 1943, there were only 355 weavers' co-operative societies having a total membership of 5,467 persons, which was only 2.3 per cent of the total number of weavers in Bengal.[130]

In the field of tanning, previous to First World War, Bengal used to export hides and skins mainly to European countries and America and very little use of these was made to turn out finished products at home.[131] But during the war, restrictions were imposed

---

Rajbalhat, Hooghly to the Director of Industries, Bengal in BSR: Bundle No. 1, PAI (Industries), B Proceedings, File No. 1*W*/3 of 1936. In the above mentioned letter, Babu Fakir Chandra stated that the demonstrations in improved processes of weaving enabled the village of Rajbalhat to win 2 silver and 3 bronze medals for their fine jacquard bordered saries, dhoties and pagries in the All-India Hand Weaving Exhibition at Patna. In addition to that he had personally received orders for those types of cloths to an extent of Rs 12,000.

[128]*RAB* 1935-36, p. 166.

[129]For details on the various problems faced by the weavers, see chapter VII, pp. 324-325.

[130]*BLCP*, 17 February 1943, First Session, p. 11.

[131]This is apparent from the export figures of hides and skins which amounted to nearly 7 crores of rupees and leather nearly to rupees one lakh only in 1910-11. See, *Report on the Maritime Trade of Bengal*, 1910-11, p. 15. Hides usually refer to undressed skins of big animals such as buffalo, cow,

on the export of hides and skins and on the import of leather manufactures.[132] As a result of which the existing few tanneries were reorganised and many new ones appeared to satisfy the demand for leather goods.[133] Munitions Board came forward to help the industry and established the Calcutta Research Tannery in 1919,[134] which was later on turned into Bengal Tanning Institute "in view of the fact that the Tannery is a training institute and a centre of research and demonstration".[135] In addition to carrying out research work, the work of the Government Tannery included the supply of technical advice and the making out of estimates and plans for tanneries; the supply of ready made treatment materials such as chrome liquors, fat liquors, etc., to facilitate the work of inexperienced and unscientific tanners; and the execution of machine work—finishing, polishing, etc., for small tanners.[136] The Institute also provided apprenticeship classes to the *mufassal chamars* and *bhadrolog* youths. These apprentices were sometimes paid allowances varying from Rs. 20 to Rs. 30.[137] In 1922, out of 16 apprentices, two were drawing an allowance of Rs. 30 and two Rs. 20 each per month.[138] Most of these apprentices later on turned to the tanning and allied professions. In 1932-33 out of 56 past students, 46 were known to be connected with this industry in one form or the other.[139] The Institute's two peripatetic tanning demonstration parties besides seeking to bring home to *mufassal chamars* the modern improved methods of tanning, also tried to create an interest in the leather trade among the educated and wealthy classes (who the Department thought could invest capital to start tanneries on modern lines) by holding demonstrations of the modern processes of tanning at different places of the province.

---

etc., and skins to those of smaller ones like calf, goat, deer and sheep. See, DOIB: *Bulletin No. 3, Handbook of Tanning* (Calcutta, 1922), p. 1.

[132] *RAB*, 1917-18, p. iii.

[133] The number of tanneries increased to 25 in 1921 against 10 in 1911, situated mainly in the eastern suburbs of Calcutta. However, the industry had not yet been a success. *Census of India, 1921*, Vol. V, Bengal, Part I, Report, p. 405.

[134] *RAB*, 1919-20, Part I, p. viii.

[135] DOIB: *Annual Administration Report*, 1926, p. 17.

[136] *Ibid., 1921*, p. 9.

[137] IOR: Vol. 11155, BRP (Industries), January 1922, No. 45, p. 71.

[138] *Ibid.*

[139] DOIB: *Annual Administration Report*, 1932-33, p. 17.

At these demonstrations, the *chamars* and *bhadrolog* youths were encouraged to do the processes involved in modern tanning with their own hands under the direction and guidance of the demonstrator.[140]

But the most fruitful result came from the actual research work done at the Bengal Tanning Institute as a result of which leather equal, for all praetical purposes, to the highest grade of imported leather was manufactured in Calcutta on a large scale.[141] This improvement was made possible due to the introduction of western processes of chrome tanning and an improved process of vegetable tanning in place of the primitive methods used by the *chamars* of Bengal.[142] Generally, most of the thick and coarse leathers such as those for sole, harness, belting were made by vegetable process while the finer varieties were chrome tanned. The principal varieties produced by chrome tanning were the shoe upper leathers, box and willow sides, box and willow calf, glace kid, chrome sheep skins and chrome patent leathers, chrome sole leathers, natural chrome sheep skins for lining and industrial leather, viz, chrome picking bands and lacs.[143]

The result of the introduction of improved processes of tanning led to the establishment of many small scale and cottage tanning industries in Calcutta which together produced fifty lakh square feet of chrome upper leather (crude box sides) valued at about twelve lakhs of rupees in 1931-32.[144] In addition to this, large

[140] *Ibid.*, *1926*, p. 21.

[141] IOR: Vol. 11988, BRP (Industries), March 1933, Nos. 1-2, p. 15.

[142] In the case of vegetable tanning, the delimed hides and akins, technically called the "prepared pelt" were treated in infusions of tanning containing vegetable matters while in chrome tanning, the delimed hipes and skins were treated in a solution of basic salt, which was called chrome liquor. DOIB: *Bulletin No. 3, Handbook of Tanning* (Calcutta, 1922), pp. 5-7.

[143] Box and willow sides were a variety of shoe upper leather made from cow hides and known for their softness and durability and their products like sandals, boots, etc., were cheap. Box and willow calf were made from small kips and calf skins, and their skin was principally used in making women's shoes for their smoothness. Glace kids were made from goat skins by chrome tanning while chrome sheep skins were used for living. Chrome patent leathers were varnished leathers made from cow hides by removing the grain surface. Industrial leathers like picking bands and lacs were used in textile looms. DOIB: *Bulletin No. 86*, *Report on the Survey of Leather Industries in Bengal* (Alipur, 1941), pp. 20-30.

[144] DOIB: *Annual Administration Report*, 1931-32, p. 20.

quantities of sole leather and varnished leather were also turned out by the cottage tanners of Tiljala—a suburb of Calcutta.[145] However, the real stimulus to the development of chrome leather industry came from the signing of the Ottowa Trade Agreement in 1932.[146] "In it the industry got an opportunity to develop to a much greater extent in three years that what it did in thirty years by private attempts".[147]

To improve other cottage industries, viz. pottery, cutlery, soap making, bell-metal, the paint and varnish industry, etc., on proper scientific lines; the Government in December 1921 appointed an Industrial Chemist[148] and next year an Industrial Engineer was also appointed.[149] The work of these officers were mainly to collect all relevent information regarding the economic and technical aspects of the existing industries other than tanning and textiles; the design, construction, and development of labour saving appliances which would eliminate drudgery from cottage industries; and the assimilation of industrial and commercial intelligence which would lead to the location of markets.[150]

[145]*Ibid.*

[146]Although separate statistical figures are not available for Bengal, the effect of the Ottawa Trade Agreement on the development of chrome leather industry in India could be seen from the following export figures:

Year	*Quantity of chrome shoe upper leather exported*	*Value (in pounds)*
1931	30,000 square feet	2,000
1932	414,000 " "	10,000
1933	3,631,000 " "	111,000
1934	4,041,000 " "	130,000
1935	6,517,000 " "	168,000

Similarly, the trade in box calf leather previous to 1934 was also small. The little that was manufactured and exported was shown under box sides. Since 1934, however, trade developed to a considerable proportion and was shown separately as box calf. The export trade in this variety of chrome shoe upper leather amounted to 533,000 square feet in 1934, and 1,000,000 square feet in 1935. See, DOIB; *Annual Administration Report*, 1935-36, pp. 23-24.

[147]*Ibid.*, p. 23.

[148]DOIB: *Annual Administration Report*, 1921, p. 2.

[149]IOR: Vol. 11293, BRP (Industries), February 1923, Vos. 44-45, p. 34. But the Industrial Engineer resigned his post on 8 July 1923 (DOIB: *Annnal Administration Report*, 1923, p. 1) and a new officer joined on 9 October 1925. LOIB: *Annual Administration Report*, 1925, p. 1.

[150]IOR: Vol, ,1988, BRP (Industries), March 1933, Nos. 1-2, p. 15.

One of the early contributions of the Industrial Engineer was the development of an improved variety of potter's wheel. The wheel which was developed could be revolved by hand at a very high speed of revolution by means of a bicycle chain and free-wheel attachment in place of the traditional potter's wheel consisting of a rough construction of wood, loaded with clay, and working on a hand wood pivot, being revolved by means of a stick.[151] The newly developed wheel was so arranged as to give uniform and steady revolutions at a high speed and for a longer duration than was possible with the indigenous crude wheel. Moreover, because of its uniformity in revolution and the higher sustained speed, the wheel could be used for moulding much larger articles with thinner walls than was usually possible to the village potter.[152] The Department also introduced a new kiln and a new process of glazing for ornamental pottery which proved beneficial to the pottery industry.[153] Attempts were also made to induce the *kumars* to adopt the glazed pottery (the market price of which was higher) to increase their earning capacity.[154]

In the field of cutlery the manufacture of Bengal was largely restricted to the manufacture of agricultural implements; the manufacture of cooking utensils and other articles of domestic use; the manufacture of tools and other articles used in various handicrafts and the manufacture of weapons.[155] This industry was carried out largely by the *karmakars* (blacksmiths) as a cottage industry and was mostly concentrated in rural areas where the techique of production remained primitive.[156] The Department investigated into the field and found the methods "very laborious and unscientific and consequently uneconomical".[157] It drew up demonstration programmes and exhibited the various aspects of improving the manufacturing process. Likewise, demonstrations and public exhibitions had also been shown in regard to shellac, bleaching of match wood, umbrella bending, etc.[158]

[151]DOIB: *Annual Administration Report*, 1930-31, p. 17.
[152]DOIB: *Annual Administration Report*, 1930-31, p. 17.
[153]*RAB*, 1934-35, p. 159.
[154]IOR: Vol. 11988, BRP (Industries), October 1933, Nos. 4-5, p. 7.
[155]DOIB: *Bulletin No. 95, Report on the Cutlery Industry in Bengal* (Alipur, 1941), p. 1.
[156]*Ibid.*, p. 6.
[157]IOR: Vol. 11784, BRP (Industries), October 1929, Nos. 10-11, p. 26.
[158]DOIB: *Annual administration Report*, 1926, pp. 5-11.

However, the most widespread demonstrations of the technique of production was carried out under the Unemployment Relief Scheme, which partially came into operation in 1932-33 for a period of three years. The main objects of this scheme were two. Firstly, to attempt to revive the fortunes of the most important and basic cottage industries of the province and secondly, to teach the unemployed *bhadrolog* youths professions along cottage industries.[159] Accordingly, 28 demonstration parties were constituted with a view to teaching them boot and shoe making, brass and bell-metal, umbrella making, soap making, cutlery making, jute and wool weaving and pottery.[160] For the successful working of the scheme, District Industrial Associations were set up consisting of the public-spirited people of the districts concerned.[161] It was the responsibility of the district associations to draw up programme of demonstrations, to look after the safety of the Government properties, to provide residential accommodation of the staff members, and also to select the condidates who would join the classes.[162] The training periods of such classes were not in excess of six months, out of which three to four months were devoted to the purely practical side of the industry, viz., teaching the art of manufacturing processes and the remaining two to three months in the commercial side of the industry[163] Under this scheme, till 1935-36 over a thousand students received training out of which 241 started independent factories and 166 students found employment (so was it claimed by the Department).[164]

The Government also attached considerable importance to industrial research. A sum of Rs. 50,000 was sanctioned in 1924-25 to build an Industrial Laboratory,[165] the work of which was completed in 1926.[166] In this Industrial Research Laboratory, the Industrial Engineer and the Industrial Chemist carried out research work in connection with intricate problems relating to industrial development. The laboratory developed, among other things, a new process of heat treatment resulting in the increased possibility of the

[159]DOIB: *Annual Administration Report*, 1932-33, p. 3.

[160]IOR: Vol. 12018, BRP (Industries), April 1934, Nos. 9-10, pp. 7-13.

[161]*Ibid.*, p. 19.

[162]*Ibid.*, pp. 19-20.

[163]DOIB: *Annual Administration Report*, 1932-33, p. 8.

[164]IOR: Vol. 12075, BRP (Industries), December 1936, Nos. 13-14, p. 22.

[165]*RAB*, 1924-25, p. xlv.

[166]DOIB: *Annual Administration Report*, 1926, p. 1.

establishment of very small cutlery factories manufacturing even razors of first quality [167] The result of all such researches were published in learned brochures of the Department of Industries.[168] However, it seems highly doubtful whether these reports were of any significance to the people at large in view of the language barrier (most of which were written in English) which according to a member of the Bengal Legislative Council was "uncomprehensible and unavailable to the general public".[169]

The engineering section and the chemical section of the Industries Department also dealt with various types of enquiries received from the public in general. The engineering section dealt with the more general enquiries and the general problems that arose in regard to the further development and improvement of cottage craft and small industries while the industrial chemical department dealt with problems of a chemical nature.[170] In the year 1938-39, the Department received a total of 989 enquiries and next year the number exceeded over 1,100.[171] Of the 989 enquiries in the year 1938-39, 356 were received from the public of Bengal, 284 from the public of other provinces, 119 from the Government of India, 183 from other provincial governments, 35 from the various departments of the Bengal government and 12 from outside India.[172] As regards the type of enquiries, 379 related to trade and commerce, 245 regarding small and medium sized industries, 90 relating to cottage industries, 33 regarding large and organised industries and 243 miscellaneous enquiries.[173]

In the field of marketing, the effort of the government was somewhat limited, and it was in this regard that the Government could be censured. In the 20's the Government tried to slove the problem of the cottagers through an annual grant to the Bengal Home

[167] *Ibid.*, 1932-33, p. 8.

[168] Such bulletions were 129 in number dating from 1920 to 1947. In addition to research publications, these also included other publications of the Department of Industries. See, India Office Library catalogue No. ST 281.

[169] *BLCP*, 28 March, 1930, Vol. XXXIV, No. 3, p. 586.

[170] DOIB: *Annual Administration Report*, 1930-31, pp. 14-15. However, from 1938-39 a new section, the Industrial Intelligence Section was established which took over the duty of industrial enquiries. *Ibid.*, 1939-40, p. 24.

[171] *Ibid.*, 1939-40, p. 25.

[172] *Ibid.*

[173] DOIB: *Annual Administration Report*, 1939-40, p. 25.

Industries Association which was founded in 1917 for the promotion and development of home industries of the Presidency. The association had also district committees, the function of which were "to circulate the objects of the Association, to collect all information with regard to home industries in their areas of operations, to act as Agents in the matter of carrying out objects of the Association".[174] But the Association did not reach a high stage of organization and, in spite of repeated warnings, had not been able to effect any appreciable improvement in its working with the result that every year a considerable sum from its capital resources had to be utilized to meet the losses accruing in its working,[175] Hence, the Government stopped the grant (which in 1926-27 was Rs 10,000) from 1927-28 as it "had failed to achieve the purpose which it had set before it, i.e., the promoting and developing of home and cottage industries, and, above all, the vital service of finding for them a market".[176] Instead, the Government decided to subsidise and give loan to the Bengal Co-operative industrial Society, Limited, with the definite object of helping in the marketing of products of cottage industries through the agency of the Central Sale Depot established in Calcutta under its auspices.[177] But it also failed to achieve any marked success due to "various difficulties".[178] In 1935-36, the Government granted a sum of Rs 250 per month to the "Good Companions", started in January 1934 under the approval and patronage of Her Excellency the Countess of Willingdon to provide a central depot for the sale of the products of Industrial Missions and Associations formed for the purpose of encouraging village handicrafts of all kinds.[179] The Department also claimed to have done everything practicable to secure facilities in marketing for

[174]See, Extract of the Rules of the Bengal Home Industries Association, in *Anglo-Indian Home Industries* (conducted by the Anglo-Indian District Committee), Calcutta, 1917, p. 6.

[175]IOR: Vol. 11630, BRP (Industries), April 1927, No. 14, pp. 21-22.

[176]*RAB*, 1927-28, p.52. The grant-in-aid to the Association was, however, renewed in 1935-36 again, in which year it received a sum of Rs. 18,000 for the purpose of finding a market in Calcutta for the products of home or cottage industries. IOR: Vol. 12049, BRP (Industries), November 1935, No. 28, p. 27.

[177]IOR: Vol. 11988, BRP (Industries), October 1933, Nos.1-2, p. 3.

[178]*Ibid.*

[179]IOR: Vol. 12018, BPR (Industries), September 1934, Nos. 12-14, pp. 21-22.

those who had applied for the same.[180] In 1933-34, the Government appointed a temporary Marketing Investigator in connection with the collection of economic information relating to demand and supply of indigenous products of small and cottage industries with a view to finding markets.[181] In 1935 a temporary marketing and publicity officer was also appointed.[182] The officer was expected to effect a liasion between cottage and small industrialists on the one hand and the markets in Calcutta and other cities and abroad on the other.[183] Till that time there was no publicity or propaganda officer to work for the benefit of cottage and small industries in Bengal.[184] As a result very few industrialists approached the Department for the solution of their difficulties.[185] Even a modest proposal to propagate ideas of industrial development amongst the rural population in Bengal through the media of cinema displays at the agricultural and industrial exhibitions and in schools and colleges could not be effected due to financial stringency.[186]

Conclusion

Having studied the limitations of the provincial government, we looked into the industrial policy of the Government of Bengal. Till 1923, the Government of India had no alternative but to follow the policy of free trade as was dictated from Whitehall, and under which goods were imported and exported virtually free of any duty. This sort of a policy was detrimental to the growth of nascent and infant industries as these had to compete with mature foreign industries which had already passed through the stages of infancy. In fact, as we have stated earlier this superiority of one country over another in a branch of production was simply because it had begun earlier and that a country had this skill and experience yet

[180]*RAB*, 1925-26, p. 87.

[181]*RAB*, 1933-34, p. 184.

[182]In view of nature and wide extent of duties discharged by the officer, the post was made permanent in 1938. See, BSR: Bundle No. 6, PAI (Industries), B Proceedings, File Nos. $\frac{8E}{8}$ 37 and $\frac{8E}{6}$ 38 of 1937-38.

[183]See, IOR: Vol. 11989, BRP (Industries), October 1933, Nos. 1-2, pp. 3-4.

[184]*Ibid.*, p. 4.

[185]DOIB: *Annual Administration Report*, 1926, pp. 9-10.

[186]*Ibid.*, *1921*, p. 7.

to acquire might in other respects be better adapted to the production than those which were earlier in the field.

In 1923 the Government of India adopted a policy of 'Discriminatory Protection' and under its influence many industries such as textile, sugar factories, iron and steel renewed their expansion. But the recommendations of the Tariff Board (which was formed in 1924 to study individual cases of industries for protection) were not in all cases accepted or only partially accepted. Examples have been cited in the case of heavy chemical industry and the glass industry. Moreover, the Tariff Board had to function under adverse circumstances, such as its temporary nature, the strict application of rules and the absence of any organization for periodical inquests.

In the case of stores purchase, the whole policy was otherwise directed and no patronage was afforded to the products of local origin. Till the 20's the stores rules were rigid and comparisons regarding price and quality had to be made with foreign products before stores could be bought in India. As such the officers empowered to purchase stores of local origin found it easier to requisition for the goods to the India Office in London than buy in India. It was only during the First World War due to restrictions placed in the movement of goods and because of the problems of finding shipping space that Indian industries received some natural protection. Under its influence, industries in India got the first big push to develop, and many new manufactures were established. In 1922 Indian Stores Department, Delhi was established but it was not till 1929 that compulsory purchase of stores of certain departments was ordered by the Government of India. A revolutionary change was brought about by the Rupee Tender System which came into operation on 1 January, 1931 and which made it compulsory for the Government of India to buy its products through the ISD, Delhi. Similarly, the provincial governments were granted the same privilege to buy their products through it or frame whatever rule they deemed fit for the purpose. The Government of Bengal allowed a limited degree of preference in respect of price to the articles produced in Bengal. Henceforth, the fortunes of the ISD, Delhi rose year by year and decline of the India Stores Department, London set in.

In the field of finance, the Government of Bengal was very roughly treated by the Government of India, both before and after the "Meston Award". The fininancial settlements before the "Meston Award" was based on culculations that the Bengal government had a low level of expenditure. The Meston Committee more or less upheld the same view. The result of these unfortunate decisions were ruinous for Bengal. During the First World War, even a modest proposal for the appointment of a Director of Industries was first turned down by the Government of India on the plea that the Government had not the resources. After the "Meston Award" when the Bengal government was faced with the realities of the creation of a new Department of Industries, the increased grant for the Decca University, and other educational institutions; the Government of Bengal was unable to sanction any large sum. In the Industries Department itself, trained officers had to be retrenched, and its policy considerably narrowed down. In the words of the Government any more cuts in the "reserved" side would have produced chaos and on the "transferred" side would have meant extinction.

In the second part of this chapter, we have studied the activities of the Government of Bengal towards the revival, regeneration and development of small and cottage industries. Till the First World War, the activities of the Government were limited to the surveys of the existing cottage and small industries and preparing monographs. But very few of the recommendations of the industrial surveys were carried out. The primary reason for this was that the Government of India was not prepared to come forward directly to develop industries, it was only prepared to familiarize the people with the technique of western production. During the First World War, the government became aware for the first time that India was vulnerable to foreign powers and was almost totally dependent on Britain for her manufactures. It led to the appointment of the IIC which in its report proposed radical changes, quite different from that of laissez faire that had come before. The Government of India accepted most of the proposals but could not carry it out due to the intervention of the Montagu-Chelmsford reforms of 1919 which transferred the industries department to the provinces.

However, in accordance with the recommendations of the IIC, the Bengal government established its permanent Department of Industries in 1920 with an Advisory Board of Industries to advice the Director on important aspects of industrial development. But due largely to the lack of finance from the very beginning the

Department became a lame duck. It had to cut its projects down and finally decided to concentrate on the development of cottage and small industries. In this respect the Government's main strategy was to demonstrate the improved methods of production and supplying information regarding it. The Government did indeed valuable work in connection with handloom cotton weaving and tanning. The Department also carried out demonstration programmes under the Unemployment Relief Scheme started in 1933. It trained no less than a thousand students in different cottage industries among whom, it was claimed, many started independent factories and many found jobs. But the Department failed to solve the basic problem of marketing, which to the village artisans were of prime importance. In this respect the occasional financial help to the different private organizations and associations were of very little use as they miserably failed to solve the acute problem of rural marketing. Moreover, the village artisans, as they were cut off from the vast market of Calcutta and other large towns were not aware of the changing fashions and fads of the day. What the government needed was probably a big scheme of rural marketing and publicity initiated and carried out under its own auspices rather than bringing in inexperienced organizations and associations to play the part.

On the whole, it can be said that the policy which the Government envisaged for the province was quite satisfactory in view of the severe limitations under which it had to function. Till the end of the First World War, in the presence of fierce foreign competition, lack of government patronage, financial stringency, and the absence of a department of industries; the process of industrialization was very slow and halting. In the 20's many of these restrictions were removed but one of the problems remained—that of financial problem.[187] It was indeed because of this that the Government of Bengal after the Reforms scheme could not carry out a "forward" or "bold" policy. Had the Government of Bengal been free to follow whatever measure it liked without restrictions being imposed on her, the economic history of the day would probably have been quite different.

[187] As late as 1935 the Industries Department of the Government of Bengal wrote that "...its work is limited, not as a matter of policy, but entirely by financial means which can be allocated by Government and placed at its disposal". DOIB: *Annual Administration Report*, 1934-35, p. 1,

3. Supply of Labour to Bengal Industries

Much has been written about the scarcity of labour supply to mills, factories, mines and plantations in India during the twentieth century. Such shortages in the labour supply have been identified with various causes. One of the commonest was the belief that the Indians were determinedly immobile and therefore to get adequate supply of labour they had to be coaxed and humoured all the time.[1] To this cause was also attributed the growing poverty of the people with which they were threatened.[2] But the myth of labour immobility does not stand up to test in view of the large emigration of indentured coolies from India to overseas colonies like Fiji, Malay States, Natal, Trinided, Jamaica, Dutch and British Guiana, Mauritius and Ceylon where labour was attracted by higher wages and better standards of life.[3] Nor was it valid to say as was claimed by Messrs. Bird and Company of Calcutta that Government of India's famine relief work competed with the supply of unskilled labour[4] or the claim that Indian labour was unresponsive to the stimulus of higher pay.[5] The fact was that, as Sir Henry Cotton

[1]*The Statesman*, 17 June, 1909, p. 6; *Ibid.*, 2 February, 1921, p. 4.

[2]*The Friend of Indian and Statesman*, 7 April, 1897, p. 19 See, Letter to the Editor by "A".

[3]The system of indentured coolies for labour outside India dated from 1842, their employment being regulated by an Emigration Act passed in 1883. The annual supply varied greatly, being dependent on the agricultural conditions prevailing in India, but it was officially estimated that some 10,000 emigrants were despatched yearly under average conditions. A considerable number of coolies settled in the countries to which they were sent after the end of their term of indenture, only 4,000 to 5,000 returning to India in any average year (*The Times*, 22 March, 1916, p. 7). The main reason for such large-scale migration was economic and their hopes were more than realized (*IPG*, 28 October, 1905, p. 525). The Government of India, however, by their Defence of India (Consolidation) Rules, 1915 prohibited the emigration, except by licence, of all unskilled labour "for the purpose of or with the intention of labouring for hire" in 1917. *The Statesman*, 30 March, 1921, p. 9.

[4]*The Friend of India and Statesman*, 26 July, 1900, pp. 5 & 19.

[5]*The Statesman*, 26 May, 1920, pp. 3-4.

pointed out, there had been no shortages of labour in India but the supply always exceeded the demand, and whatever difficulty there might have been among capitalists in obtaining labour was due entirely to their own reluctance to pay higher market rate of wages which the increased cost of living had made inevitable.[6] In this regard, the *Times* also pointed out:[7]

> It is often said that, whereas in many countries the supply of labour exceeds the demand, in India the demand exceeds the supply. But this is not strictly accurate. India has an immense mass of potential labour, and the supply is probably more elastic than in countries in a more advanced stage of industrial development. An increase in the rewards offered to labour does not fail to evoke a fairly rapid response, and the rewards offered have not always been the highest that the industry could bear.

In addition to wages, labour supply also to a very great extent depended upon the conditions of work. Such conditions included a host of factors—a more kindly and sympathetic management, better housing, congenial working hours, the healthiness of a place, the supply of good and sufficient filtered water, accessibility to a good bazar, and freedom from interference.

In sections I and II of this chapter we, therefore, propose to study the question of labour supply in the three principal industries of our period; jute, tea and coal in relation to wages and conditions of work and will endeavour to find out how far those factors were conducive to the supply of labour and to what degrees. Section III shows the composition of the labour force in those industries in relation to its origin, caste, age and sex composition.

SECTION I

The purpose of this section is to show that the supply of labour in a particular industry depended to a very great extent on the question of proper remuneration; and the one which offered most

[6] *IPG*, 1 August, 1914, p. 174.
[7] *The Times* (Supplement), 17 November, 1921, p. xi.

attractive terms got all the labour it wanted while others suffered from its deficiency. Labour not unlike capital went to places where it was most profitable to go. For our purpose of analysis, we have selected three major industries; jute mills which employed one-third of the total labour force, the tea gardens of Jalpaiguri and Darjeeling which employed nearly another third, and the coal mines.[8]

In our study, however, we are handicapped from the start by the lack of proper statistical data on the cost of living and wages as no useful record was maintained either by the local government or by the Government of India. The Government of India prepared an All-India index number of prices (almost entirely wholesale prices) for 39 articles from 1861 onwards and that of wholesale index numbers for each of the five ports (Calcutta, Bombay, Karachi, Madras and Rangoon) since July 1914; these index numbers were of little, if any, practical value for our purpose. This is mainly because they included articles which did not enter into the workman's budget, while they excluded the expenditure on house rent. These index numbers, moreover, did not allow for the relative importance of cereals, pulses, other articles of food, fuel and light, clothing, and house rent in the expenditure of the industrial classes. Similarly, in the matter of wages, other than the quinquennial wage census collected by the Agricultural and Industries Department for agricultural workers as also for selected artisans, e.g., blacksmiths and carpenters, we have no useful data.[9] Hence, we have to rely on whatever fragmentary data we have been able to obtain from occasional government reports and proceedings as well as newspapers and journals and on the qualitative evidence we have been able to muster to back up our assertions.

Of the official documents, the most valuable was perhaps that of K.L. Datta, a senior and experienced officer of the Finance Department, who was appointed by the Government of India in 1910 to conduct an enquiry into rise in prices in India. In doing so,

[8] *The Statesman*, 31 July, 1913, p. 5.

[9] That this was so could be understood from the fact that when John Davison, MP, asked in the House of Commons on the 10 March, 1920 with regard to the rate of wages of workers in the principal industries of India, the Secretary of State for India could not give any satisfactory reply and had promised to enquire on the matter which ultimately led to the collection of some fragmentary data. IOR: Vol. 10749, BFP (Commerce), June 1920, No. 35. p. 77.

he also went into evaluating the effect of the rise in prices on labourers, including that of industrial workers; and examined how far wages had increased for the various classes of labour and what the increases in "real" wages had been in comparison with the money wages. From his report we have some data on jute and coal. Datta, however, ignored Darjeeling and Jalpaiguri labour. Moreover, his data are available only up to 1912. In 1960, K. Mukerji also prepared a wage census of jute mill workers. In preparing the average wage rates he depended upon the Government of India's publication, *Prices and Wages in India* and some other sources like that of the *Report on the Royal Commission on Labour*. The working-class cost-of-living index was also constructed from the wholesale and retail prices available from *Prices and Wages in India* and from the *Calcutta Municipal Gazette*. Although we shall be using Mukerji's findings, we need not however be blind to their limitations in view of marked differences in wages existing according to the particular district the factories were located in, i.e., Sealdah group, Titaghur group, Howrah group, Kankinarrah group, Bradreswar group and Budge Budge group.[10] Wages also differed according to the fabrics produced and the type of accommodation provided.[11] Such limitations arise as Mukerji's findings were based upon a slender basis, particularly for the period from 1900 to 1914 where he relied on the wage data of one single jute mill representing the whole jute mill industry in India.[12]

Mukerji's findings could be found in Table 3.1 which represents the average wages of jute mill workers and in Appendix II, Table 1 we can see the average number of persons employed in the industry from 1900 to 1939. From Table 3.1, we can see that the average monthly money wages of jute mill workers was Rs. 12 in the early years of this century. The money wages continued to go up till 1927, whereafter industrial disputes and depression intervened to reduce the money wages of workers. However, it must be stressed that in spite of increases in money wages, it did not mean any increase in real wages until the depression lowered the prices of agricultural foodstuffs sufficiently to allow the workers a real increase in wages. Nevertheless, in comparison with the other two

[10] IOR: Vol. 10749, BFP (Commerce), June 1920, No. 37, pp. 81-100.
[11] *Capital*, 8 August, 1929, p. 306.
[12] A.K. Bagchi, *Private Investment of India* (Cambridge, 1972), p. 123.

large-scale organized industries of Bengal—tea and coal, money wages in jute mills were through out relatively higher. It was about three times what the tea industry workers could earn in the beginning of this century and more than double the amount of an average colliery worker (as we shall see later).

Although such wage differentials between industries narrowed down considerably since the end of the World War I, jute mill labour was better paid than almost any other industry in Bengal. The higher rates of wages prevailing in the jute mill industry were not, however, due entirely to the philanthropic disposition of the employers but was due to two probable reasons. Firstly, jute mill industry was easily the most profitable industry in India and as such it could pay higher rates of wages to their workers than others. Being also the largest organized industry in Bengal, public attention was always focussed on it and hence, employers had to be vigilant against possible charges of exploitation as was so often directed against it by nationalist politicians from within and vested interests from Dundee and elsewhere. Secondly, in comparison with coal or tea, trade union organization (registered or otherwise) in the jute mill industry was stronger. It was the jute mill industry which launched the biggest ever industrial strike till then in Bengal in 1929 on account of certain unfavourable wage alterations by the IJMA and which ultimately led to the victory of the Bengal Jute Workers' Union under the able leadership of its President, Probhabati Das Gupta.[13]

The comparatively better pay offered by the jute mill industry did not fail to get a sufficient response from the labouring classes. From Appendix II, Table 1 we find that the number of workers doubled in the first decade of this century from over one lakh to over two lakh workers. With the exception of 1912, the rise continued unabated till 1925 in which year the industry employed 338, 297 workers or more than three times that of the year 1900-01. The reason for the decline in 1912 was possibly due to the agreement of the mills to work five days a week with some variations with the result that many workers left those mills working only four days a week unless they could obtain work in mills working five days. Similarly, a limited drop which took place in

[13]IOR: Vol. 11866, BFP (Commerce), April 1930, No. 16, 555-589; *RAB*, 1928-29, pp. xxii-xxiv.

the number of workers in the years 1926 and 1927 which was due mainly to the change-over of large number of mills (17 in 1926 alone)

TABLE 3.1

AVERAGE MONTHLY MONEY WAGES AND REAL WAGES IN THE JUTE-TEXTILE INDUSTRY, 1900-1939

Year	*Wages in Rs. per month*	*Working class cost of-living index number for Calcutta 1944=100*	*Index of real wages 1951=100*
	1	*2*	*3*
1900	12.0	33.5	62.3
1901	12.0	34.1	61.2
1902	12.0	34.6	60.3
1903	12.0	30.7	68.0
1904	12.7	32.3	68.4
1905	12.8	34.4	64.7
1906	12.8	38.4	57.9
1907	12.8	41.8	53.2
1908	13.5	48.2	48.7
1909	13.5	43.9	53.6
1910	13.5	40.3	58.3
1911	13.7	37.6	63.3
1912	13.2	41.8	55.0
1913	14.4	45.9	54.6
1914	14.5	45.8	55.1
1915	14.6	47.8	53.0
1916	14.6	48.2	52.7
1917	14.8	45.9	56.0
1918	14.8	49.5	52.0
1919	16.4	61.2	46.9
1920	18.4	65.8	48.7
1921	19.9	64.7	53.6
1922	19.9	63.6	54.4
1923	19.6	62.2	54.8
1924	19.4	62.5	53.9
1925	19.8	57.5	59.8
1926	19.2	54.5	61.2
1927	19.3	55.8	60.2
1928	17.7	55.0	56.0
1929	16.5	54.6	52.5
1930	14.3	48.8	51.0
1931	16.2	42.1	67.0
1932	15.4	43.0	62.3
1933	14.6	41.1	61.7
1934	14.6	37.5	67.7
1935	14.6	38.8	65.4
1936	16.9	37.4	78.6
1937	18.3	38.3	83.0
1938	19.6	39.3	86.8
1939	19.6	39.0	87.5

SOURCE: K. Mukerji, 'Trends in real wages in the Jute Textile Industry from 1900 to 1951', *Artha Vijnana*, Vol. 2, No. 1, March 1960.

from multiple shift system to single shift system.[14] The dramatic drop in 1931 was due to the abolition of the multiple system of shifts by the existing mills with effect from March 1931.[15] During the period from 1926 onwards, we also find the gradual decline in child labour till it was almost extinct by the year 1936. This had, however, nothing to do with the non-availability of children but was due to the policy of the mills to dispence with them on account of its exploitation by time keepers and sirdars, the responsibility for which had to be shouldered by the managers.[16]

The qualitative evidence that we have also shows that labour had been plentiful in the jute mill industry. In 1895, the Bengal National Chamber of Commerce writing on the conditions of labour in mills and factories commented:[17]

> ...though no compulsion is brought to bear on them, they spontaneously seek the employment and invariably perfer it to other occupations of the kind...Labourers from all directions flow into those places for employment, and this, more than anything else, clearly shows that they find their tasks both remunerative and delightful.

Writing a report on trade in jute manufacture in 1900-01, the managing agents of the Shamnagar Jute Factory Company, Limited, also commented that "labour has been plentiful all through the period."[18] A. Wighton, Chairman of the IJMA in his evidence before the Factory Labour Commission (1908) expressed his confidence that if two or three new mills were started they could be staffed without any trouble[19] and in 1926 similar views were forthcoming from the then Chairman of the IJMA that the supply of labour was almost invariably more than the mills could absorb.[20] The complaint that jute mill labour was generally scarce in the hot weather months also does not seem to be absolutely true, as replace-

[14] *AFR*, 1926, p. 4.
[15] *Ibid.*, *1931*, p. 10.
[16] *Ibid.*, *1930*, p. 19; and *RAB*, 1925-26, p. 91.
[17] *The Friend of India and Statesman*, 30 July 1895, p. 19.
[18] IOR : Vol. 6087, BGP (Misc.), November 1901, Nos. 15-16, p. 404.
[19] *The Friend of India and Statesman*, 6 February 1908, p. 9.
[20] *The Statesman*, 4 February 1926, p. 16.

ments could be found not only from Bengal but also from other parts of India.[21]

Among the organized industries of Bengal, tea ranked only second to jute in the number of persons employed. The two principal districts which contained virtually all the tea plantations were Darjeeling and Jalpaiguri. Ever since tea plantations started in Bengal in the 1850's, its growth had been phenomenal (the industury was first started in Bengal as a commercial enterprise in Darjeeling in 1856). In 1870, there were only 56 gardens with 11,000 acres under tea cultivation, employing some 8,000 labourers in Darjeeling district and by 1905, there were 148 tea gardens with an acreage of over 50,000. The number of persons employed in 1901 amounted to 64,000 coolies.[22] The growth of Jalpaiguri gardens was even more spectacular. From 13 gardens with an acreage of 818 in 1876, the total number of gardens rose to 235 in 1901 with an acreage of 76,403 and employing some 90,000 persons.[23]

In the early stages of its development, however, the tea gardens of Bengal did not face much of a difficulty in securing adequate supplies of labour. Darjeeling could always count on the Nepali coolies while Dooars recruited aborigins from the Chota-Nagpur division in addition to its local supplies. As years passed, this equilibrium was however tilted against it by severe competition for labour supply from private and public bodies, including the government. As one correspondent commented regarding Dooars in 1900:[24]

> Good coolies, as any one who keeps his eyes open can see, are yearly becoming more and more difficult to get. Railway and other contractors are competing for the same class of labour as the tea gardens employ, and their competiton is even more seriously affecting the very limited sources of supply, than Assam or other tea districts.

Against this sort of competition, the only alternative was to pay sufficiently attractive wages, which however the tea industry was

[21] B. Foley, *Report on Labour in Bengal* (Calcutta 1906), pp. 15-16.
[22] Bengal District Gazetteers, *Darjeeling* (Calcutta, 1907), pp. 74-75.
[23] Bengal District Gazetteers, *Jalpaiguri* (Allahabad, 1911), pp. 102-03.
[24] *IPG.*, 15 December 1900, pp. 596-97. See, Letter to the Editor by "Share holder".

not willing to offer or as was claimed "the scarcity of money has hitherto acted as something of a set-off to the scarcity of labour."[25] The actual rate of money wages was already low as could be seen from Table 3.2. Even this nominal amount could not be earned

TABLE 3.2

ACTUAL PREVAILING MONTHLY MONEY WAGES IN THE TEA GARDENS OF BENGAL, C. 1900

	Darjeeling *Rs. As.*	*Terai* *Rs. As.*	*Duars* *Rs. As.*
Men	5 8	6 0	6 0
Women	4 8	4 8	4 5

SOURCE : IOR Vol 5851, BGP (Emigration), October 1900, No. 29, p. 187.

by an average coolie as was reported by the Deputy Commissioner of Jalpaiguri, Mr. Forrest. According to him, the average earnings of a male coolie amounted to Rs. 4-14 annas which included over-time payment of Rs. 1-0-3 pies or in other words the mean percentage of his extra earnings on *hajiri* earnings was 26. Similarly, women coolies earned on an average Rs. 3-2-7, which included overtime payment of Rs. 0-8-5. On the other hand, the average earnings of a child was Rs. 1-3-3 and overtime of Rs. 0-2-9, or a total of Rs. 1-6-0.[26] In calculating their average earnings it must also be remembered that they also paid the expenses of their journey from their own pocket. The rate of wages prevailing in 1900 did not undergo any major changes till 1914 when it was resolved in a meeting of the Dooars Planters' Association that "greater liberality in recruiting terms seems called for in view of the extension of free labour in other tea districts, and the consequent increase in competition", and it was left to the individual garden to decide for itself what further inducements it could offer to its labour.[27] But next year it was finally agreed by the Dooars Planters' Association that 4 annas, 3 annas and 1½ annas *ha jiri* should be considered as a maximum which should be exceeded by no garden save by general

[25]*Ibid.*, 9 February 1907, p. 151.
[26]IOR: Vol. 5851, BGP (Emigration), October 1900, Nos. 24-25, p. 190.
[27]*IPG*, 15 August 1914, p. 254.

agreement.[28] The rates fixed in 1915 appear to have remained stationary till 1919. On the other hand, the changes in the wage structure in Darjeeling and Terai, if anything was nil or insignificant. The Darjeeling rate of wages for men which was below that of Dooars and Terai was made at par at Rs. 6.[29]

While money wages in the tea gardens remained almost stationary, the real wages of the coolies had been dropping fast, specially since 1906 owing to the high prices of foodgrains. Rice formerly obtainable at Rs. 3 per maund was now usually as high as Rs. 7, and had even touched the famine rate of Rs. 10.[30] Likewise, *bhoota* price which was about Rs. 12 per maund at thre cheapest season rose to Rs. 2-4 during similar period.[31] Under these conditions it was naturally impossible for a family earning perhaps Rs. 16 to Rs. 20 per month, and consisting of four working members, with say two non-working children, to live on their pay.[32] The result was that due to the inability of the coolies to earn a living wage, there was a great exodus of labour to Nepal, Sikkim and Bhutan to grow crops for which there was a demand in the Indian market. As was rightly pointed out:[33]

> The terms on which work is to be had are no longer tempting enough to bring coolies of the right stamp from Nepal, for the increase in necessary expenditure is such as to leave them no better off on tea gardens than they would be in their own homes.

[28]*Ibid.*, 20 November 1915, p. 549.

[29]Bengal District Gazetteers, *Darjeeling* (Calcutta, 1907) p. 84.

[30]*IPG*, 7 March 1908, p. 309.

[31]*Ibid.*, 26 September 1908, p. 445.

[32]To off-set the effect of price spiral, many of the tea gardens like the Teesta Valley, gave the coolies small plots of *khets* to cultivate which not only gave an increase to their wages but attached them to the soil. But such concessions were severely opposed by a good number of tea gardens which did not have sufficient land to give and as a result of which they already faced additional, difficulty in procuring labour.

[33]See, "A Note of the Crying Evils of Darjeeling Labour and their necessary Remedies", *IPG* 7 March 1908, p. 309. In effect on account of the difficulties of transport the price of foodgrains in Nepal was exceedingly low—as low as 12 annas a maund for rice. It was therefore not unnatural that the Nepalese in their own valleys should have preferred to stay at home. IOR: Vol. 8139, BGP (Emigration), October 1909, No. 30, p. 102.

Theoretically, such a state of affairs—demand for labour on the one hand and scarcity of supply on the other—should have led to higher wage rates, until by the extinction of the least profitable gardens and an increase in the supply of labour, an equilibrium were established. That this did not take place was due to a number of reasons—the imperfect mobility of labour, combination of a formal or informal character among the managers, and finally the "superintendent" system which was almost universal in the Dooars.

The imperfect mobility of labour in the tea estates can be assigned to the facilities offered in individual gardens. Although a certain percentage of coolies moved freely enough from garden to garden, there was a very considerably residium, more especially in the long-established gardens, who did not find it necessary to move. In these gardens one found number of coolies who had become permanent residents. They had been living in the same plot of land for a number of years and had a house superior to those found in the coolies lines, with a well cultivated plot of land of their own on the garden property. Migration to another garden would have entailed the loss of all this, and naturally it took a great deal of inducement for them to move. Another factor which militated against movement was that most of the garden coolies were indebted to their sirdars (who obtained loans from *mahajans* or garden proprietors) and therefore could not go elsewhere till such loans were cleared. Moreover, it was also a common practice in most gardens to provide advances to their coolies on recruitment. To protect the industry against fraud on the part of the indebted labour (and to project gardens from enticement of labour by their neighbours), the various tea district associations also drew up "Labour Rules" which ensured the gardens against the movement of coolies.[34] The monopoly powers claimed by the Darjeeling

[34]A typical "Labour Rules" was that of the Darjeeling Planters' Association, which was as follows:

1. Coolies bolt from garden called 'A' to a garden called 'B'.
2. (a) A writes within three months requesting the coolies to be returned. B must return the coolies. If they refuse to go, B must see that they are not allowed to work on his garden.

(b) A writes within three months, but says that if the coolies are not willing to return, he will accept the money owed by them. B may then turn the coolies out or pay the money owed, whichever he prefers, but he must do one or the other.

Planters' Association made matters worse. This they claimed in view of the fact that since labourers from the plains were unwilling to come to the hills for outdoor work of any kind, Nepal had been the only recruiting ground possible from which they could obtain their labour.[35] But the Nepalese saw it otherwise, as a result of which "the district is seething with dissatisfaction, the coolies at not being allowed to go to the, as promised, El Dorado and the planters are losing their labourers".[36]

When we turn to formal and informal combinations, we find that the wages of coolies were fixed by the Calcutta agency houses in conjunction with the members of planting organizations. Those which did not belong to such organizations usually had an understanding with the neighbouring gardens as to this. Therefore, it was virtually impossible to act alone in the matter of wages even if one wished so. In this regard, the Deputy Commissioner of Jalpaiguri had this to say:[37]

> Managers of neighbouring gardens as a rule tacitly or explicity agree to give a certain rate for a certain quantity of labour, and this is usually adhered to; and of course those gardens which belong to the Duars Tea Association have to conform to the general rates fixed by this body. The greater number of gardens in the Duars do belong to the Association.

Not only did the planters keep the wages low and uniform throughout the tea districts by combined action, they even did not like others (i.e., government) to recruit from within the tea districts and

3. A does not write until more than three months have elapsed. B may pay the money owed or turn out the coolies, whichever he perfers, but he must do one or the other.

4. If more than six months elapse before A writes, B is not bound to assist in any way.

5. Should any case come up which is not covered by the fore-going rules, or should the two parties concerned not be able to agree, the question is to be referred to the Members of the Committee elected in the Sub-District concerned from whose decision there is to be no appeal." See, *IPG*, 8, May 1909, p. 626.

[35] IOR : Vol. 8139, BG*P* (Emigration), October 1909, Nos. 28-29 p. 97.

[36] *The Statesman*, 19. December 1912, pp. 7-8. See, Letter to the Editor by "A Darjeeling Planter".

[37] IOR: Vol. 5851, BGP (Emigration), October 1900, Nos. 21-22. p. 185.

thereby cause labour discontentment as government rates were far better than theirs.[38]

The "superintendent" system was most prevalent in the Duars. A company owing 10 to 20 different gardens, or a combination of private proprietors, appointed a planter of experience and ability on a large salary to superintend a number of gardens and put him in a position of authority over the individual managers. The superintendent was constantly travelling and inspecting the gardens in his charge, he compared the *nirikhs* of one garden with another, and this comparison enabled him to cut down expenses to the lowest possible limit. The system was a great check on the effect of competition for labour among managers, as any attempt on the part of an individual manager to raise the price of labour in his garden was severely scrutinized by the superintendent who required a full explanation of any difference in the *nirikhs* of the various gardens under his superintendence.

After the war, however, some changes in the wage structure seemed called for. Already the coolies were feeling the effect of the rise in prices which war brought about in the daily necessities of life like cloth and salt and which often led to the looting of private and government bazars by garden coolies.[39] To off-set rising costs of living, new scales were introduced in the Duars with effect from 1 January, 1920, enhancing wages to a daily rate of four annas for men and three annas for women.[40] Likewise, in Darjeeling rates were also improved.[41] The wages went up further in the 1920's as the Royal Commission on Labour (1931) found the average monthly earnings in Duars in 1929 to be Rs. 14-4-1 for men, Rs. 10-5-8 for women and Rs. 2-14-5 for children. In Darjeeling the minimum earning of an ordinary worker was about 7 annas 6 pies a day for men, 6 annas for women and 2 annas 9 pies for children.[42] These

[38] See, Minutes of the proceedings of an extraordinary meeting of the Committee of the Darjeeling Planters' Association, *IPG*, 6 June 1914, p. 880.

[39] *IPG*, 9 February 1918, p. 158.

[40] *Ibid.*, 20 December 1919, p. 732.

[41] *The Statesman*, 1 June 1922, p. 15.

[42] *Report of the Royal Commission on Labour in India* (PP XI of 1930-31), p. 1013. After 1920, the *hajiri* rate of payment at least so far as Duars was concerned remained stationary—4 annas for a man and 3 annas for women and children. The increased average earnings was due to the policy of the gardens to decrease the tasks by introducing a system of second and even a third *hajiri*. Percival Griffiths, *The History of the Indian Tea Industry* (London, 1967), p. 310.

later wage increases were probably on account of increased cost of living and more effective competition for labour from all quarters, including Assam which now recruited upon the same free labour sardary system under the control of a semi-official organization with a senior government official as its chairman. The inbreased rate of wages also seemed to have minimised the problem of labour scarcity so often complained of by the planters till the middle of the 1920's.[43]

The growth of the coal industry was no less spectacular than that of tea. From 77 mines in 1891, the number increased to 206 in 1899 and to 458 in 1908.[44] Such large increases in the number of mines obviously required large numbers of additional labour force. But as one of the miners pointed out "there is the greatest difficulty in getting a supply of labour for the collieries...outside the Santals and Banris (sic) we have no available supply of labour..."[45] Such shortage as was complained of by the coal mine owners was confirmed by the Labour Commission of 1896, which among other things, undertook to ascertain the extent of the labour requirements of the coal mining industry, and the reason why, the employers of labour had not succeeded in getting a sufficient supply of it. It attributed labour scarcity, however, to comparative sparseness of population in the mining districts and that of increased competition for labour in the tea gardens of Assam.[46] What it ignored or failed to point out was the question of proper remuneration on which the supply of labour largely hinged.

In no other large-scale organized industry except tea were the wages so depressed as that of coal. Even after considerable wage

[43]In 1924, the Dooars and Terai agency houses also made arrangements under which the task of recruiting was delegated to the Tea Districts Labour Association and the industry placed itself voluntarily under the supervision of a Committee of Control in Calcutta with ample powers to put a stop to anything in the way of recruiting that was not entirely satisfactory (*The Statesman*, March 19, 1925, p. 12). Earlier only a few Dooars concerns used to recruit through this Association. One of the principal deterrents that influenced certain Dooars interests from joining the Association was that they were not willing to pay higher recruiting costs involved in such operations. *The Statesman*, October 12, 1921, p. 19.

[44]*The Friend of India and Statesman*, 18, August 1896, p. 18; *AMR*, 1899, p. 18 and *Ibid.*, *1908*, p. 40.

[45]*The Friend of India and Statesman*, 10, July 1893, p. 15,

[46]*Ibid.*, 18, August 1896, pp. 18-19.

increases in the 1890's[47] the average daily wages of the principal categories of workers in the "Bengal Southern and Western" Circle (which included the districts, among others, Birbhum, Burdwan, Bankura, Hooghly, Howrah and Midnapore) were as follows (see Table 3.3). Women workers earned even less—one anna and a half for

TABLE 3.3

AVERAGE DAILY MONEY WAGES OF CERTAIN CATEGORIES OF COLLIERY WORKERS IN THE YEARS 1900, 1904, 1908 AND 1912

Category of worker	*1900*	*1904*	*1908*	*1912*
	Rs. a. p.	Rs. a. p.	Rs. a. p.	Rs. a. p.
Surface coolie	0 3 3	0 3 6	0 4 0	0 4 6
Miner (underground)	0 8 0	0 8 0	0 9 0	0 10 0
Skilled surface labour	0 7 0	0 7 0	0 8 0	0 8 0
Miner (above ground)	0 6 0	0 7 0	0 7 0	0 7 6

SOURCE : K.L. Datta, *Report on the Enquiry into the Rise of Prices in India*, Vol. III (Calcutta, 1914), pp. 68-69.

surface and two annas for underground work in *hajiri* or daily labour system.[48] From Table 3.3, we find that the underground miners were the highest wage receivers in the coal industry but even their wages compared unfavourably with that of weavers in the jute textile industry and also somewhat lower than spinners, beamers and winders.[49] After the war, although there had been an increase of miners' wages, it was no more than was justified by the rise in the cost of living.[50] In comparison with other colliery workers of India, the average wages of Bengal miners were lower and if a comparison was made with that of miners employed in gold, tin, lead, and salt; it was not half as much (see Table 3.4). It was perhaps more than

[47] *AMR*, 1903, p. 5.
[48] *Ibid.*, *1902*, p. 3.
[49] K.L. Datta, *Report on the Enquiry into the Rise in Prices in India*, Vol. III (Calcutta, 1914), pp. 28-29, 66-67.
[50] *Capital*, 11, July 1929, p. 88.

TABLE 3.4

HOURS WORKED AND WAGES PAID AT A LARGE REPRESENTATIVE MINE IN EACH IMPORTANT MINING FIELD IN BRITISH INDIA, 1923

Mining Field	*Miners*		*Underground Males other than Miners*		*Underground Females*		*Surface Males*		*Surface Females*	
	Hours worked	*Weekly Earnings*	*House worked*	*Weekly Earnings*	*Hours worked*	*Weekly Earnings*	*Hours worked*	*Weekly Earnings*	*Hours worked*	*Weekly Earnings*
Jharia Coalfield (Bihar and Orissa)	40	4-12-0	52	3-12-0	48	2-8-0	60	3-15-0	60	2-7-0
Raniganj (Bengal)	48	3-8-0	48	3-4-0	48	2-0-0	48	2-10-0	48	1-12-0
Giridih (Bihar and Orissa)	48	4-0-0	48	3-4-0	48	2-0-0	48	3-4-0	48	2-0-0
Assam	48	7-8-0	48	6-0-0	—	—	48	4-8-0	48	2-10-0
Punjab	54	7-15-9	60	7-5-9	—	—	60	6-3-9	—	—
Baluchistan	48	7-8-0	48	6-8-0	—	—	54	5-0-0	—	—
Pench Valley (C.P.)	35	4-1-6	50	3-0-0	50	2-8-9	55	2-10-0	55	1-11-0
Bihar and Orissa Mica	56	4-12-0	56	2-14-0	56	1-8-0	56	2-14-0	56	1-8-0
Madras Mica	42	2-3-0	42	1-15-6	42	1-5-0	42	2-3-0	42	1-5-0
C.P. Manganese	48	3-8-0	48	4-8-0	48	2-4-0	48	2-8-0	48	1-8-0
Madras Manganese	56	2-4-0	—	—	—	—	56	3-8-0	56	1-0-0
Burma Ruby	54	6-0-0	54	6-0-0	—	—	54	8-0-0	—	—
Madras Gold	48	10-8-0	48	4-0-0	—	—	48	11-8-0	42	1-5-0
Bihar and Orissa Iron	44	2-8-3	—	—	—	—	44	4-4-0	38	2-0-0
Burma Lead	43	9-0-0	52	18-0-0	—	—	51	9-4-0	—	—
Burma Tin and Wolfram	36	9-4-0	—	—	—	—	42	8-5-0	—	—

SOURCE: *Report of the Chief Inspector of Mines in India, under the Indian Mines Act (VIII of 1901) for the year ending 31st December 1923* (Calcutta, 1924), p.3.

coincidental that the coal and mica mining industries were chiefly controlled by local firms of managing agents, whilst the gold, tin, lead and salt mines were financed and directed by larger corporations with head-quarters in England; in the case of salt, by Government.[51]

The low wages prevailing in the coal mining industry was not condusive to the evolution of a mining class. The majority of the miners regarded mining only as a means of adding to their income, and which work they were prepared to perform if it were in accordance to their own time and convenience. They frequently travelled long distances from their villages, worked off and on for a certain number of hours or days until the required sum of money had been earned and then went away for two or three days. The majority of them were in effect cultivators or agricultural labourers who commonly occupied a plot of land upon which he could raise enough food to provide for his modest wants. The result was that the labour supply in mines varied according to the season. Thus in the Asansol subdivision labour supply in the months of July and August was poor owing to the cultivation of winter rice and hence collieries were severely affected by a shortage of labour in those two months. There was again a good supply from September till the beginning of November, but again, there was an appreciable shortage in the latter part of November and in the two following months owing to the cutting and harvesting of the paddy crop.[52] Not only did labour supply vary according to seasons but also from year to year on the state of the harvest. A good harvest meant a diminished supply of labour, and if there was a failure it meant a temporary over-supply of labour, leading to lack of employment. On this, the Government of Bengal commented:[53]

> In the coal-mining areas...the supply of labour varies inversely with the quantity of the harvests. A good harvest means a bad

[51]*Ibid.*

[52]Apart from cultivators, a substantial portion of its work force deserted mines during cultivating seasons in search of higher wages. On this the Commissioner of Burdwan observed: "In the mining area of the Asansol subdivision of the district of Burdwan the supply of labour was fairly good except during the cultivating season when the labourers generally migrate to other places in search of higher wages." IOR: Vol. 11691, BFP (Commerce), December 1932, No. 43, p. 69.

[53]IOR: Vol. 11866, BFP (Commerce), April 1930, No. 9, p. 21.

labour supply, as there is less need for the villager to seek extra means of sustenance, and a bad harvest the opposite. Famines and bad harvests thus lead to unemployment in the sense that ther is a surplus of labour asking of employment.

Nor were the colliery owners unaware of the factors affecting the supply of colliery labour. But the employers simply choose to ignore the reality and followed a short sighted policy of convenience not the least because wage increases involved a reduction in profits for themselves and their investors. It was also principally because of this reason that the colliery owners time and again opposed the government proposal to put a stop to the employment of women underground.[54]

SECTION II

While wage differentials remained the principal arbiter in differential labour supply, conditions of work also determined the flow of labour into industries. However, it must be emphasised at the beginning that the three industries under study—jute, tea and coal were differently affected and in various degrees by those conditions; sometimes one significant factor playing a larger part than all the rest put together as was in the case of the tea industry.

Not only were the average wages better in the jute textile industry than tea or coal; it was also claimed by J.C. Kydd that the conditions of labour generally were also superior in this industry than in any other in India.[55] The same sentiment was also expressed by D.P. McKenzie, Chairman, IJMA, when he proclaimed at its annual meeting "...we pride ourselves on the fact that in no industry in India is labour better cared for than at our mills...."[56]

Although in the matter of housing the jute mill industry was handicapped due to its urban location which invariably raised the price of land to almost prohibitive rates, several mills took measures from the early parts of this century in constructing "excellent pucka built quarters".[57] The profits which the jute mills gained dur-

[54] *AMR*, 1927, pp. 6-7; and IOR: Vol. 11632, BFB (Commerce), August 1927, No. 14, p. 39.

[55] *The Statesman*, 18 August, 1920, p. 7.

[56] *The Statesman*, 2 February, 1922, p. 18.

[57] C.A. Walsh, Special Inspector of Factories to the Secretary, Government of Bengal, General Department. See. IOR. F. 5. VII. 1904.

ing the First World War were also reflected in the construction of additional quarters of a good sanitary type for the housing of their coolies. In the year 1916-17, it was estimated that dwelling accommodation was provided for 100,000 workers by the larger textile factories as compared to 80,000 in 1915.[58] A.R. Murray reported in 1919 that the mills in four different municipalities up the river alone had also agreed to spend Rs 800,000 on *bustee* improvement in the very near future[59] and in 1929 it was estimated that the jute mill industry accommodated approximately 50 per cent of the total mill operatives.[60] "Practically all the houses are pucca; one or two mills only have kutcha houses, and a few have both pucca and kutcha. Excluding 5 mills, the rents charged for pucca houses range from "rent free" to Re 1 per month, the average being approximately 12 annas per month.[61] But it must, however, be remembered at the same time that the other half of the workers lived in *bustees* in the most unhygenic conditions. "The conservancy, ventilation and general sanitary conditions are, in most instances, extremely bad, though the rents are higher than the companies' quarters".[62]

As regrads sanitation of the place, the jute mills did not have to face particularly unhealthy conditions like that of the tea districts or the collieries which suffered from malaria and cholera respectively in an intense form. Moreover, the frequent visits of the factory inspection staff kept the mill sanitation upto the mark, although surrounding villages were constant sources of outbreaks of epidemics. Furthermore, with increasing prosperity the mill dispensaries were modernized by bringing in surgical instruments, microscopes, diathermy and X-ray apparatus.[63] As a result of these factors, the general mortality rate of the jute mill population appears to have been low.[64]

Working conditions as laid down by the Factories Acts, however, did not go far enough. The Indian Factories Act, 1891 did not limit any working hours for men as a result of which large numbers of operatives were being regularly worked for fifteen hours a

[58]*RAB*, 1916-17, p. 68.
[59]*The Statesman*, 5 February, 1919, pp. 17-18.
[60]*AFR*, 1929, p. 9.
[61]*AFR*, 1929, p. 9.
[62]IOR: Vol. 11938, BFP (Commerce), April 1931, No. 9, p. 43.
[63]*AFR*, 1927, p. 12.
[64]IOR: Vol. 11866, BFP (Commerce), April 1930, No. 12, p. 117.

day or even longer.[65] This caused physical deterioration owing to the severe strain thrown on the constitution of the workers and was probably responsible for the high rate of absenteeism and labour turnover.[66] Similarly, children's health was also probably affected as no special provision was made as to the hours of commencement of work by them, and as such they had to leave their homes daily at 4.30 a.m. in order to commence work in the mills at 5 O'clock whether in the hot or cold season.[67] The Indian Factories Act, 1911 which came into force from July 1912, however, made it illegal to employ children before half-past five or after 7 O'clock in the evening.[68] Likewise, provision was also made whereby no person could work for more than 12 hours in any one day.[69] The Indian Factories (Amendment) Act, 1922 (II of 1922) was a further improvement in the right direction. It made it illegal to employ any child below the age of 12 years and for a period of more than 6 hours in any one day (whereas till then children of 9 years or above were allowed to work as part-timers).[70]

As regards actual working conditions inside the factories, those were generally pleasant. In this regard G.M. Broughton, who had studied the subject, had this to say:[71]

> The workers have, at any rate, on the whole a healthy environment in which to work. The mills, unlike those in Bombay, are built only one storey high. Ventilation and lighting can therefore be more easily arranged. These are not always entirely satisfactory, but are a great improvement on what one finds in Bombay. The jute mills are generally situated in large spaces of open ground. A good drinking water-supply is provided and the sanitary septic tanks that have been installed have been found to be satisfactory.

[65]IOR: Vol. 8416, BGP (Misc.), January 1910, Nos. 81-84, p. 64.

[66]*Report of the Indian Factory Labour Commission*, Vol. I, Report and Appendices (PP 74 of 1908), pp. 636-39. See, Note of dissent by Dr. T.M. Nair.

[67]C.A. Walsh to Secretary, General Department, Government of Bengal. IOR. F. 5. VII. 1904.

[68]See, *Indian Factories Act, 1911* (XII of 1911).

[69]*Ibid*.

[70]*The Indian Factories (Amendment) Act, 1922*, section 2.

[71]G.M. Broughton, *Labour in Indian Industries* (Bombay, 1924). p. 132.

On the other hand, conditions of work in the tea plantations were not always pleasant. The single most predominent factor, apart from wages, which militated against the supply of labour was undoubtedly the question of the sanitation of the place. The tea districts of Darjeeling and Jalpaiguri had been regarded as particularly unhealthy districts due to widespread prevalence of malaria. To the superficial observer the connection between malaria and inadequate labour supply might not be apparent, but planters who had studied the question, and the general body of medical men, were convinced that one of the main reasons for this inadequacy was the intensely malarious nature of the climate in the principal tea growing districts.[72] "Among the permanent residents", observed the Dooars Planters' Association "attacks of malarial fever are frequent; among visitors to the Duars in the malaria season there are but few who can boast that they got scathless away... even if a fatal termination be avoided, result in constitutional debilitation or permanent loss of health".[73] This, from an economical point of view was more important than deaths, for it was the amount and duration of sickness rather than the mortality that tell on the prosperity of a community.[74]

In addition to malaria, there existed other fevers, probably enteric fever, kala-azar, pneumonic and even phthisis for which there had been no specific remedy till then.[75] All these diseases, together with others like dysentry and cholera brought a heavy death toll on the coolies (see Table 3.5) which acted as a deterrent on the minds of others "for no man comes gladly to a district of such evil repute; and this cause must militate against efficiency of administration and industrial development. The prevalence of the feeling of alarm, the widespread notoriety of the Dooars, are facts too

[72]*The Friend of India and Statesman*, 10 December, 1908, p. 5.

[73]Memorandum by the Dooars Planters' Association to His Honour the Lieutenant-Governor of Eastern Bengal and Assam, *IPG*, 19 January, 1907, p. 75.

[74]*Census of India, 1911*, Vol. V, Bengal, Bihar and Orissa and Sikkim, Part I, Report (Calcutta, 1913), p. 70. In some of the gardens, an overwhelming proportion of the coolies were afflicted with malaria (like that of Chalouni, Debpara, Gurjangjhora, Moortee, Toorsa) as could be seen from the statistics of malarial treatment. See, *Annual Report on the Working of the Jalpaiguri Labour Act, 1912, for the year ending 30th June 1915*, Appendix, Table III, pp. vii-viii. The series is henceforth referred to as Jalpaiguri Labour Report.

[75]*Jalpaiguri Labour Report*, 1913-14, p. 3.

patent to demand confirmation".[76] If Dooars mortality rate was high, Darjeeling's was only higher as the hill coolies (Paharias) were more susceptible to diseases than the Madesis (Plains' coolies).[77]

TABLE 3.5

ANNUAL MORTALITY RATE (PER MILLE) IN THE TEA DISTRICTS OF JALPAIGURI AND DARJEELING, 1898 TO 1904

Year	*Provincial death rate*	*Jalpaiguri*	*Darjeeling*
1898	26.57	33.40	39.73
1899	31.21	34.45	40.30
1900	36.63	45.20	49.67
1901	31.04	33.05	39.15
1902	33.43	33.67	36.10
1903	33.33	33.15	39.20
1904	32.45	34.85	39.54

SOURCE: IOR. V/14/76, Twenty Years, Statistics' V.-Sanitation, pp. 2, 28-29.

To improve the health conditions of the Dooars, the Government of Bengal passed the Jalpaiguri Labour Act, 1912 which came into force in April 1913 and under which the civil surgeon of the district was made the Inspector of tea estates. From his annual reports, it appears that public health had gradually improved, especially in the years from 1920 onwards by the appointment of medical personnel in most gardens and by regular treatment of malaria and other fevers. The death rate which had been appreciably higher started to climb downwards.[78]

[76]*IPG*, 19 January, 1907, p. 75.

[77]*Jalpaiguri Labour Report*. 1914-15, p. 3.

[78]This could be seen from the figures of mortality (per mille) noted below:

Year	*Deaths in tea gardens*
1918-19	47.86
1919-20	31.75
1920-21	29.15
1921-22	24.93
1922-23	25.54
1923-24	29.21
1924-25	26.72

See. *Report on the Working of the Jalpaiguri Labour Act for the year ending 30th June 1919* (Calcutta, 1919) and subsequent annual issues till 1924-25.

Working conditions in the tea industry were also not always pleasant. In the rainy months, wet grounds caused ulcers of the feet and legs which resulted in more sickness than malarial fever and an enormous loss of labour.[79] There was also the cruel practice fortunately not general, of keeping labour out all day, when it was excessively wet or cold. This greatly disheartened the coolies and the resultant sickness distressed and frightened them.[80] Nor were the conditions of work within the factories entirely satisfactory. In many cases, the atmosphere was impregnated with tea dust and fluff and the women and children employed therein worked with a cloth tied round their mouths and nostrils. These conditions obtained more in hill factories where windows had to be closed on account of mist and dampness which would otherwise spoil the tea. Such dust, acting as an irritant, probably caused throat and lung diseases.[81] Other factors affecting labour supply were probably the bad state of housing in Jalpaiguri, which were in effect nothing but primitive huts without plinth; and interference in their way of life, i.e., working labour on bazaar day, restricting leave on festivals, etc. The explanation for the desertion of a large numbers of coolies, sometimes in batches just after despatch could perhaps be found in the prevailing conditions of work in the tea estates.

However, of the three industries under study, conditions of work was probably the worst in the case of coal mining industry in Bengal. Unlike in the West where mechanical appliances had been in use in the coal mines, miners in Bengal had to do all their functions physically.[82] This meant a tough day's job for all concerned—

[79]*Jalpaiguri Labour Report*, 1913-14, p. 58.

[80]*IPG*, 21 January, 1905, p. 58.

[81]*AFR*, 1928, p. 7.

[82]Although the question of securing mechanical appliances as a panacea for labour shortage had been raised as early as 1898 at the sixth annual general meeting of the Indian Mining Association, little progress was made in this directiod till the middle of the 1920's (*The Friend of India and Statesman*, 4 August, 1898, p. 20). The principal reason which went against its use had been the high cost of production and this was "not unnatural" as the Chief Inspector of Mines in India commented as "machines in use in England do the work of men earning eight to twelve shillings a day, while in this country they replace men earning only eight annas a day at the most" (*AMR*, 1909, p. 21). Mechanical and electrical equipments, however, began to be installed at mines in the 1920's with increasing labour costs and greater depths at which coal had to be mined. *Capital*, January 9, 1930, p. 51.

men, women and children. The physical conditions of work inside the mines was made worse by inadequate ventilation facilities as a result of which smoke from the kerosene oil filled the galleries to such an extent that it was impossible to see, and the want of sufficient air and the effects of other emanations were sometimes so terrible that a light would not burn and a man felt that he could not long live in such a place.[83] When such were the general conditions inside the mines, it does not need much of an explanation to see why labour shunned collieries unless driven to despair. Failing to attract sufficient local labour, colliery owners even tried to import miners but experiments in this direction also proved a complete failure in view of the new and startling nature of the work.[84] The hard and suffocating environment under which coal cutters had to work was equalled if not surpassed by the rigour of duties performed by their wives, who usually carried the coal to the surface in baskets. In this regard the Chief Inspector of Mines wrote:[85]

> The miner and his wife commonly work together, the man cutting the coal, and the woman carrying it to the surface in baskets. The man will only cut 13 cwts. of coal for the day's work—a very poor result—but the woman will carry the coal to the surface up a road-way 750 feet long with an inclination of 1 in 10. She will thus walk over five miles, and for half the distance carry a load of 80 Ibs., and will have raised 13 cwts. to a height of 75 feet. This is a remarkable day's work for a woman.

Nor were there any consideration for the children (many of whom only seven or eight years of age) who were employed by the hundred as water-balers, gate-boys, etc., and generally in shifts of 12 to 24 hours. Again, there were the miners' children whom their parents took with them underground to help to carry the coal. The appalling physical hardship which these children had to bear at this tender age is best described by a contemporary:[86]

[83] *AMR*, 1899, pp. 6-7.
[84] *The Statesman*, 25 May, 1921, p. 20.
[85] *AMR*, 1905, p. 2.
[86] *The Statesman*, 7 August, 1913, p. 7. See, Letter to the Editor by "A Chota Sahib".

> As for the children, one sees these mites staggering and panting along with a huge basket of coals on their heads, with a flickering oil lamp to see their way with, or worse still, a quarter-candle-power safety lamp. This they have to keep up hour after hour, so long as there is any ready-cut coal at the face... He, the inhuman brute, squats down and rests most of the time, and is apparently quite indifferent to the sufferings of his offspring.

These physical conditions in the mines were equalled by the ill-treatment and oppression which some colliery owners and their understrappers perpetrated on their workers. Such unfair treatment included assaults on labour by those in authority at the collieries; the stopping of pay; and defrauding them of a portion of their earnings.[87] Indeed, some contemporaries ascribed the inadequacy of labour supply in mines to this particular cause. "If the staff treated the men like men", observed one "they would have ample labour on the spot; but when an ignorant Englishman is permitted to stop the pay of a poor miner who has worked for six full days to earn a single rupee, simply because he is a "sahib", it is obvious that abourers (sic) will shun such tyrants".[88]

There was also the lack of proper housing facilities in the mining concerns. The few that existed did not conform to the tastes and desires of the tenants, and in most cases, the almost necessary verandah was not provided.[89] Moreover, the rooms were so small that it was virtually impossible for a worker and his family (consisting probably of 5 or 6 persons) to stay together.

> Small wonder then that the coolies turns his nose in disgust on finding that he and his family... will be crowded into a small dingy hut no bigger than a sentry box, with the usual leaky roof, without windows, and without a door unless the cavity through

[87]See, the presidential speech of J.H. Pattison at the Annual Meeting of the Indian Mining Association, in the *Statesman*, 23 March, 1922, p. 21; *The Friend of Indian and Statesman*, 27 November, 1895, p. 11; and the proceedings of a special general meeting of the Indian Mining Federation, in the *Statesman*, 7 December, 1917, p. 20.

[88]*The Friend of India and Statesman*, 10 February, 1898, p. 11. See, Letter to the Editor by "Capital".

[89]*AMR*, 1906, p. 4.

> which the occupant has to crawl in monkey fashion may be distinguished by that title.[90]

The general standard of housing probably began to improve only in the 1920's owing to the insistence of the Asansol Mines Board of Health for the construction of quarters according to their own standard specifications. Even then a census taken three years later in 1925 showed that only 14 per cent of the houses conformed to the standard plan.[91] Another return covering 104 mines and employing 37,738 labourers showed that collieries provided accommodation to 59 per cent of their labour force.[92]

On the top of all these, there was the great question of public health and sanitation caused by a lack of good supply of filtered water at the mines. Some collieries put down installations to filter the water down from the wells and tanks but their number was few and far between. The vast majority of the workers had no choice but to drink and use water as they got it from the tanks. The result was that in years of drought, the scarcity of water was reflected in outbursts of cholera which killed or drove away the labour from the mines. In 1906, in the case of one of the largest mines, 75 per cent of the workpeople left owing to the cholera, and the desertion in many other cases were most serious. The loss of output was estimated at no less than 200,000 tons of coal.[93] But probably the worst outbreak came in the year 1908 and of which the Chief Inspector of Mines had this to say:[94]

> At the collieries alone nearly 5,000 deaths occurred, and in the adjoining villages, from which it is impossible to obtain any reliable statistics, the loss of life was probably much more. Work was stopped at mines because the labour fled. About the middle of May while inspecting one mine I found only 250 people employed; a few weeks before the number at work was 2,000. This state of things was reflected all over the Jharia coal-field, and the

[90] *The Friend of India and Statesman*, 31 May, 1906, p. 11 See, Letter to the Editor by A.F. Bramley.

[91] *Royal Commission on Labour in India*, Vol. V, Part I, Evidence (London, 1931), p. 181.

[92] IOR: Vol. 11632, BFP (Commerce), May. 1927, No. 6, pp. 17-18.

[93] *AMR*, 1906, p. 16.

[94] *Ibid., 1908*, p. 17.

gruesome sights that were witnessed are not likely soon to be forgotten.

Along with deaths and desertion, alarming rumours about unhealthy conditions of the mining districts were quickly spread over large tracts of recruiting grounds, and thus increasing the difficulty of obtaining labour for the mines enormously. To combat such deadly occurances and to improve the general healthiness of the place, the Asansol Mines Board of Health was constituted under (Bengal) Act II of 1912 and it finally came into active existence in the early part of 1916.[95] With its establishment, things seemed to have improved a great deal.[96]

SECTION III

Looking at the composition of the labour force, the fact which at once strikes the attention of an observer is the relative disproportion of the outsiders to Bangalis in the principal organized industries of the province. According to the Census of 1921, in the jute mill industry, less than a quarter of the labour force were Bengalis. Similarly, in the tea industry, 68,912 were locals against a grand total of 215,611 or the percentage of locals was only 31.96. In the coal mining industry, which was the third largest organized industry of the province, native-born labourers numbered 22,904 out of a total labour force of 40,343 or 56.77 per cent (see Table 3.6). This disproportional participation of the Bengalis in their own province is perplexing in view of the fact that Bengal itself was a heavily populated province. Why was it that the Bengalis shunned industrial life? Was it simply prejudice or there were deeper reasons peculiar to Bengal itself which motivated such an action on the part of the Bengali population?

The aversion of the Bengalis to manual labour is incomprehensible in view of their early association with the jute mill industry. The real reason, therefore, seems to lie in the relative economic prosper-

[95]IOR: Vol. 11866, BFP (Commerce), April 1930, No. 12, p. 125. The Mining Settlement Area covered 413 square miles of territory in the district of Burdwan and included the greater part of the Asansol subdivision.

[96]During the years 1926-27 and 1927-28, the death rate, for example, in the Asansol Mines Board Area were 18.48 and 17.14 per mille respectively. Ibid., p. 137.

ity of the Bengalis in comparison with immigrants from other parts of the country. Early in the century, the development of the jute manufacturing industry gave a considerable encouragement to the cultivators which not only brought an increased return for themselves but also for agricultural labourers.[97] With the possible betterment of the standard of living it was perhaps sufficient to enable him to live from harvest to harvest without adding to his earnings elsewhere. Therefore, to attract Bengali labour, he had to be paid higher wages than other parts of the country.[98] The only exception in Bengal which supplied industrial workers to the metropolitan manufacturing area were Midnapore and, to a smaller extent, Bankura. "The exodus from Midnapore is evidence of the very heavy pressure of the population on the soil in that district. The bulk of emigration from the Bankura district arises from agricultural reasons", observed the Government of Bengal.[99] In addition to the higher standard of living of the Bengali population; the fixity of the tenure and of rent stood in the way of an adjustment between the supply and demand for labour in the province.[100] He could not be expected to sacrifice these rights and go in search of work to industrial centres except in the last extrimity. The recruitment policy followed by some mills was also to a certain extent responsible for the gradual decrease in the percentage of Bengali population in the

[97]As a matter of fact, the higher wages prevalent in the agricultural districts of Eastern Bengal brought large numbers of upcountrymen into Bengal every year. These emigrants especially went to the jute districts of Dacca and Mymensingh and remitted back home substantial sums of money. See IOR: Vol. 7036, BGP (Emigration), August 1905, Nos. 27-28, p. 34. Not only were they employed in the jute fields but also in the paddy fields, railway construction and earth work under railway, in assorting and pucca baling, etc., as unskilled labourers. The precise reason for such employment was that foreign labour was cheap and amenable. IOR: Vol. 10503, BFP (Commerce), May 1919 Nos. 4,6,7, pp. 9, 15-17. On the relative prosperity of the Bengalis also see, *Census of India, 1911*, Vol. V, Bengal, Bihar and Orrisa and Sikkim, Part I, Report (Calcutta, 1913), pp. 168-69; *IIC*, Vol. II, Evidence (PP XVIII of 1919), p. 142; and *Report of the Land Revenue Commission*, Bengal, Vol. I (Alipore, 1940), p. 111.

[98]It was also found that females of Muhammadans, as a rule, and also those of the Bengali Hundus were mostly dependents and not wage earners. Hence, for their maintenance they required still higher wages which the employers were not willing to pay in view of cheaper sources of supply. IOR: Vol. 11938, BFP (Commerce), April 1931, No. 9, pp. 24-25.

[99]IOR: Vol. 11866, BFP (Commerce), April 1930, No.9, p. 23.

[100]*Census of India 1921*, Vol. V, Bengal, Part I (Calcutta, 1923), p. 383.

jute mills.[101] It was alleged that the Bengali was slack in his attendance, had not the application and would not work in the heat.[102] Whether such allegations were justified or not is difficult to prove or disprove due to lack of statistical data but the fact remains that some mills pursued a preferential policy towards men from the United Provinces and Bihar against Bengali population and which in its turn must have had also a discouraging effect on them towards industrial vocation. The poor communication existing in this period between Calcutta and much of the province is also sometimes blamed for the restricted rate of migration to the city by Bengali population.[103]

On the other hand, the explanation for the predominance of the non-Bengali population in the industrial labour force of this province must be sought mainly in their own economic background. The land from whence they came (mainly U.P, Bihar and Orissa and Chota-Nagpur plateau) was relatively less fertile; pressure of population was high; and the cumulative result was large-scale immigration from those areas into Bengal. They were furthermore attracted by the growing economic opportunities which Bengal offered, and which were better known because of the communication system existing between those areas and the metropolitan districts. Bengal received an accession of population from Bihar and Orissa of 1,086,987 in 1911, 1,110,657 in 1921 and 981,326 in 1931. From the United Provinces, she received a net accession of 379,877 in 1911,324,461 in 1921 and 317,449 in 1931. From the Central Provinces she received a net total of 15,179 in 1911, 51,536 in 1921 and 38,898 in 1931. The increasing immigration from the Punjab resulted in a net accession of strength to Bengal of 20,466 in 1931 against 12,654 in 1921, although the figure of 1921 was less than that of 1911 when it reached 14,557.[104] It must not be, however, implied that all those

[101] In the early mills, the workers were mostly Bengalis (Foley, *Report on Labour*, p. 14). In 1902, Bengalis formed 28 per cent of the whole labour force in certain mills (*The Statesman*, 12 March, 1919, p. 20) and in 1921, they formed only 24.07 per cent of the jute mill labour in Bengal.

[102] Foley, *Report on Labour*, p. 15, and the *Friend of India and Statesman*, 6 February, 1908, p. 9. See, evidence of D.K. Wallace before the Factory Labour Commission.

[103] Kenneth MC Pherson, *The Muslim Microcosm: Calcutta, 1918 to 1935* (Wiesbaden, 1974), p. 3.

[104] *Census of India, 1931*, Vol. V. Bengal and Sikkim, Part I Report (Calcutta; 1933), p. 92.

people were engaged in employment in the organized industries. But that a substantial number did could be seen from Table 3.6 which shows the birth-place of skilled and unskilled labourers in the jute, tea and coal industries of Bengal. In the jute mill industry, for example, out of 279,854, 32.25 per cent of the total labour force were Biharis, 23.23 per cent from the United Provinces and 11.43 per cent from Orissa. Among the skilled labour, no less than 74.12 per cent were from outside Bengal, Bihar and the United Provinces contributing 38.8 per cent and 24.35 per cent respectively. In the tea industry, Chota-Nagpur plateau contributed 46.36 per cent of the grand total and "other parts of India" (almost all from Nepal and employed mainly in the Darjeeling district) contributed 18.95 per cent. Chota-Nagpur plateau also supplied a third (31.64 per cent) of all the colliery workers of Bengal, almost all as unskilled labourers.

From the above figures, we find that labourers from Bihar and Orissa and the United Provinces were to be found mainly in the jute mills of Bengal. On the other hand, labour from the Chota-Nagpur plateau flowed towards the coal mines of Burdwan and the tea districts of Darjeeling and Jalpaiguri. The employment policy of industries in general coupled with the socio-economic background of the recruits was mainly responsible for such a spatial distribution. Mr. Foley in his Report on Labour in 1906 mentioned that jute mills would not employ certain classes of labourers and that they had a preference for "Hindustanis from the United Provinces and Bihar. These men have been found more regular, stronger, steadier and more satisfactory generally, so that at present in most of the mills two-thirds of the hands are composed of up-country-men. In many mills it is the custom that the hessian weavers should be up-country Muhammadans".[105] In some jute mills it was also found that a large body of labourers came from a very closely circumscribed area, often a few adjoining villages only, in some up-country district. The recruitment policy of jute mills was again responsible for such agglomeration. A sirdar, whose home was in one of those districts would bring with him a gang of recruits from among the poorer of his co-villagers. He maintained some sort of a control over them while they were employed and generally

[105]B. Foley, *Report on Labour*, p. 14.

TABLE 3.6

PLACE OF ORIGIN OF SKILLED AND UNSKILLED LABOURERS, 1921

Industrial Establishments and class of workers			Birth Place										
			Bengal										
	Males	*Females*	*Dt. of Enumeration*	*Adjoining dts.*	*Other dts.*	*North Bihar*	*South Bihar*	*Chota-Nagpur Plateau*	*Orissa*	*U. P.*	*Madras*	*Others parts of India*	*Out side India*
Collieries (Skilled)	3130	45	2024	118	37	9	238	639	11	74	1	24	—
Collieries (Unskilled)	24702	12466	17671	2973	81	431	2253	12128	18	653	10	950	—
Jute Mills (Skilled)	115121	9100	28434	5972	4484	25088	19597	1031	8762	28030	2062	600	161
Jute Mills (Unskilled)	117652	37981	21429	5287	1782	15947	29607	2358	23218	36988	10786	8226	5
Tea Garden coolies	107940	107671	65327	2784	801	1918	1370	99966	950	761	884	40848	2

SOURCE: *Census of India, 1921*, Vol. V, Bengal, Part I, Report (Culcutta, 1923), pp. 436-37.

looked after them till he retained or sent them away.[106] Tea gardens of Darjeeling, on the other hand, had no choice but to recruit whatever labour they could procure on account of their low wages. Darjeeling Planters' Association had, however, another explanation:[107]

> Experience has proved that labourers from the plains are unwilling to come to the hills for outdoor work of any kind involving manual labour. Under these circumstances, Nepal has been the only recruiting ground possible from which to obtain labourers for the tea estates.

It was precisely because of low wages that Jalpaiguri tea gardens had also no alternative but to import various aborigins from the Chota-Nagpur plateau who had a lower standard of living than other plains people and who by nature also preferred outdoor agricultural life. On the other hand, in spite of their choice for North West Provinces and Oudh labour, the coal mines had to employ aboriginal people from Chota-Nagpur as the imported labour from those places "did not take kindly to the work".[108]

Of the castes or races engaged in the organized industries, Muhammadans formed a substantial number in the jute mill industry. In 1911, the four groups—Sheikhs, Pathans, and Jolahs together formed 32.78 per cent of the labour force.[109] The proportion of Muhammadans, however, seems to have fallen in 1921 when they numbered 80,096 out of 269,854 or 28.62 per cent. Among the skilled workmen, they were more numerous, forming 37.8 per cent in 1921 and were mainly engaged in the weaving and spinning departments (see Table 3.7). Among the numerous Hindu castes, the most important ones in 1911 were the Chamars and Chasi-Kaibarttas who were principally engaged as unskilled labourers. Brahmans formed the third largest group, numbering nearly 9,000

[106] *Census of India, 1921,* Vol. V, Bengal, Part I, Report (Calcutta, 1923) p. 143.

[107] IOR: Vol. 8139, BGP (Emigration), October 1909, Nos. 28-29, p. 97.

[108] *IPG*, 3 March, 1900, p. 189.

[109] The respective numbers in each group were as follows: Sheikhs 41,029; Saiyads 1,824; Pathans 3, 118; and Jolahas 19,745. Together they numbered 65,716 out of a total labour force of 200,446 in 1911. See, *Census of India*, 1911, Vol. V, Bengal, Part II, Tables (*Calcutta*, 1913), pp. 343, 383.

TABLE 3.7

CASTE OR RACE OF INDUSTRIAL WORKERS IN BENGAL, 1921

Caste, Tribe or Race	Coal Mines				Jute Mills			Tea Gardens		
	Skilled		Unskilled		Skilled	Unskilled		Skilled	Unskilled	
	No.	%	No.	%	No.	%	No.	No.	No.	%
Muhammadan	324	10.2	1084	2.9	4617	37.8	33179	21.3	4466	2.07
Brahman	78	2.5	391	1.1	2154	1.7	4614	2.9	1013	.5
Chasi Kaibartta	—	—	22	—	4022	3.2	2219	1.4	64	—
Jali Kaibartta	1	—	66	—	3489	2.9	3978	2.6	16	—
Pod	—	—	4	—	1311	1.1	1094	.7	—	—
Chamar & Muchi	117	3.7	1110	2.9	6941	5.6	21883	14.1	411	.2
Teli	51	1.6	190	.5	3677	2.9	6143	3.9	345	.2
Dosadh	28	.9	381	1.0	1528	1.2	1279	.8	211	.1
Goala	109	3.4	753	2.0	2739	2.2	4454	2.9	2632	1.2
Sadgop	8	—	16	—	674	.5	445	.3	—	—
Napit	17	.5	37	—	957	.8	1377	.9	27	—
Kahar	28	.9	232	.6	1822	1.5	3554	2.3	390	.2
Jugi	1	—	16	—	758	.6	470	.3	950	.4
Tanti	7	—	78	—	4811	3.9	8612	4.4	382	.2
Santal	455	14.3	14243	38.3	22	—	268	.2	9422	4.4
Oraon	—	—	51	—	1	—	63	—	57342	26.6
Munda	4	—	439	1.2	178	.1	457	.3	20149	9.3
Bagdi	36	1.1	179	.5	3546	2.8	4429	2.8	37	—
Bauri	755	23.8	7906	21.3	70	—	329	.2	433	.2
Unspecified	1156	36.4	9952	26.8	38604	31.1	58586	37.7	116989	54.3
Total	3175		37168		124221		155633		215611	

SOURCE: *Census of India, 1921*, Bengal, Vol. V, Part II, Industrial Statistics, pp. 422, 424, 431-32, 438, & 444.

in 1911 but their number had fallen by 1921 to nearly 7,000 and were numerically superseded by such castes as the Jali Kaibarttas, Teli, Goala, Tanti and Bagdi.[110]

Oraons, Santals and Mundas were the three principal *jats* of coolies to be found in the tea gardens of Jalpaiguri. Together they numbered 84,142 out of a total Jalpaiguri labour force of 134,041 or 62.77 per cent in 1911.[111] On the other hand, the three principal Nepalese castes in Darjeeling in that year were the Jimdars (or Khambus), Murmis and Mangars, who accounted for over 20,000 or nearly two-fifths of the workers.[112] The principal caste and race composition of the year 1921 for the tea gardens of Bengal could be seen in Table 3.7. It still shows the predominance of the Oraons who constituted over a quarter of all the tea garden labour of the province. Mundas were a remote second with 9.3 per cent and Santals 4.4. per cent. Although the Table does not give the percentage figures of the principal Nepalese castes, we know (from elsewhere in the Census Report) that Jimdars and Murmis numbered nearly 15,000 and 10,000 respectively in 1921 in the Darjeeling district and Mangars just over 5,000.[113]

In the coal mining industry at Ranigunge, the earliest miners were the Bauris, a native low caste of mixed Hindu origin. They had been cutting coal for several generations "so much so that they are begining to look upon it as their traditional occupation".[114] Although possessed of great skill and mental ability, they were as a rule very thriftless, lazy and found of drinking and were gradually replaced by hardier types of miners, the most attractive of the latter were the aboriginal Santals.[115] They displayed many of the same defects as the Bauris, but were found to be steadier as a result of which they were "preferred to any other kind of labour by the majority of Managers".[116] The preponderance of these two castes could be seen from Table 3.7. Among the unskilled labourers, these two castes

[110]*Ibid.*, p. 383, and Table 3.7 of this Book.

[111]*Census of India, 1911*, Vol. V, Bengal, Bihar and Orissa and Sikkim, Part I, Report, p. 538; and Ibid., *Vol, II*, p. 342.

[112]*Census of India, 1911*, Vol. V, Bengal, Bihar and Orissa and Sikkim, Part I, Report, p. 538.

[113]*Ibid.*, *1921*, Vol. V, Bengal, Part II, Tables, p. 438.

[114]*Ibid.*, Part I, Report, p. 351.

[115]Foley, *Report on Labour*, p. 30.

[116]*Ibid.*

formed 59.59 per cent, while among the skilled workmen they constituted 38.11 per cent in 1921. Among other Hindu castes, mention may be made of the Chamars and Muchis, and Goala. In addition, there was also a small leavening of Muhammadans, locally known as Meahs or Julahas. The proportion of the latter was so small that no communal disturbances had been experienced in the coalfields.[117]

As regards the age and sex composition of the workers, we have much less information; and those statistics that have survived suffer from ambiguity on account of its uneven classification. Thus in the jute mills, there were till 1910-11 four categories of workers—adult males, females, young persons and children. The mode of classification was changed to adult males, females and children from 1912 onwards till 1934 and again from 1935 a fourth category of workers called "adolescents" was introduced. That such changes in the classification procedure bring unnecessary and unexplainable shifts in in the data could be seen from Table 3.8. From this Table, however, the general trend that emerges is clear. The percentage of adult male workers was overwhelming. It had increased from about 67 per cent in 1904-05 to over 86 per cent by 1939. This increase in the adult male popultation of the labour force was undoubtedly at the expense of the children whose share fell very sharply from about 17 per cent in 1904-05 to around 1 per cent or below by the year 1931. The decrease in the amount of child labour could partly be attributed to stringent measures adopted by the Government of Bengal.[118] A partial explanation lay in the raising of the age of children from 9 to 12 years with effect from July, 1922. The proportion of women also seems to have fallen, but only to a limited extent from around 16 per cent to 13 per cent. In this industry, children were mainly employed for the shifting work on spinning frames on account of their height.[119] On the other hand, women were to be found mainly in the preparing, sewing, batching and

[117]*Capital*, 11 July, 1929, p. 88.

[118]For example, till 1908 the Special Inspector of Factories, Bengal was the only person who was solely entrusted with the task of factory inspection not only of Bengal but also of the United Provinces. In between 1908 and 1912, two more factory inspectors and a certifying surgeon was added to the factory inspection staff. IOR: Vol. 9139, BGP (Misc.), July 1913, Nos. 29-34, p. 55.

[119]*AFR*, 1930, p. 19.

TABLE 3.8

AVERAGE DAILY EMPLOYMENT OF MEN, WOMEN AND CHILDREN IN THE JUTE MILL INDUSTRY, 1904-05 TO 1939[120]

Year	*Men%*	*Women%*	*Children%*
1904-05	66.95	16.52	16.52
1905-06	67.61	16.19	16.20
1906-07	67.69	16.56	15.75
1907-08	67.88	16.14	15.98
1908-09	67.94	16.13	15.94
1909-10	66.75	16.03	17.22
1910-11	65.41	15.74	18.85
1912	72.79	15.69	11.52
1913	73.14	15.72	11.14
1914	72.78	15.96	11.26
1915	72.95	16.35	10.70
1916	73.25	16.16	10.59
1917	73.71	15.84	10.45
1918	73.80	15.97	10.23
1919	73.70	15.81	10.50
1920	73.93	15.89	10.17
1921	73.77	15.86	10.37
1922	75.56	15.53	8.91
1923	75.23	15.97	8.80
1924	75.32	16.37	8.31
1925	75.77	16.40	7.83
1926	77.53	16.13	6.35
1927	77.85	16.24	5.91
1928	78.44	16.17	5.39
1929	78.82	16.10	5.09
1930	80.57	15.88	3.55
1931	82.96	15.75	1.29
1932	83.56	15.84	0.60
1933	84.41	15.13	0.46
1934	84.97	14.67	0.36
1935	84.83	14.24	0.92
1936	85.15	14.00	0.84
1937	15.76	13.05	1.18
1938	86.47	13.09	0.44
1939	86.04	13.35	0.61

[120]See, Appendix II, Table 1 for absolute figures and sources.

winding departments as unskilled workers.[121]

The age and sex composition of the tea garden labour are difficult to come by. From the fragmentary reports that we have on the subject, it appears that the male-female proportion on the whole was more evenly balanced than in the jute industry. According to the 1901 Census, out of 154,120 labourers and subordinates engaged in the Jalpaiguri and Darjeeling districts, 72,209 or 48.15 per cent were females, although the proportion of females was slightly higher (50.43 per cent) in the latter.[122] The proportion of female labourers continued to be more in the Darjeeling district according to the next two Census reports but in 1931 they formed only 38.57 per cent.[123] The increased supply of male labourers in the district was probably a reflection of the higher unemployment problem of the period coupled with improved pay and conditions of labour. In the Jalpaiguri district there were 100,532 males and 86,421 females in 1931. The proportion of children under 14 in those two districts were 23.03 in 1911 and 34.83 in 1921. The work of women and children was mainly plucking as they were quicker with their hands than men, but men were employed when there was a rush of leaf and it was important to get it off the bushes quickly.[124]

Unlike in the West, in view of the labour scarcity, the employment of women and children in the mines was considered a neces-

[121]M.I. Balfour, who conducted a survey on women workers in jute mills in 1931-32 found the proportion of female employees in the various departments as follows:

Preparing Department	roughly		53	per cent	
Sewing	,,	,,	18	,,	,,
Batching	,,	,,	12	,,	,,
Winding	,,	,,	8	,,	,,
Spinning	,,	,,	4	,,	,,
Sweeping	,,	,,	3	,,	,,

See, IOR: Vol. 11961, BFP (Commerce), June 1932, No. 6, 98. At the beginning of this century, according to another report, women were only employed in the preparing, sewing and winding departments, See, IOR: Vol. 7861, BGP (Misc.) November 1908, Nos. 143-44, p. 510.

[122]*Census of India, 1901*, Vol. VIA, the Lower Provinces of Bengal and their Feudatories, Part II, the Imperial Tables (Calcutta, 1902), pp. 344-45.

[123]For absolute figures, see, *Census of India, 1911*, Vol. V, Bengal, Part II, Tables (Calcutta, 1913), p. 342; *Ibid.*, *1921*, Vol. V, Bengal, Part II, Tables (Calcutta, 1923), p. 438; and *Ibid.*, *1931*, Vol. V, Bengal and Sikkim, Part II (Calcutta, 1933), pp. 84-85.

[124]Bengal District Gazetteers, *Jalpaiguri* (Allahabad, 1911), p. 106.

sity. The arguments against the prohibition of women and children from the mines is clear from Mr. Grundy's (who was then the Chief Inspector of Mines) remarks:[125]

> Labourers are already scarce, prohibition would lessen the number, and it is probable that the prohibition of females would, at least temporarily, lessen the number of male workers as well as females. The employment in mines of wives and dependents is a great inducement for males taking to this kind of work.

The arguments advanced by Mr. Grundy were propagated no less enthusiastically by the employers and the press. In 1899, when the Government of India introduced its Mining Bill, the clauses restricting the employment of women and children came under fire and those had to be withdrawn.[126] As late as 1925 the Indian Mining Federation opposed the prohibition of employment of women in mines on the ground that under a family system, her labour was only complementary and not additional to the labour of the man and hence its withdrawal from the mines would mean "an entire breakdown of the industry".[127]

Hence, in the Bengal coal mining industry, females and children constituted a significant proportion of the labour force. In 1911, women constituted 28.09 per cent of the entire colliery labour of Bengal, and their proportion among unskilled labour (above 14 years of age) was 51.50 per cent.[128] The number of children below 14 years of age was 3,288 or 8.72 per cent.[129] Due probably to outside pressure, the Government of India by its Indian Mines Act, 1923 (Act IV of 1923) banned the employment of children below the age of 13 with effect from 1 July, 1924.[130] Amidst severe opposition, the Government of India also finally decided that after 1 July, 1929,

[125] *The Friend of India and Statesman*, 26 December, 1894, p. 19.

[126] *Ibid.*, 7 September, 1899, p. 4; and IOR: Vol. 11422, BFP (Commerce), January 1924, No. 10, pp. 13-14.

[127] *The Statesman*, 30 July, 1925, p. 15.

[128] *Census of India, 1911*, Vol. V, Bengal, Part II, Tables (Calcutta, 1913), p. 342.

[129] *Ibid.*

[130] One of the recommendations of the International Labour Conference held in Washington in 1919 and of which India was a participant was that age of children should be raised. *RAB*, 1919-20, p. xi; and *the Statesman*, 5 November, 1919, p. 4.

the percentage of women working underground would annually be reduced by 3 per cent till it was completely eradicated by July, 1939.[131] Under the circumstances, the proportion of females to males fell progressively, but was by no means eliminated as women continued to work on the surface and in the areas not situated beneath the superjacent grounds.[132]

Summary and Conclusion

From the above discussion, it is abundantly clear that the supply of labour in Bengal depended essentially on the question of proper remuneration. Jute mills where average wages were better than either coal or tea had little difficulties in attracting sufficient labour. On the other hand, there were perennial shortage in the coal and tea industries. To earn their living, colliery workers had combined their work with that of agriculture, and, therefore, labour supply in mines was irregular and seasonal. On the other hand, tea gardens which offered the lowest wages had to resort to all kinds of measures akin to serfdom (i.e., Labour Rules, Monopoly powers of employment in Darjeeling, etc.) and in spite of all these, could not command the full complement of coolies. While wage differentials remained the principal arbiter in differential labour supply, conditions of work also affected the supply of labour into industries. In this regard also, conditions on the whole were better in the jute manufacturing industry than either tea or coal. Although in the matter of housing, the jute manufacturing industry failed to

[131] *AMR*, 1929, p. 7.

[132] That it fell considerably could be seen from the figures below which were compiled by the Chief Inspector of Mines in India on a selected day in February of each year:

Year	*Grand total in the register*	*No. of males*	*No. of females*
1934	58,942	48,313 (81.97%)	10,629 (18.03%)
1935	66,066	55,304 (83.71%)	10,762 (16.29%)
1936	72,028	61,371 (85.20%)	10,657 (14.80%)
1937	57,182	49,310 (86.23%)	7,872 (13.77%)
1938	76,199	69,111 (90.70%)	7,088 (9.30%)
1939	77,079	69,647 (90.36%)	7,432 (9.64%)

Figures from the *AMR*, 1933, pp. 96-97 and subsequent annual issues till 1938.

provide residential accommodation to all its employees, the quarters built were superior to those built either by the tea or coal industry. In the matter of sanitation, while collieries suffered from periodic outbursts of cholera and tea districts from that of malarial climate; jute manufacturing industry did not suffer from any particular disadvantages of this nature. Actual working conditions were also superior in this industry than the appalling conditions of dust and filth existing inside the collieries or the exposure that the coolies in plantations had to undergo in the rainy seasons resulting in ulcers of the feet and legs. Cruel practices, including that of physical assualts in some of the collieries on their labour force, must also had its adverse influence on the supply of labour. It was only from about the middle of the 1920's when wages and other conditions of work had substantially improved in the tea and coal industries that the problem of inadequate labour supply seems to have been overcome.

A striking feature in the composition of the industrial workers of Bengal had been its non-Bengali predominance. This was principally due to better economic conditions of the people of this province than those from which labour generally migrated into Bengal industries, i.e., United Provinces, Bihar and Orissa, Nepal and Central Provinces. The flow of labour from those regions into various industrial centres, however, depended on the employment policy of industries and the socio-economic background of the recruits. Of the principal castes or races, Muhammadans could only be found in large numbers in the jute mills while most other workers in the same industry were from the lower Hindu castes like Chamars, Muchis, Chasi-Kaibarttas, Teli, Bagdi, Goala, Jali-Kaibarttas. In the tea industry, aboriginal tribal people constituted the largest segment, the most important of which were the Oraons, Mundas and Santals. Nepalese castes like Jimdars, Murmis and Mangars were in a majority in the Darjeeling tea estates. In the collieries, Bauris and Santals predominated. As regards age and sex composition of the workers in the jute mills the overwhelming proportion of the labour force remained adult males from the beginning, and their proportion increased gradually till it reached 86 per cent of the labour force in 1939. This gradual increase was due to the abolition of child labour from most of the mills. The sex distribution in the tea industry was, however, much more even especially in the Darjeeling gardens. In the collieries, on the other hand, the proportion of adult females which was substantial was brought down to around 10 per cent of the labour force by 1939 by legislative interference on the ground that underground employment of women involved a risk.

4 Problems of Profitability and Capital Supply

Ever since the question of industrial development came to the forefront of public attention, it had been a constant complaint of the Bengali industrialists that sufficient capital was not forthcoming for this purpose. The various committees and commissions set up to investigate the question of industrial development also came out with the same view. Thus Swan in his Report on the industrial development of Bengal pointed to "insufficient capital" as one of the two major bottle-necks for the failure of industries in Bengal.[1] The Indian Industrial Commission also pointed out that money for investment in industries "whether on loans or by way of subscription to capital, is not readily forthcoming".[2] However, it was quick to point out that this was not due to the insufficiency or inaccessibility of money but due to "the opinion which its possessors hold of the industrial propositions put before them".[3] The opinion expressed by the investors, it need not be elaborated, was that industrial investments in general were risky and less attractive than other alternative avenues open to them. This proposition at once raises the question of profitability and security of industrial investments, which we propose to study in Part I of this chapter.

Financial institutions and capital markets play an important role in making available the supply of capital to industries. In Part II, therefore, we shall be analysing the role of the principal financial institutions that existed in Bengal and see how far those were adequately developed to meet the needs of industry. These agencies were the banks, the state and the managing agency system. In Part III, we shall discuss in detail how the various industries raised their fixed capital expenditure and working capital.

[1]J.A.L. Swan, *Report on the Industrial Development of Bengal,* Part I. The other deficiency was inefficient management.

[2]*Report of the IIC* (PP XVII of 1919), p. 214.

[3]*Ibid.*

PART I

Profitability and Security

Private investment essentially depends upon two factors—(*a*) the rate of return and (*b*) security. In this section, an attempt has therefore been made to find out the rates of return in various industries and the security it offered to the investors.

(*a*) *The rate of return*

Most of the data on the rate of return has been compiled and computed from the section on the "Calcutta stock and share list", in *Capital*, a weekly commercial and financial paper published from Calcutta. In the tables, which we would soon be analysing, the rate of return has been shown in two columns—dividends and yields. This has been done to avoid a commonly-held but mistaken idea that a high dividend necessarily meant a high profit. In actual effect, dividends were only a convenient term of reference for values and were expressed on the par value of shares and were thus not a measurement of the shares value except at a time when a company was formed and shares issued. The real value changed with each day's profits and loss. As such it is a misleading idea to assume that a dividend rate of, say 40 per cent in any year was a big profit without a concurrent reference to the percentage return that the dividend represented on the value of the ordinary shareholder's actual property and assets in the business at the beginning of the year. If he was a new shareholder, he had probably to pay for his share chiefly on the basis of that value. On the other hand, if he was one of the original shareholders, the difference between that value and par value represented additional capital that he had put into the business from time to time.

This difference between the dividend rates and yields could be seen from the tables. The yields, which represented the true rate of return have been calculated from the market quotations and par value of ordinary shares and from dividend rates in the following manner :

$$\text{The yield} = \frac{\text{D of SP}}{\text{MQ}} \times \frac{100}{1}$$

where, D=dividends declared SP=share price, and MQ=market quotation.

For our purpose of analysis, we have selected two periods, 1914-19, and 1928-33. The first period coincides with the First World

War when industry was believed to be in general prosperity; and the second period covers two normal years, that of 1928 and 1929, and four years of economic depression, 1930-33 when industry was rather in a low key.

Jute Mill Industry

To find out the rate of return, we have randomly selected 11 jute mills of various sizes for the period 1914-19 (Albion, Alexandra, Alliance, Auckland, Standard, Union, Empire, Fort Gloster, Kinnison, Naihati and Reliance). The smallest of these was the Albion Jute Mills which represented only 340 looms and the biggest one Fort Gloster had 1,350 looms in 1919. The total loomage of these mills varied from 8,263 in 1914 to 8,393 looms in 1919 which represented 21.67 per cent and 21.27 per cent respectively of the total loom capacity of jute mills.[4] For the next period 1928-33, we added three more mills—Birla, Hukumchand and Anglo-India, so that the number of mills analysed stood at 14. Their combined loomage formed 27.15 per cent in 1928 and 26.95 per cent in 1933. The biggest of these mills—Anglo-India had a total loom capacity of 2,561 in 1933 or 4.24 per cent of the entire jute mill loomage.[5]

From Table 4.1, we can form a general idea of the jute industry's profitability. It can be distinctly seen that the return was highest during the war years, reaching a maximum yield of 26.57 and 26.44 per cent in 1918 and 1919 respectively and declining gradually during the economic depression of the 1930's when it reached as low as 3.93 per cent in 1933. On the average, the yield was 12.06 per cent which could be said to be a good rate of return. On the other hand, if we count the average dividend rate, the return on par value was much higher, reaching as high as 57.74 per cent, almost five times the actual yield of shares. In some years the average dividends declared was over 150 per cent as was in 1918

[4]Loomage of individual jute mills could be found in the Calcutta stock and share list vide *Capital*, 2 July, 1914, 2 July, 1915, 7 July, 1916, 6 July, 1917, 28 June, 1918 and 4 July, 1919. The statistics relating to the total loomage of jute mills obtained from *IIYB,1921*, p. 140.

[5]For the loomage of individual jute mills see, Calcutta stock and share list in *Capital*, 5 July, 1928, 4 July, 1929; 3 July, 1930; 2 July, 1931; 7 July, 1932 and 29 June, 1933. Grand total of jute mill loomage obtained from *IIYB*, 1929-30, p. 193; *Ibid*, 1935-36, p. 185.

and 1919 when it amounted to 169.54 and 158.63 per cent respectively. In no year did it fall below 10 per cent.

TABLE 4.1

AVERAGE RATE OF RETURN IN THE JUTE TEXTILE INDUSTRY, 1914-19, 1928-33

Year	*Average dividend*	*Average yield*
1914	7.31	5.07
1915	27.09	11.87
1916	65.00	19.05
1917	71.59	17.73
1918	169.54	26.57
1919	158.63	26.44
1928	72.02	10.95
1929	52.26	9.52
1930	26.19	5.17
1931	14.82	4.20
1932	11.96	4.24
1933	16.50	3.93
Average	57.74	12.06

SOURCES: The average yield has been calculated from the share price and market quotations as shown in the Calcuttta stock and share list, vide, *Capital*, 2 July, 1914, 2 July, 1915; 7 July, 1916; 6 July, 1917; 28 June, 1918 and 4 July, 1919 for the period 1914-19 and 5 July, 1928, 4 July, 1929, 3 July, 1930; 2 July, 1931, 7 July, 1932 and 29 June, 1933 for the period 1928-33. The rate of dividends have been obtained from *Capital*, 3 July, 1920 and 5 July, 1934.

Tea Industry

For the period 1914-19, we have analysed the rate of return of 13 tea companies (Darjeeling Tea and Chin, Gielle, Margaret's Hope, Nagri Farm, Okayti, Banarhat, Baradighi, Birpara, Carron, Choonabhutti, Ellenbarrie, Atul and Gungaram) which together produced on the average 7.5 per cent of the total tea production of Bangal.[6] The tea companies were selected at random from all the

[6]For production of individual tea gardens, see, Calcutta stock and share list, *Capital*, 6 July, 1917 and 3 July, 1920. The statistics relating to total production of Bengal obtained from the *Indian Tea Statistics*, 1930, pp. 20-21.

mjaor tea producing areas, and they varied in size and output greatly. For the next period 1928-33, our list consisted of 16 tea companies which included all the former ones in addition to three more—Lingia, Ambari and New Terai. Their contribution to the total tea production of Bengal varied from 7.42 per cent in 1933 to 8.59 per cent in 1928, the average for the whole period being 7.83 per cent.[7]

The rate of return of the tea companies could be seen from Table 4.2. A glance at the table would show the great variation in the rates of return for the various years. Taking first the dividend rates, we find that in the war years of 1914-19, the tea companies had declared a dividend of no less than 23.19 per cent on the average

TABLE 4.2

AVERAGE RATE OF RETURN IN THE TEA INDUSTRY, 1914-19, 1928-33

Year	*Average dividend per cent*	*Average yield per cent*
1914	22.30	6.48
1915	30.19	12.47
1916	26.15	10.49
1917	19.61	7.74
1918	23.46	10.24
1919	17.45	6.13
1928	26.90	4.86
1929	23.64	5.70
1930	15.21	4.27
1931	7.18	2.97
1932	6.71	2.64
1933	21.50	6.28
Average	20.03	6.92

SOURCES: The average yield has been calculated of from the share price and market quotations obtained from *Capital* in the issues mentioned in Table 4 1. Devidends obtained from *Capital*, 3 July, 1920; 29 July, 1933; and 5 July, 1934.

[7]Production figures of the tea gardens could be found in the Calcutta stock and share list vide *Capital*, 3 July, 1930; 7 July, 1932; 5 July, 1934. The grand total of tea production of Bengal obtained from *Indian Tea Statistics*, 1930, pp. 20-21; and *Ibid*, 1938, p. 17.

but for the next period which also covered a part of the economic depression 1930's, it fell to 16.86 per cent. This difference in the rate of return could also be marked in the actual yield of the shares. The yield of the war years were much higher than the later period. For the first period 1914-19, it averaged 9.42 and for the later period only 4.42 per cent, the average for the two periods being 6.92 per cent.

Coal Industry

The rate of return of 8 joint-stock colliery companies (Bengal, Equitable, Dhemo Main, Aldih, New Beerbhoom, North Damuda, Seebpore and Katras Jherriah) have been calculated for the period 1914-19. But due to lack of statistical data regarding the output of each colliery company, it has not been possible to know their share of output to Bengal's total coal production. For the next period, 1928-33, we analysed the rates of return of 10 colliery companies (the eight mentioned a little earlier and West Jamuria and Khas Kajora) whose total output averaged between 42.03 per

TABLE 4.3

AVERAGE RATE OF RETURN IN THE COAL INDUSTRY, 1914-19, 1928-33

Year	*Average dividend (per cent)*	*Average yield (per cent)*
1914	35.92	6.25
1915	34.13	6.02
1916	39.67	6.98
1917	32.83	4.81
1918	35.17	5.02
1919	42.14	5.70
1928	13.10	3.99
1929	14.57	3.31
1930	17.53	4.09
1931	13.35	8.99
1932	10.13	6.27
1933	6.11	3.23
Average	24.55	5.38

SOURCES: As in Table 4.1.

cent in 1930 to 49.29 per cent in 1933.[8] The rate of return of all those colliery companies could be seen from Table 4.3. For the first period 1914-19, the average dividend rates varied from 32.83 per cent in 1917 to 42.14 per cent in 1919. As regards the actual yield of shares, it varied from 4.81 per cent in 1917 to 6.25 per cent in 1914, the average being 4.79 per cent. Both the average dividend rates and yield would have been as high as 45.81 per cent and 7.19 per cent respectively but for the inclusion of Dhemo Main and North Damuda which did not declare dividends for the entire period.

The next period 1928-33 does not appear to have been economically prosperous years for the coal industry. The average dividend never rose above 17.53 per cent and went as low as 6.11 per cent in 1933. The average for the period being only 12.46 per cent against 36.64 per cent for the earlier period. The yield of the shares were likewise depressing, varying from 3.23 per cent in 1933 to 8.99 per cent in 1931, the average being only 4.98 for the period against 5.79 for 1914-19. If we add the two periods together, the average dividends come to 24.55 per cent and yield to 5.38 per cent only.

In actual effect, the rates of return of the coal industry as a whole was possibly much lower as a result of the existence of hundreds of small private collieries whose individual coal production was insignificant. Since the cost of production of those collieries was relatively higher, they could only survive if the price of coal was remunerative. Such concerns, the Indian Industrial Commission remarked, "are readily closed down if prices fall too low, and are as readily started again when the market improves".[9] But as the coal industry was suffering from severe depression from about the mid-twenties due to the "loss of equilibrium of demand and supply",[10] prices tumbled[11] and a large number of small collieries closed down.[12] The case of small joint-stock colliery

[8]These percentages have been worked out on the basis of production of individual coal companies working in Bengal obtained from the *Indian Coal Statistics*, 1930, pp. 39-42; *Ibid*, 1933, pp. 39-42. Total coal production of Bengal obtained from the *Indian Coal Statistics*, 1933, p. 19.

[9]*Report of the IIC* (PP XVII of 1919), p. 45.

[10]IOR: Vol. 12019, BFP (Commerce), April 1934, No. 4, p. 36.

[11]Prices of coal fell from Rs. 9-2 annas per ton in 1923 to Rs. 3-4 annas in 1932. IOR: Vol. 12019, BFP (Commerce), August 1934, No. 68. p. 251.

[12]Ibid., p. 190.

companies were no better. According to one estimate, out of 114 coal companies in Bengal in May, 1918 while 8 were new companies, 49 made no distribution of dividends at all, 20 distributed 5 per cent and under, 14 distributed between 5 and 10 per cent, 11 between 10 and 20 per cent, 6 between 20 and 30 per cent, 4 distributed between 30 and 40 per cent and 2 distributed over 40 per cent.[13] If this was true, the condition of the smaller joint-stock colliery companies must have been worse during the economic depression which lasted almost throughout the 1930's in Bengal.

Cotton Mill Industry

The average rates of return for the cotton mill industry in Bengal have been calculated from 4 mills (Bengal Luxmi, Bowreah, New Ring and Dunbar) for the period 1914-19 and from 6 mills (the four preceding and Kesoram and Mohini) for the period 1928-33. This limitation is because of the fact that only the shares of these cotton mills from Bengal were quoted by the Calcutta Stock Exchange and as such statistical data regarding the vest are not available. The average rates of return for the cotton mill industry have been calculated for the various years and these could be seen in Table4.4.

TABLE 4.4

AVERAGE RATE OF RETURN IN THE COTTON TEXTILE INDUSTRY, 1914-19, 1928-33

Year	*Average dividend*	*Average yield*
1914	3.25	2.98
1915	7.50	4.96
1916	2.50	1.70
1917	11.00	10.05
1918	17.50	15.90
1919	65.00	31.28
1928	0.50	0.28
1929	3.13	2.60
1930	0.83	1.28
1931	2.50	2 64
1932	1.87	2.02
1933	Nil	Nil
Average	9.63	6.31

SOURCES: As in Table 4.2.

[13] *Capital*, 7 June, 1918, p. 1309.

However, great caution is necessary in interpreting these figures as both the dividend rates and yields were extremely uneven throughout. A glance at the table shows that the most abnormal years were the period 1917 to 1919 when both the dividend rates and yields soared very high. The explanation behind this high profitability of the mills during these years was the abnormal rise in the prices of cotton goods[14] due to the scarcity of tonnage and increase in prices of ocean freights for both piece-goods and yarn.[15] As such, the rates of return of these three years should not be taken to reflect the profitability of the cotton mill industry in Bengal. If these years are omitted, the average dividend of the remaining years come to 2.45 per cent only and yield 2.05 per cent. This rate of return was much less than all the three major industries in Bengal—jute, tea and coal.

Engineering and Metal Industry

For our purpose of analysis, we have examined the rates of return of 9 engineering and metal industries for the period 1928 to

TABLE 4.5

AVERAGE RATE OF RETURN IN THE ENGINEERING AND METAL INDUSTRY, 1928-33

Year	*Average dividend*	*Average yield*
1928	7.77	6.09
1929	6.38	4.28
1930	3.61	3.12
1931	1.78	3.94
1932	2.85	2.91
1933	0.83	0.52
Average	3.87	3.47

SOURCES: Yield calculated with the help of the share price and market quotations as shown in the Calcutta stock and share list, vide *Capital*, 5 July, 1928; 4, July 1929; 3 July, 1930; 2 July, 1931; 7 July, 1932 and 29 June, 1933. Dividends obtained from *Capital*, 2 July, 1931, 29 June, 1933, and 5 July, 1934.

[14]Taking the rate of July, 1914 as 100, the wholesale price of cotton cloths had risen to 261 by the end of December, 1917. IOR: Vol. 10298, BFP (Commerce), March 1918 No. 9, p. 12. The rise for the later periods was still higher. See, IOR: Vol. 10298, BFP (Commerce), November 1918, No. 5, p. 11.

[15]IOR: Vol. 10298, BFP (Commerce), October 1918, No. 2, pp. 3-4.

1933.[16] The earlier period has been omitted as engineering industry in Bengal was only at its infancy during that time. An analysis of Table 4.5 clearly shows that the industry was not doing well during the depression of the 1930's. While in the two years preceding the depression, the average dividend paid was 7.07 per cent and yield 5.18 per cent; it fell sharply from 1930 onwards. The average dividend of the firms in the period 1930-33 was only 2.26 per cent and yield 2.62 per cent. Taking the whole period, the average dividend of the engineering and metal industry in Bengal comes to 3.87 per cent and yield to 3.47 per cent only, which was far less than other major industries of the province.

Apart from these large-scale industries on which statistical data are available, we are absolutely in the dark regarding the profitabi-

TABLE 4.6

PROGRESS OF RICE MILL INDUSTRY IN BENGAL, 1903-39 (WITH INTERVALS IN BETWEEN)

Year	*Numbered registered*	*Total employed*
1903	1	33
1916	35	1,531
1918	40	2,039
1920	80	3,604
1922	101	4,023
1924	132	6,185
1926	235	9,711
1928	286	10,778
1930	315	12,225
1932	—	—
1934	343	13,509
1936	381	16,305
1938	411	18,635
1939	400	18,742

SOURCE: B. P. Adarkar. *Report on Labour Conditions in the Rice Mills* (Delhi, 1946), pp. 28-29.

[16]These were the Bridge and Roof Co. Ltd; Britannia Building and Iron; Britannia Engineering; British India Electric Construction; Burn and Company Ltd; Indian Iron and Steel; Indian Standard Wagon; Hooghly Docking and Howrah Docking.

lity of medium sized and small-scale industries in Bengal. One of the reasons for this was that these being mostly proprietorships or partnerships, their shares were not quoted in the stock exchange nor were these industries well organized in themselves like the larger ones and published no yearly reports or bulletins from which some idea could be had of their economic health. If, however, the establishment of large number of concerns in any one industry over a period of time is a measure of its success and profitability, the rice mill industry of Bengal could be said to be one of those. The industry was first established in Bengal in 1903 with only 33 employees. Over the period it had increased its number, and in 1939 there were 400 rice mills working in Bengal and employing some 18,742 persons on the average. The phenomenal development of rice mills could be accounted for by the large supply of raw materials and a ready local market for finished products in addition to the requirement of small investment of capital on fixed assets.[17]

(*b*) *Security*

To the investor, security of his investment was probably as important as that of rates of return, if not more. It would be quite natural for him to put his money only on those avenues where these was relative security and comparatively high yield. It is for this reason that we would like to find out how secure industrial investments were in Bengal. This we intend to do from Table 4.7, which shows among other things, the total number of factories brought annually under the Indian Factories Act in Bengal and the number of factories struck off annually from the said register on account of their closure for more than two years consecutively or having reduced their number of workers to below twenty.[18] If we add up column (3), we find that from 1901 to 1939 (with the exception of the years 1905 and 1908 for which figures are not available), no less than 2,538 factories were brought under the Act. On the other hand, column (4) shows that during the same period (with the exception of 1905), 1,005 factories were removed from the register, almost in all cases factories so removed were closed down permanently.[19] In other words, taking the whole period, we

[17]DOIB: *Bulletin No. 33, Rice Milling Industry* (Calcutta, 1928), 3, 8-10.

[18]From 1936 onwards, however factories which remained closed for more than twelve months consecutively were removed. See, *AFR*, 1936, p. 2.

[19]*Ibid., 1923*, p. 1; *Ibid., 1924*, p. 1; *Ibid. 1927*, p. 1.

TABLE 4.7

NUMBER OF FACTORIES ANNUALLY REGISTERED AND LIQUIDATED, AND ALSO THE TOTAL NUMBER OF FACTORIES TOGETHER WITH THEIR WORKFORCE IN BENGAL, 1901-1939

Year	*Total No. at work (Perennial and seasonal)*	*No. of workers employed*	*No. brought under the Factories Act*	*Number removed*
	1	2	3	4
1901	253	200,019	38	2
1902	259	205,152	10	4
1903	259	213,014	18	18
1904	267	234,802	34	26
1905	185	234,725	—	—
1906	190	266,205	9	4
1907	204	293,490	16	2
1908	223	301,727	—	3
1909	250	309,680	32	5
1910	256	—	12	6
1911	258	—	8	6
1912	322	320,087	14	12
1913	347	341,820	35	10
1914	361	354,886	20	6
1915	383	378,235	28	6
1916	492	407,318	113	4
1917	522	410,769	36	6
1918	570	439,961	52	4
1919	614	446,541	57	13
1920	680	464,713	82	16
1921	720	465,412	51	11
1922	975	517,080	271	16
1923	1,040	523,635	91	26
1924	1,104	543,123	94	30
1925	1,215	551,342	129	18
1926	1,293	550,923	119	41
1927	1,384	559,759	120	29
1928	1,446	571,079	93	31
1929	1,482	589,860	71	35
1930	1,555	563,877	100	27
1931	1,603	480,439	72	24
1932	1,615	454,007	62	50
1933	1,649	455,018	69	35

	1	*2*	*3*	*4*
1934	1,672	479,388	84	61
1935	1,739	513,199	113	46
1936	1,667	531,235	97	169
1937	1,694	566,458	108	81
1938	1,735	562,791	91	50
1939	1,752	571,539	89	72

SOURCES AND NOTES: *AFR* (tabulated from annual issues). The above mentioned figures do not not include mines as these were subject to the operation of the Indian Mines Act while tea factories were included only from 1922 onwards. See, *The factories Act* (XXV of 1934), Chapter 1, 2 (j) and *AFR*, 1922, Statement II, pp. viii-ix.

find that out of every 100 factories registered in Bengal from 1901 to 1939, no less than 38.54 per cent of the factories were closed down. The number of removal was maximum during the period of the economic depression of the 1930's when a total number of 615 factories were removed against 885 being brought under the Act. From the figures shown above, it is quite clear that industrial ventures were far from steady and secure and were subject to extreme uncertainities.

Apart from vicissitudes of trade cycles, the various reasons which contributed to the unsteadiness of industrial ventures were voluntary winding up according to pre-determined plan, insufficient capital, inefficient or dishonest management, lack of technical knowledge and experience.[20] No less was the want of business morality giving rise to 'adventure companies' which were inevitably closed down within a few years of their inception. Such concerns, according to the Bengal National Chamber of Commerce, not only entailed loss involving crores of rupees to the unwary investors but also "acted as a definite hindrance to the commercial and industrial development of the country through joint-stock enterprie."[21]

Having studied the rates of return and the security of industry, it now remains for us to see its effect upon the investing class of Bengal. From our analysis, we have found that jute, tea and coal

[20] DOIB: *Bulletin No. 83, Report on the Growth of Joint-stock Companies in Bengal* (Alipore, 1939), p. 32.

[21] IOR: Vol. 12077, BFP (Commerce), August 1936, No. 17, p. 290.

industries were the most profitable ones among those. In reality also, we find that these were the most developed industries in the region and their shares were often quoted at a premium in the stock exchange. Moreover, these industries were also considered to be relatively secure and hence the investing public had little hesitation in purchasing their shares and debentures. On the other hand, industries like cotton textile and engineering and metal workers had yet to prove their success. Public naturally felt shy to subscribe in such risky enterprises as these, more so when the rates of return were in general lower than the existing bank rates[22] and where people were traditionally bound to land purchase and in money-lending.

PART II

Institutions of Industrial Finance

The close relationship between financial institutions and industry needs no emphasis. Without a sufficient supply of capital—both long term and working—there could be no industrial development and hence no economic progress. In this section, therefore, we propose to study the principal financial institutions that existed in Bengal and see how far those were adequately developed to meet the needs of industry. These agencies of industrial finance were the (*a*) Banks (*b*) the State and (*c*) Managing Agents.

Banks and Industry

Among the commercial banks, the Presidency Bank of Bengal (amalgamated in 1921 with the other two Presidency Banks of Madras and Bombay to form the Imperial Bank of India) occupied the premier position in the banking system of Bengal. Although formed in accordance with the Presidency Banks Act of 1876, the Bank of Bengal was an ordinary commercial bank with private shareholders and it competed in business with all other banks for dividends. However, since the Government of Bengal, native states and semi-

[22]The Allahabad Bank Ltd gave 4½ per cent on Savings Bank; the Central Bank of India—4 per cent; and the Bengal National Bank Ltd—4½ per cent. See, *Thackers Indian Directory*, 1927, pp. iii-v. The Post office Savings Bank allowed at 3 per cent per annum on all deposits at call. *Ibid.*, p. 16. On fixed deposits for a year, the rates of interest varied from 6 per cent to 8 per cent. Thus the Chittagong Commercial Bank gave 8 per cent and Rangpur and Jessore Loan Offices 6 per cent. *BPBEC*, Vol. II (Evidence, Part I) (Calcutta, 1930), p. 378.

government bodies kept their money with this bank for little or no interest (because of its stature), it could offer terms which were far more advantageous than other Indian banks. But it is only necessary to glance at the records relating to the Bank of Bengal (and later that of the Imperial Bank) to realize how inconsistent their official policy on loans was. Despite its access to cheap capital, directors of the bank pursued an ultra conservative policy making little or no effort to assist new enterprises. The Imperial Bank gave loans to established industries only.[23] No facilities were available at the initial stages of an enterprise, while such facilities as were given were liable to be withdrawn by the bank at any moment.[24] Moreover, the advances made by the bank had always to be secured by stocks of raw and other manufactured goods. Before such loans was granted, the Imperial Bank also needed by their Act, the signatures of at least two persons or firms unconnected with each other to promissory notes.[25] This meant that before industrial concerns (however sound and flourishing they might have been) could get any advance, they had to get a guarantor, which in this particular case invariably was that of managing agents. As a result, smaller and medium sized firms on partnership of proprietory ownership were at a disadvantage regarding loan facilities. Further, in advancing loans, distinctions were made between industries for reasons unexplained. In the case of jute mills, the Imperial Bank did not require a mortgage of the block agains loans but in the case of cotton mills such a mortgage was deemed essential.[26] Another limitation was that loans by law were given for a period of six months only[27] and in 1934 extended this to nine months but made this a procedure applicable only to special cases.[28]

Next in importance were the exchange banks. These banks whose main business were to finance the import and export trade of India in addition to carrying out the ordinary banking business. Numbering 18 in 1929, they financed their foreign trade with Indian money

[23]*ICBEC*, Vol. II (Evidence) (Calcutta, 1931), p. 528.
[24]*Ibid.*
[25]*ICBEC*, Vol. I, Part I, Majority Report (Calcutta, 1931), p. 23.
[26]*Ibid.*, Vol. II (Evidence) (Calcutta, 1931), p. 528.
[27]*The Imperial Bank of India Act, 1920* (XLVII of 1920), Schedule I, Part II.
[28]*The Imperial Bank of India* (*amendment*) *Act, 1934* (III of 1934), Clause 15, Sub-clause 2 & 3.

deposited with them in the course of ordinary banking business but would not give loans for construction of factories however, as they thought it highly improper for such banks to lock up any large part of their funds in such capital expenditure.[29] They would finance industries only with a part of the working capital for short periods on the security of stocks of raw materials or other stores. Even here they kept an eye on the industrialist lest he should turn such capital as they advanced into channels not specified and sink it into capital goods like machinery or buildings. They would also not give capital required to start an enterprise nor would they underwrite industrial concerns as they considered such activities beyond the scope of banks.[30] Their main emphasis was upon giving loans on such securities as would sell easily in the market in case they failed to realize the loans on the due date.

Detailed statistical data relating to joint-stock banks working in Bengal are not available but it is known that such banks other than loan offices were few in number. Although these banks had enough capital to finance industries, they would not take upon themselves the element of risk which was involved in lending for long periods.[31] Their view was that if government would guarantee to help banks to the extent they had invested they might then put their money into industry.[32] Since no such guarantee was available, the joint-stock banks preferred to invest a large part of their deposit in government and "other securities".[33] But it is quite unlikely that "other securities" involved any large amount of industrial investments, especially in the light of the above remarks. However, such banks advanced short-term loans against various kinds of securities, mainly that of stock-exchange shares; discounted bills of exchange and also opened cash credits. But as most of the industries other than the larger ones did not possess attractive securities, they failed to obtain short-term loans more so as many banks insisted upon an additional security.

[29] *IIC*, Vol. II (PP XVIII of 1919), p. 747.

[30] *ICBEC*, Vol. III (Oral Evidence) (Calcutta, 1931), pp. 327-28.

[31] *IIC*, Vol. II (Evidence) (PP XVIII of 1919), p. 132.

[32] *IIC*, Vol. II (Evidence) (PP XVIII of 1919), p. 132.

[33] In the year 1938, for instance, the 43 Indian joint-stock banks having a minimum paid-up capital and reserves of Rs. 5 lakhs and over invested a sum of Rs. 41.71 lakhs in government and other securities. See, *Statistical Tables relating to Banks in India*, 1938 (Delhi, 1941), p. 2.

Numbering more than a thousand in 1935,[34] the loan offices of Bengal were scattered throughout the length and breadth of the province. These were owned by the Bengali-speaking people and their chief business consisted in lending to landholders, mainly on the security of their landed property and other valuables and hence cannot be said to have served the interests of indigenous industries. Moreover, these indigenous banks had small paid-up capital, so small that in 1929 all but 13 offices had less than Rs. 100,000.[35] With the oncoming of the depression in the 1930's, the loan offices were "in a state of suspended animation, hovering between liquidation and the possibility of survival"[36] as the agriculturists to whom they gave long term loans failed to repay their debts and the loan offices on their turn failed to pay back the deposit of their creditors.

At the bottom of the scale were the indigenous bankers. These bankers were of two classes—the *mahajans* and the *shroffs*.[37] The *mahajans* were usually the petty village money-lenders and mainly dealt with small loans to agriculturists. But there were also some Marwari *mahajans* who carried on their money-lending business along with their retail trade, both in Calcutta and in the *mufassal*.[38] On the other hand, the *shroffs* mainly confined their business operations to Calcutta and the main towns. In the City of Calcutta, the principal indigenous banking firms were,[39] Tarachand Ghanshyamdas, Bansidhar Abirchand, Sadasukh Gambhirchand, Hursukhdas Balkissendas, Kanayalal Daga, and Ramkissen Bajri.

Their main business consisted of receiving deposits and dealing on *hundis* or lending money. Besides, they also financed the internal trade of the province and provided the necessary banking facilities to small industries like oil mills, hosiery manufactures, saw mills, rice mills, tanneries and foundries—in all cases secured by the personal securities of the proprietors. The two main indigenous firms of Dacca, Budhunath Sukhlal Poddar and Late Jagabandhu Poddar and his sons, however, did not finance any industry.[40] Their main

[34]*BLCP*, 19 August, 1935, Vol. XLVI, No. 2, pp. 165-66.

[35]M.L. Darling, *Report on the Loan Offices in Bengal*, p. 1. The Report is available in the IOR: Vol. 12077, BFP (Commerce), May 1936, No. 44, pp. 61-74.

[36]*Ibid.*, p. 3.

[37]*BPBEC*, Vol. II (Evidence, Part I), p. 359.

[38]*Ibid.*, p. 384.

[39]*Ibid.*, p. 421.

[40]*BPBEC*, Vol. II, (Evidence, Part I), pp. 410 & 412.

business was financing cloth and hide merchants. As a whole, the main criticism against the *shroffs* was that their services were more readily available to their own class of people than to others and that they failed to come out of this narrow limit, perpetuating their monopolistic hold over the province. They did not pull their resources together to form any joint-stock company but preferred to deal upon an individual level. Moreover, the rate of interest was also high, usually between 15 and 36 per cent per annum.[41]

It is clear from our discussions above that banks in Bengal did not stretch their hands far enough. No money was forthcoming whatsoever for block capital expenditure. Even in the case of short-term borrowings there were numerable obstacles before the industry was in a position to secure advances. The result was that industry was starved for finance. This was quite in contrast to the great commercial banks of Germany and that of France and Japan where closer relationship between industry and banking existed.[42]

State Aid to Industries

In the absence of a well developed banking system and such institutions as Investment Banks, Investment Trusts, Issue Houses, Acceptance Houses, etc., small and medium class industrialists found it extremely difficult to raise sufficient financial resources. To remove this difficulty, the Indian Industrial Commission in its report proposed the setting up of an industrial bank which it considered "would be a potent means of removing these difficulties and of affording help to industrialists".[43] With this aim in view, a committee was supposed to be appointed which would, among other things, consider the question of Government assistance and control. But before the recommendations of the Commission could be carried out, industrial development was made a provincial subject by the Montagu-Chelmsford Reforms of 1919.

The Government of Bengal in its turn tried to handle the question of industrial finance through state aid. But due to financial and

[41] *Ibid.*, Vol. I, Report (Calcutta, 1930), p. 122.

[42] See, Hubert F. Schiffer, *The Modern Japanese Banktng System* (New York, 1962), pp. 17-19; Phra Sarassas, *Money and Banking in Japan* (London, 1940), pp. 256-58; J.H. Clapham, *The Economic Development of France and Germany, 1815-1914* (Cambridge, 1945), p. 390; and Bertrand Gille, 'Banking and Industrialisation in Europe 1730-1914', Carlo M. Cipolla (edited), *The Industrial Revolution, 1700-1914*, Vol. 3 (Harvester Press/Barnes Noble, 1976).

[43] *Report of the IIC* (PP XVII of 1919), p. 217.

practical difficulties in framing the rules, it was not before 1931 that the Bengal State Aid to Industries Act was passed. This Act made provisions for aid to be given in the form of (*a*) loans (*b*) guarantees of cash credit, overdraft or fixed advance with a bank (*c*) taking the shares or debentures (*d*) guarantees of interest on perference shares or debentures (*e*) guarantees of a minimum return on the whole or part of the capital of a joint-stock company (*f*) grants on favourable terms of land, raw materials, firewood, water or any other property of the local government (*g*) payments of a subsidy for conduct of research, purchase of machinery and (*h*) supply of machinery on hire purchase system.[44]

To enquire into the various applications, a Board of Industries was formed in October 1932; and certain rules were framed by the Board in November, 1932. These were sent up to Government for sanction, and these rules, as amended by Government were published in July 1933.[45] However, when these rules came up to the Board, it found grave objections to the procedures which required, for instance, that every application for aid to be advertised in the *Calcutta Gazette* and the daily newpapers and that every application had to be sent up for final acceptance or rejection by Government.[46] The Board was of the opinion that some measure of financial responsibility might reasonably be given to them. In this connection they noted that in the United Provinces the local government had decided with the approval of the legislative council to place a sum of money at the disposal of the Board of Industries of that province for non-recurring grants-in-aid to industries. In the absence of any financial power, the Board was more or less a committee for the disposal of loan petitions. Moreover, the length of time taken by the Government to reconsider the recommendations of the Board, and then the length of time again taken to arrange the preliminaries, mortgage, etc., simply disheartened the applicants. To the end of January, 1935, nearly 27 months after the first sitting of the Board, not a single applicant had received any aid[47] and by 1938-39 only just over two lakhs of rupees had been given

[44]*The Bengal State Aid to Industries Act, 1931* (Bengal Act III of 1931), Section 19.

[45]*BLCP*, 28 March, 1935, Vol. XLV, No. 2, pp. 678-80.

[46]*Ibid.*, p. 680.

[47]*BLCP*, 28 March, 1935, Vol. XLV, No. 2, p. 678.

as financial help (see Table 4.8) and in no case had the sanctioned amount exceeded Rs. 10,000 to an individual or a company.[48]

TABLE 4.8

GRANT OF LOANS UNDER THE STATE AID TO INDUSTRIES ACT IN BENGAL, 1933-34 TO 1938-39 (FIGURES IN RS.)

Year	*No. of applications received*	*Total amount asked for*	*Number sanctioned*	*Total amount sanctioned*
1933-34	9	589,000	3	6,900
1934-35	41	262,000	11	59,600
1935-36	28	129,001	11	41,125
1936-37	55	631,725	20	39,200
1837-38	28	117,675	8	38,600
1938-39	52	321,700	22	31,650

SOURCE: *BISC* (Alipore, 1948), p. 166.

The Government of Bengal had also established a state-assisted industrial bank—the Industrial Credit Syndicate, Limited, to make finances available to small and cottage industries in general. The Syndicate was incorporated on 1 March, 1937 and it commenced business on 6 May, 1937 with a paid-up capital of just over Rs. 150, 000.[49] The general features of the Syndicate were as follows:

(*a*) The Syndicate was registered under the Indian Companies Act for the purpose of making loans to approved applicants to enable them to establish small industries in Bengal.

(*b*) Government was to contribute towards the administrative expenses of the Syndicate a sum of Rs. 20,000 for a period of five years.

(*c*) Government undertook to make good one-half of any loss, up to an amount not exceeding Rs. 10 lakhs, in respect of the first loans issued from public funds. The government similarly accepted the liability for one-half of the loss incurred for subsequent loans which would be paid from the sums set free by those to whom the first loans were sanctioned.

[48]Rs. 10,000 was sanctioned to Visva Bharati, Santiniketon, Birbhum, for running a cotton and silk factory. DOIB: *Annual Report of the Board of Industries, Bengal for the year 1936-37* (Alipore, 1938), p. 3.

[49]BSR: PAI (Industries), November 1940, Nos. 19-20, p. 18.

(*d*) Undertakings established with the assistance of loans were to be systematically inspected under arrangements to be agreed upon between the Government and the Syndicate; such inspection to include the giving of technical advice and guidance.

(*e*) The position of the Syndicate to be reviewed after ten years with a view to a decision whether it should be continued with or without government assistance or be wound up.[50]

Unfortunately, however, the objects for which the Syndicate was established were not being fulfilled. By the close of its financial year ending on 31 March, 1938 the Syndicate had financed nineteen industries only with just over Rs. 90,000 of which Rs. 18,211 (including the amount of interest for the period up to date) remained outstanding.[51] Furthermore, in no case had the loan to a single individual exceeded Rs. 15,000 and in a large number of instances it was just above Rs. 1,000.[52] The failure of the Syndicate to serve its purpose has been attributed by the Bengal Industrial Survey Committee to organizational deficiency.[53]

The Managing Agency System

The system of managing agency in industry is a unique contribution of India to institutional developments. In the absence of Issuing Houses and firms of underwriters, they performed valuable service to the cause of Industrial development, especially in the early years of its existence. Among their manifold finctions the three principal ones were, first, the pioneering of new enterprises, secondly, financing of industries in respect of both fixed and working capital and thirdly, the day to day management of industries. But here we are concerned only with its second function, viz., managing agency system as an institute of industrial finance.

In Bengal, financing of industry by the managing agents was done by the purchase of shares and debentures, by the grant of loans from their own resources and by obtaining loans from banks on their signature to the promissory notes. So far their contribution to the share capital is concerned, it appears, however, that the managing agents did not contribute any significant amount on this score. An analysis of the list of principal shareholders of the 42 jute

[50]*RAB*. 1935-36, p. xxii; and *BISC*, p. 326.
[51]BSR: PAI (Industries), November 1940, Nos. 17-20, pp. 16-18.
[52]BSR: PAI (Industries), November 1940, Nos. 19-20, p. 18.
[53]*BISC*, p. 326.

TABLE 4.9

SHARE OF MANAGING AGENTS TO THE TOTAL CAPITAL ISSUED AND SUBSCRIBED IN CERTAIN TEA COMPANIES, 1927

Name of the Tea Co.	*Total No. of shares*	*No. of shares held by Managing Agents*	*Percentage of total capital held by Managing Agents*
(1) Killcott Tea Company (Messrs. Duncan Bros. & Co., Ltd)	45,000	4,498	10.00
(2) Ranicoherra Tea Company, Ltd (Messrs. Begg, Dunlop & Co., Ltd)	48,000	2,240	6.13
(3) Singell Tea Co., Ltd (Messrs. Hoare Miller & Co., Ltd)	6,250	105	1.68
(4) Jaybirpara (Dooars) Tea Co., Ltd (Messrs. Andrew Yule & Co., Ltd)	35,000	900	2.57

SOURCE: Pat Lovett, *The Mirror of Investment* (Calcutta, 1927), pp. 445-46, 448-49, 468-69. 457-76.

mills contained in the *Mirror of Investment* shows that although they held the largest individual shareholdings in Alliance, Bally, Fort Gloster, Fort William and Hukumchand and the second largest in Gourepore, Khardah, Nuddea and Waverly; their total shareholdings on the whole were not high.[54] Basu who studied this aspect of the managing agents in the case of the Calcutta jute mills also came to the same conclusion.[55] In the case of the tea companies also, the situation was more or less the same. This is borne out from Table 4.9. The table shows that in none of these companies did the managing agents' had a share-capital of more than 10 per cent and in the case of

[54]See, Pat Lovett, *The Mirror of Investment, 1927* (Calcutta, 1927), Section IV, pp. 257-312.

[55]Saroj Kumar Basu, *Industrial Finance in India* (Calcutta, 1939), pp. 168-69.

Singell it was as low as 1.68. It is somewhat unlikely that the general picture would be any different in the case of other industries in Bengal. But it is quite possible that in the initial stages of their floatation, the managing agents might have contributed substantially and then gradually unloaded those during boom periods when prices of shares rose high as was during the World War I.

However, the managing agents did also provide loans to their client-concerns in times of need. This financing they did out of their own private resources or by helping to secure the necessary advances from the banks on the strength of their signatures to the promissory notes. As regards the extent of their self financing, we have no information due to lack of proper statistical data. But it is believed that such advances made by the managing agents in normal times were "considerable".[56] In periods of distress also, like that of the economic depression of the 1930's they saved many companies from definite ruin.[57]

But since the capability of extending such monetary help essentially depended on the financial strength of individual managing agents it was seen that in bad times many agents failed to cope with the requirements of companies under their management. Moreover, in such times the managing agents quite often disregarded the interests of their investors and converted such loans advanced into debentures as a result of which many concerns had passed into their hands causing shareholders to loose all their money.[58]

Another acknowledged defect of the managing agency system was the practice of inter-investment of funds. This meant that the surplus funds, or funds raised on the credit of one company were sometimes invested in other companies under the same managing agent. There was no inherent disadvantage so far as these funds were cautiously invested in sound companies, but in many cases just the opposite was done. Thus, for example, Messrs. Mackinnon Mackenzie, the managing agents of the India Jute Company, Limited, invested no less than Rs. 50,68,500 in Megna Jute Mills Limited, another firm under its own management.[59] But the investment sustained great loss as the shares of Megna considerably depreciated in value.[60] This

[56] *ICBEC*, Vol. I, Part I, Majority Report (Calcutta, 1931), pp. 279-80.
[57] IOR: Vol. 12077, BFP (Commerce), August 1936, No. 17, p. 292.
[58] *ICBEC*, Vol. I, Part I, Majority Report, pp. 279-80.
[59] See, Pat Lovett, *op. cit.*, pp. 285-86, 296-79.
[60] Saroj Kumar Basu, *op. cit.*, pp. 183-84.

questionable method of finance practiced by some managing agents entailed serious unfairness to share-holders in the concerns whose funds were thus transferred and at the same time perpetuated thoroughly insolvent concerns which it would have been better in their own interest and in the interest of the industry as a whole to have closed down.

In conclusion, we can say that although the managing agency system as a financial institution performed valuable services to the cause of industry, it was far from perfect. It tended to disregard the interests of shareholders and was overcautious about their own money. Moreover, their funds being limited, financial support could not always be relied upon especially in times of distress when it was needed most. The importance of the managing agency system in Bengal rather seems to lie in their function as company promoters rather than as financiers.

PART III

Raising of Capital

As we observed earlier, industries required capital mainly for two purposes—for its fixed capital expenditure or block, and working capital to finance floating assets. Block capital was required for newly started industries for fixed assets; such as land, buildings, machinery and other appliances of a durable and permanent character. It was also required for purposes of extensions and replacements. Working capital, on the other hand, was required to defray its current expenses such as the purchase of raw materials and stores, the payment of wages, salaries, rents and rates, expenditure for marketing the manufactured goods and other incidental charges like taxes, repair and maintenances, insurance, etc. The relative proportion between the block and working capital, however, differed greatly from one industry to another. As industrial enterprises become more 'roundabout' or capitalistic, the proportion of its block capital tends to increase in relation to its working capital. It is because of this fact that the modern industrial entrepreneurs of Bengal found it very difficult in most cases to raise sufficient capital to finance their projects.

In Bengal, as a general rule, the fixed capital was raised out of the paid-up capital. Most of this paid-up capital was made up of ordinary shares of various denominations varying in the main from

Rs. 5 to Rs. 500, but usually shares of Rs. 100 were the most common. Debentures were issued only in exceptional cases to raise a part of the working capital or for extensions. An analysis of the capital issued and subscribed by the 47 jute mills having rupee capital[61] shows that 55.67 per cent of the capital issued and subscribed was raised from ordinary shares. Preference shares were issued by no less than 40 jute mills and which formed 27.69 per cent of the capital issued and subscribed. In this particular industry, debentures were also common, and in 1920, no less than 24 jute mills had issued debentures which formed 16.64 per cent of the capital. One of the probable reasons for the relative popularity of debentures in this industry was the nature of its security and the attractive yield of its shares.[62] As to the subscribers, they belonged to both the communities—Indians and British. However, in the absence of statistical data, it is not possible to estimate the relative percentage of shares held by the two communities.[63] But it is generally believed that the Indian share in this industry would be over 60 per cent by the middle of the 1920's.[64] The Indian capitalists in this industry belonged mostly to the Marwari and other upper Indian trading communities in addition to some rulers of princely states.[65]

[61]A short summary of the various component elements of the capital issued and subscribed are as follows:

Total No. of Companies having rupee capital—	47	
Paid-up capital ordinary—	Rs. 10,20,55,305	
Per cent to total capital—	55.67	per cent
Preference shares—	Rs. 5,07,52,950	
Per cent to total capital—	27.69	per cent
Debentures issued—	Rs. 3,05,07,800	
Per cent to total capital—	16.64	per cent

Figures computed from *Capital*, 28 August, 1920, pp. 576-77.

[62]*ICBEC*, Vol. II (Written Evidence), p. 682.

[63]This is so as the shareholders' lists which were deposited in the Office of the Registrar of Companies, Calcutta, have been destoyed because of lack of space; lists are now preserved for ten to fifteen years preceding the current date. Bagchi, *Private Investment*, p. 192.

[64]Pat Lovett, *op. cit.*, p. 245. Some, however, put the total share of the Indians in the jute industry to about 75 per cent. *Capital*, 5 May, 1932, p. 667.

[65]See, List of Principal Shareholders in the Jute Mill Industry, Pat Lovett, *op. cit.*, pp. 257-312.

There was also hardly any problem as regards the working capital of jute mills. Most of the established jute mills had substantial reserve funds accumulated over the years. This money, together with the financial backing of managing agents made them virtually free from all worries as regards their current expenditure. Moreover, as the jute mills could offer good security of stock and other liquid assets built up by the industry, they could always secure short-term borrowings from various joint-stock banks including the Imperial Bank of India.

The initial expenses of tea gardens which was required for the acquisition of land, laying out the garden, construction of buildings and quarters and purchase of machinery was raised from paid-up subscription of shares and from admission fee charged on the shareholders or by the system of providing money on private account by an individual or partnership. Of the capital stock of 62 tea companies of Bengal whose names appear in *Capital*[66] no less than 91.32 per cent of the amount was raised from ordinary share capital. Preference shares amounted to 8.68 per cent of the capital issued and subscribed while not a single tea company issued any debentures. One of the likely reasons for the non-issuance of debentures could perhaps be the failure of the gardens to provide reasonable security in any liquid form so that the money could be realized in case of non-payment of loans or in case of liquidation or it could well be the fact that as temporary loans for tea gardens were easier to secure, the promoters did not wish to issue debentures. The admission fee raised from the shareholders, likewise, was also used for block and was realized along with the application money. This amounted from 20 per cent to the full face value of the share, and was treated as a sort of loan and generally repaid before distribution of any interest.[67] The idea behind this admission fee was not to make the capital of the company too high. As

[66]The details of the capital stock of the 62 tea companies are as follows:

Total Capital stock (including debentures)—	Rs. 2,19,54,454
Paid-up capital ordinary—	Rs. 2,00,49,454
Per cent to total capital—	91.32 per cent
Preference shares—	Rs. 19,05,000
Per cent to total capital—	8.68 per cent

Figures computed from *Capital*, 31 March, 1938, pp. 494-95, 500-01.

[67]*ICBEC*, Vol. II (Written Evidence), p. 658.

regards private gardens, these depended for their block capital on the proprietors and directors themselves, and their close associates, friends and relations. The raising of working capital of tea gardens for the older concerns was no problem. But in the case of new gardens some difficulty was faced in the initial years as it was not till the expiry of at least four years that production commenced and income started flowing. Naturally money had to be borrowed till then, and this was obtained from diverse sources such as managing agents, moneylenders, and other capitalists on the mortgage of the gardens and appurtenances at a rate of interest varying from 9 to 15 per cent.[68] From the fourth year onwards, however, money could be obtained on the hypothecation of crop from the managing agents, various joint-stock banks including the Imperial Bank of India and from firms of tea brokers on the guarantee of managing agents. The rate of interest charged for such finances was from 1 per cent to 2 per cent over the bank rate with a minimum of 7 to 8 per cent. Frequently, when money had to be secured promptly and finances were not available, the promoters and directors had to resort to money-lenders and Marwari merchants in which case the interest rates were higher than those of banks and loan offices, varying from 9 to 25 per cent.[69]

The joint-stock coal companies like that of jute and tea companies raised their initial expenses or block from the paid-up capital of shares and debentures. The average capital stock of the 62 coal companies quoted in *Capital* in 1938 amounted to Rs. 10,60,277.[70]

[68]*ICBEC*, Vol. II, p. 658.

[69]*BPBEC*, Vol. I, Report, p. 120.

[70]The break-down figures of the capital stock of the coal companies are as follows:

Total capital stock of 62 coal companies—	Rs. 6,57,37,185
Paid-up capital Ordinary—	Rs. 5,85,76,385
Percentage to total capital stock—	89.11 per cent
Preference share—	Rs. 38,11,800
Percentage to total capital stock—	5.80 per cent
Debentures—	Rs. 33,49,000
Percentage to total capital stock—	5.09 per cent

Figures computed from *Capital*, 31 March, 1938, pp. 496. All the coal companies were not necessarily working in Bengal but due to the indivisibility of each company's capital which worked in more than one province, we had no alternative but to work out the entire list. We have also excluded from our computation 'East India' which had sterling capital.

Out of this amount, 89.11 per cent was raised from ordinary shares of the value between Rs. 2½ and Rs. 100, shares of Rs. 10 being common. Preference shares were issued by only 7 companies and their aggregate amount formed only 5.80 per cent compared to 27.69 in the case of jute and 8.68 for tea. Debenture issues were also somewhat unpopular in this industry and amounted to Rs. 33,49,000 or 5.09 per cent of the total capital. This unpopularity of debentures indicates that the investing public were very cautious as regards their choice of investments, and preferred only sound debentures like that of jute mills which had an attractive yield, and a very large margin of safety in addition to its property being readily saleable. The working capital or current expenses of colliery companies were usually met from their reserve funds which in some companies ran to over crores of rupees. Thus Bengal Coal Company and Burrakur's reserve and depreciation funds amounted to over two crores of rupees and that of Equitable to one crore.[71]

However, as most of the enterprises in this industry were either proprietory or partnership as distinguished from public limited companies, their resources were slender. In such enterprises the initial expenses, e.g., lump sum considerations payable to the royalty receivers, cost of machinery, rails, tubs and buildings, etc. was found by the owners and partners of the colliery. But as coal mines required constant capital on block to keep the extracting facilities unimpaired, quite occasionally money had to be borrowed from the indigenous moneylenders at a rate of interest varying from 12 to 18 per cent per annum.[72] These enterprises also faced considerable strain on their working capital as it was not uncommon for trade bills to be left unattended for four to six weeks as the banks, according to the Bengal National Chamber of Commerce, were reluctant to handle these, and where cash credits were given, these did not exceed 70 to 80 per cent of the accounts of the bill. This reluctance on the part of the banks, according to them, was on the plea that the drawers were not parties of standing.[73]

Apart from these three large-scale industries—jute, tea and coal which had a number of successes, most other industries found it

[71]*Capital*, 31, March 1938, p. 496.

[72]*ICBEC*, Vol. II (Written Evidence), p. 504. See, 'A Note by the Bengal National Chamber of Commerce on the finance of the Coal Industry'.

[73]*Ibid.*, pp. 504-05.

exceedingly difficult to raise their fixed capital expenditure or block. One of the examples was that of the cotton mill industry in Bengal. According to the Bengal Industrial Survey Committee, the minimum economic size of a cotton mill was 500 looms and 17,500 spindles and a capital of at least Rs. 20 lakhs.[74] Smaller units than this, according to it, were at a disadvantageous position as regards purchase of raw materials and stores, and the sale of finished goods. Moreover, the cost of smaller units were bound to be high as it would not be able to secure the services of a properly trained and well-paid technical staff. Besides, the establishment costs and other expenses were also proportionately higher. An analysis of the Bengal cotton mills in 1937 shows, however, that only seven mills—Bengal Luxmi, Bowreah, Dhakeswari, Dunbar, Kesoram, Mohini, and Sree Radha Krishna had the requisite number of looms and spindles and in the case of Acharya Profullah Chandra, it was working with only 50 looms and Victoria had only spindles.[75] As regards their capital, the picture was more dismal—only Dhakeswari, Kesoram and Sree Radha Krishna had over Rs. 20 lakhs and many were working with a total capital of less than Rs. 5 lakhs as was in the case of Acharya Profullash Chandra, Bangeswari, Bangadaya, East India and New Ring.[76] In many cases, the promoters could not even proceed with their constructional work due to inadequacy of funds.[77] However, it should be stressed that this inadequacy of capital was not due to the poverty of the people but due to the failure of the promoters to create confidence in the minds of the investing public.

The cotton mill industry also faced problems as regards their current expenditure or working capital. This was due to two factors, firstly, in the case of new mills they did not have sufficient reserve funds and secondly, the banks followed a policy of discrimination as regards the granting of loans to cotton mills unlike that of jute or tea. Thus in the case of jute and tea, the principal security was the hypothecation of stocks but in the case of cotton mills, the

[74] *BISC*, p. 40.

[75] DOIB: *Bulletin No. 75, Cotton Mill Industry in Bengal* (Alipore, 1937), pp. 18-19.

[76] *Ibid.*

[77] *BISC*, p. 41.

Imperial Bank, for example, demanded the mortgage of the block also.[78]

The middle-sized industries like that of mills for husking rice, pressing oils, match factories, printing presses, soap and chemical works, etc., faced, however, greater problems as regards their block capital expenditure and working capital than the larger ones. This problem was acute as most of the enterprises in this category were either proprietary or partnership with some joint-stock companies of course.[79] In the case of partnerships or proprietory ownership, capital being limited, many entrepreneurs even failed to raise sufficient initial expenses and hence were unable to start their concerns or were working with an uneconomic plant. Thus Babu M. N. Ghose, manager and proprietor of Jessore Comb, Button, and Mat Manufacturing Company, Limited, testified before the Indian Industrial Commission that with great difficulty he was able to raise a sum of Rs. 25,000 only in three years when he required a sum of Rs. 50,000.[80] Again, Babu Bhupendra Nath Basu, who claimed to possess considerable experience in raising capital for indigenous concerns including the Bengal Hosiery, Limited, the Bengal Luxmi Cotton Mill, Limited, found great difficulty in raising capital for those concerns as people in general preferred to invest in alternative channels like land.[81] Only the more enlightened among the masses, claimed Babu Rajani Kanto Bhattacharjee, supported financially the cause of industrial development. They included, according to him, people following the learned professions, i.e., legal and medical; service holders, government pensioners; and the educated middle class gentlemen.[82]

The problem of raising working capital for these industries, be it proprietary or partnership or joint-stock company was by far the worst. The IIC in its report remarked :[83]

> . . .the difficulties in obtaining loans and financial assistance which are felt—and of the reality of these we have plenty of evidence—

[78]*ICBEC*, Vol. III, p. 385.
[79]*BPBEC*, Vol. I, Report, p. 121.
[80]*IIC*, Vol. II (PP XVIII of 1919), p. 88.
[81]*IIC*, Vol. II (PP XVIII of 1919), p. 141.
[82]*Ibid.*, p. 71.
[83]*Report of the IIC* (PP XVII of 1919), p. 213.

> are experienced chiefly in the case of the middle-class industrialists, who are unable to offer the security of approved names, or of stocks which could be readily disposed of. Indians suffer in a special degree from this deficiency; for, among other reasons, they find in difficult to satisfy a bank, whose directorate and superior staff are entirely European, as to their financial position.

In the virtual absence of existing banking facilities, owners had to borrow money from indigenous moneylenders who charged much higher rates of interest than the banks would have allowed. Usually the rates of interest in such cases varied from 15 to 36 per cent per annum and was obtained by the personal security of the owners.[84] S. N. Dutt of P. N. Dutt and Company (mechanical engineers and bucket manufacturers), however, complained of some Marwari money-lenders who sometimes charged even higher rates of interest than 36 per cent per annum.[85]

This difficulty in raising adequate capital for middle-sized industries led to the liquidation of many industrial enterprises and in many others cut the margin of profits and unduly delayed the dividend-earning stage. The Industries Department of Bengal, for example, reported in 1922 the closure of a steel factory which had just started manufacturing high grade steel on account of financial difficulties.[86] The Boolbool Soap Factory of Dacca could not be worked for want of funds and the Indian Soap Factory of Nimtoli could not even purchase the necessary plant for want of capital.[87] In another case, "a company" was floated with a share capital of rupees four lakhs. Of these, Rs. 85,000 was subscribed and only Rs. 65,000 was paid-up. The plant was purchased but from the outset it had to borrow money "at high rates of interest". Thus the enterprise was hampered from the onset, and it had never been able to free itself from the incubus of debt.[88]

Conclusion

From our study, we find that industries which were long established and relatively profitable had little difficulty in attracting public

[84] *BPBEC*, Vol. I, Report, p. 122.
[85] *IIC*, Vol. II (PP XVIII of 1919), p. 61.
[86] DOIB: *Annual Administration Report*, 1922, Appendix I, p. 1.
[87] IOR: Vol. 9780, India Commerce and Industry Proceedings (Industries). 1915, No. 12, p. 38.
[88] J.A.L. Swan, *Report on the Industrial Development of Bengal*, Part I, p.1.

deposits irrespective of their ownership. Thus jute, tea and the larger coal companies which were earning between 5 per cent and 12 per cent had little difficulty in tapping their resources. Not only that, their shares were also selling at a premium at the stock exchange. On the other hand, the rest of the industries including the cotton mill industry and engineering industry which were paying only 2 to 4 per cent annually found it extremely hard to attract sufficient capital.

In the absence of adequate public subscription and specialized financial institutions, banks were expected to play an important role by advancing liberally to the cause of industry. But these followed a very conservative approach as regards their grant to industries. They advanced but only short-term loans, that too after satisfying themselves regarding their numerable laid down procedures. Naturally, the demand for state aid became urgent. But the Bengal government, probably because of its financial plight followed a delaying tactics and till 1938-39 sanctioned no more than just over Rs. 2 lakhs by way of state aid to industries. The state assisted Industrial Credit Syndicate which was established in 1937 also failed to serve its purpose to any great extent. However, in the absence of properly developed financial institutions, the managing agency system played an important role. Although their share in the fixed capital expenditure could not be said to be substantial, it is probable that they contributed quite liberally in times of economic distress by providing short-term loans. But being mostly partnerships their funds were also limited. In short, it can be said that there was no well developed financial institution to meet the needs of industry. The result of such absence was disastrous—many companies in need of money had to be closed down and many more could not even see the light of day.

5 Supply of Industrial Entrepreneurship in Bengal

Whether manufacturing industry is likely to establish in a country or not depends essentially on the presence or absence of a special factor—the spirit of enterprise.[1] British officials and others in India alleged that this factor of enterprise (the pre-requisites of which are energy, venturesomeness, the faculty of organization and good economic judgement[2]) was more or less absent amongst the natives of Bengal. This absence of enterprise, they further alleged was accountable for the limited degree of industrial development of the region, and the main cause of Bengal's economic ills. Thus in 1890, Collin in his *Report on the Existing Arts and Industries in Bengal* accused the capitalists of Bengal for "wanting in enterprise" and failing to introduce "new manufactures".[3] The same theme was voiced later on by *Capital*, which in 1929 commented that "the Bengalee, owing to his lack of interest in, and lack of proficiency for, industrial pursuits" was wholly responsible for his poverty.[4] Still later, a member of the Bengal Legislative Assembly commented that the "inhabitants of this territory is not industrially inclined" as they were in the past[5] and in 1942 another member finds that "the indurtrial instinct has become dead" and calls upon the Government to infuse that spirit in them.[6] But before we censure the inhabitants of Bengal for their disinterest in industrial pursuits, we ought to question ourselves: Were the natives best fitted by education and training to be industrial leaders? Were there sufficient opportunities and inducements for them to venture into industrial fields? In this chapter, therefore, an attempt will be made to find out the answers to the above queries and in the light of it a general study will be made to

[1]*Capital*, 19, April 1928, p. 844.
[2]*Ibid.*
[3]E.W. Collin, *Report on the Existing Arts and Industries*, p. 14.
[4]*Capital*, 21, February 1929, p. 389.
[5]*Bengal Legislative Assembly Debates*, 13, March 1940, Vol. LVI. No. 4, p. 43.
[6]*BLCP*, 27, February 1942, First Session, No. 9, pp. 259-60.

bring out the share of native participation in various major organized industries in Bengal.

According to Alfred Chatterton, the qualities of an industrial leader could be acquired in three stages, firstly, he could acquire scientific and technical knowledge, then practical experience in technology and finally, business experience and aptitude in handling affairs.[7] To him the Education Department provided the first though science colleges and technical institutions; the second could be obtained only in workshops, mills and factories; while the third was usually picked up in a haphazard way in the office of industrial concerns or was obtained, in the course of conducting business.[8]

In Bengal, the opportunities for industrial and technical education were very limited.[9] The Government of Bengal emphasised its importance in the education curricula, but could not decide whether the desired objects could best be attained by the creation of a separate branch of the Education Service or otherwise.[10] It took no less than ten years before a decision was taken to transfer the control of technical and industrial education to the Department of Industries in 1920.[11] The net result was that technical education was treated until then as branch of general education and was entrusted to the regular educational authorities. They naturally concentrated on the literary type of education in which they possessed expert knowledge, and even when they realized the importance of technical education, their complete unfamiliarity with the needs and methods of industry made it impossible for them to guide the

[7]Sir Alfred Chatterton was Director of Industries, Madras, 1908; Director of Industries and Commerce, Mysore, 1913-16; and a Member of the Indian Industrial Commission, 1916-18.

[8]Sir A. Chatterton, 'Indian Industries', *Capital*, 13, February 1929, p. 327.

[9]The words "technical education" and "industrial education" were loosely used. What was described as a technical school in one province would be classified as an industrial school in another; and even within the same province there were cases of a "technical school" in one district giving precisely the same training as an "industrial school" in another. See, A.G. Clow, *The State and Industry* (Calcutta, 1928), p. 45. However, in general, "technical education" meant "the instruction necessary for the foreman and the manager, the employer or the director; while "industrial education" was that which was necessary for the artisan. See, J.G. Cumming, *Technical and Industrial Instruction in Bengal, 1888-1908*, Part I of Special Report, p. 1.

[10]*BLCP*, 21, March 1908, Vol. XL. p. 21.

[11]DOIB: *Annual Administration Report*, 1920, p. 4.

movement along practical lines. Even after the transfer of the technical and industrial schools, most of these institutes remained merely preliminary training grounds for various professions like blacksmithy and carpentry. After passing out from these schools, their pupils were engaged in coal jobs as they did not even get the proper training to make a saleable article except for the roughest products of the village artisans.[12]

At the advanced level, as late as 1939, there existed only two engineering colleges in Bengal, the Bengal Engineering College, Sibpur[13] and the Ahsanullah School of Engineering, Dacca where only overseer and sub-overseer courses existed.[14] Higher engineering training leading to B.E. degree confined to the Sibpur College only, where a course of four years was followed by one year's practical training.[15] In the year 1938-39, in all thirty-four students had obtained B.E. degree in Civil, Electrical and Mechanical Engineering.[16] In the field of commerce, advanced education was imparted by the two universities of Calcutta and Dacca and by a Calcutta College. Science education was more common but arts was the rule.

[12]DOIB: *Annual Administration Report*, 1926, p. 4.

[13]The Sibpur College was originally built in Calautta in 1856 by the Public Works Department with the object of training engineers and subordinates for their service. In 1864, it was placed under the Education Department and transferred to the Presidency College. In 1880, it was removed to the site of the old Bishop's College at Sibpur in Howrah district. See, J.G. Cumming, *Technical and Industrial Instruction*, p. 11. The Bengal Engineering College, Sibpur opened its degree course in Civil Engineering in 1880 and that of Mechanical Engineering in 1932. In addition to these, it had Diploma courses in Mechanical and Electrical Engineering (opened in 1922) and that of Associated Course in Mechanical Engineering (opened in 1923). See, 'Memorandum furnishing particulars of Industrial Development, etc., in the Presidency of Bengal from 1928 to 1934' in IOR: Vol. 12049, BRP (Industries), September 1935, No. 22, p. 43. The three senior technical schools, Kanchrapara (in connection with the Eastern Bengal Railway); Calcutta Technical School (in connection with the Calcutta firms); and Kharagpur Technical School (in connection with Bengal Nagpur Railway) acted as its feeder institutions. DOIB: *Annual Administration Report*, 1926, p. 25.

[14]*Ibid., 1928-29*, p. 29. Sub-overseer classes were also held at Pabna, Rajshahi and Burdwan.

[15]*Progress of Education in Bengal, 1917-18 to 1921-22*; *Sixth Quinquennial Review* (Calcutta, 1923), p. 50.

[16]*Report on Public Instruction in Bengal, 1938-39* (Alipur, 1940), p. 17.

In the year 1932-33, for instance, 661 students had obtained science degrees in Bengal as against over 2,100 in arts.[17]

TABLE 5.1

TECHNICAL TRAINING INSTITUTES IN BENGAL ON 1 JANUARY, 1935

Type of institute	*Total No.*
A. Engineering Colleges	2
B. Other specialized institutions of collegiate rank	2
C. Technical and industrial schools owned by Government	49
D. Technical and Industrial schools owned by local bodies	5
E. Private-aided technical and industrial schools	76

SOURCE: IOR: 12049, BRP (Industries), September 1935, No.22, p. 42.

But the opportunites of paractical training were again virtually nil. Even the students of the Bengal Engineering College, Sibpur found very little encouragement from the employers of industries. It was the opinion of the large employers that the Sibpur youth usually forgot quickly all that he learnt in the workshop and that he was afraid of hard work and hence not suitable for a responsible position.[18] Even the railways where they provided training facilities, followed a policy of discrimination. Thus in 1920, out of seventy-two Indians who applied to the Kanchrapara Railway Workshop, only one was admitted as against three Anglo-Indians out of eight who applied.[19] The workshop's pay-scales were also unfair to

[17]*Ibid., 1932-33* (Alipore, 1934), p. 80. The totals are that of B.A./B.Sc. (Pass and Honours) and M.A./M.Sc.

[18]J.G. Cumming, *Review of the Industrial position and prospects in Bengal in 1908, Part II of Special Report*, p. 5.

[19]*BLCP*, 19, December 1921, Vol. VI, pp. 23-24. The fact that seventy-two students applied for higher technical training demonstrates that the Bengalis were not unwilling to acquire technical knowledge. The same trend was marked at the Dacca School of Engineering, as a result of which seats had to be increased. *Quinquennial Report of the Ahsanullah School of Engineering, Dacca for the years 1922-23 to 1926-27* Calcutta, 1927), p. 2. This was contrary to popular belief that the natives were prejudiced towards such education. See, for example, DOIB: *Annual Administration Report*, 1926, p. 36.

the Indians (see Table 5.2). The Bengal Nagpur Railway Technical School was even more discriminatory. Until 1931, only Anglo-Indian apprentices (thirty-five annually) were trained to the complete exclusion of all others.[20] In that year it was decided to admit Indians as well and the number of intakes was increased to seventy, thirty-five for Anglo-Indians and thirty-five for Indians.[21]

TABBE 5.2

STIPENDS OF ANGLO-INDIAN AND INDIAN APPRENTICS (PER MONTH IN RUPEES) IN THE KANCHRAPARA RAILWAY WORKSHIP IN THE YEAR 1921

Year	*For Anglo-Indian apprentices*	*For Indian (1st Class) apprentices*
1st	50	22
2nd	60	26
3rd	70	30
4th	80	34
5th	100	38
6th	120	N.A.

SOURCE: *BLCP*, December 19, 1921, Vol. VI, pp. 23-25. See, answer to Question No. 11 (h) of Rai Radha Charan Pal Bahadur by the Hon'ble the Nawab Saiyid Ali Chaudhuri Khan Bahadur.

The third ground of management training was in the offices of industrial concerns and in the course of conducting business. This practical training was of vital importance to the world-be-entrepreneur as it acquainted him with the real facts of life, helped him to form sound business judgement and at the same time gave him the chance to learn the processes at first hand. But the opportunity for a Bengali to acquire such practical training in the offices of industrial concerns was very restricted indeed. In fact, a constant theme against the employment of foreign capital in Bengal had been this: that they provided little or no chance to the natives and preferred their own men as directors and supervisors.[22] However, the Bengalis

[20] *Eight Quinquennial Review on the Progress of Education in Bengal for the years 1927-1932* (Calcutta, 1933), p. 117.

[21] *Ibid.*

[22] *Repott of the External Capital Committee* (Simla, 1925), p. 8; *The Bengalee*, 27, May 1932, p. 7; and also, *Report of the Indian Fiscal Commission*, 1921-22 (PP II of 1922, Second Session), p. 488.

could gain some practical experience from conducting trade and commerce, as the Marwari and some other up-country communities like the Bhatias, and the Chettiars, the Borahs and the Parsis did, and who became highly successful in this line. But the Bengalis would not go into trade and commerce after their initial failure in the first half of the nineteenth century.[23]

With limited technical knowledge, commercial education, and practical experience the native entrepreneurs had to face modern technology. They had not only to acquire efficient technological equipment, secure adequate financial resources, develop a market for their products and maintain an efficient organization, but also to devise new products to meet anticipated consumer demands and maintain good public relations. They had to take decisions as regards the size of the plant and install new machinery when those become obsolete, calculate costs of production, and not the least surmount innumerable obstacles as regards supply of skilled labour power plant, transportation links and repair shops. Naturally from the beginning the native entrepreneurs were at a disadvantage compared to their European counterparts who had years of practical experience and knowledge in the field in addition to technical knowledge.

The smallness of the market also somewhat restricted the entry of entrepreneurs into industries. Since most of the people living in the villages of Bengal were economically poor, their demands were also limited, perhaps restricted to such consumer products as cotton goods, salt and kerosene—the products for which there were no substitutes. In cases, where substitutes existed as in the case of sugar, ordinary people used those. Thus *gur* and *rub* were in general use as a sweetening ingredient in food and drink, and Bengal manufactured these (from the juice of the date palm) to an estimated extent of 100,000 tons a year.[24] The

[23]The reasons for the failure of the Bengalis in these lines were that of fraud and deception and over-speculation on the part of their British partners. Thereafter, according to N.K. Sinha, "Bengali businessmen practically withdrew from any adventurous business activity in Calcutta. . .a distrust among European Business became a part of Bengali thinking". See, N.K. Sinha, 'Indian Business Enterprise: Its Failure in Calcutta (1800-1848)', in *Bengal Past and Present* Diamond Jubilee Number, 1967), p. 120.

[24]*Report of the Indian Tariff Board on the Sugar Industry* (Delhi, 1938), p. 24.

price of *gur* was also lower than sugar.[25] The demands for other such simpler products like socks, mufflers, combs, buttons, stationery and the like were also small. Many such factories producing these goods, like Messrs. Dass and Co. of Calcutta (producers of office stationery), the Calcutta Knitting and Woollen Mills Company, Limited (producers of socks and stockings, mufflers, etc.,) or that of Calcutta Box Manufacturing Company had to obtain the help of the Department of Industries to secure markets for them.[26]

A handful of foreigners, some twenty-thousand, living in Bengal[27] plus a few more high ranking government officials and businessmen and the bigger landlords possibly required such advanced industrial products as electric fans, bulbs, knives and forks, radios, bicycles and cars and the like. The establishment of manufacturing industries for such goods were economically unsound or only limited as the Government of India, various local governments, and other administrative bodies used to purchase their products by indent to the India Office (till the end of the 1920's). Such industries as cement also suffered from the lack of sufficient demand, and the few that were established in India, competed with each other for the market.[28]

The only way by which entrepreneurs could be made interested in industrial development was by raising the demand of their products. This could be done in two ways; either factory costs were lowered, an extraordinarily difficult proposition in view of the already low level of wages and taxation, or the purchasing power of the rural community had to be increased. Lord Linlithgow very rightly pointed out:[29]

> The prosperity of India rests, in the main, upon her agriculture, and her commerce and industry are both founded on that same

[25]In 1935-36, *gur* price per maund in Calcutta was Rs. 4-5 annas (*Ibid.*, p. 52) and the price of sugar per maund (wholesale) Rs. 9. See. *Ibid.*, *Vol, II*, p. 290.

[26]DOIB: *Annual Administration Report*, 1923, p. 15; and *Ibid.*, *1924*, pp. 12-13.

[27]Out of this number, over two-thirds lived in Calcutta. See, IOR: Vol. 12019, BFP (Appointments Department), July 1934, No. 14, p. 19.

[28]Economic and Overseas Department Collections, File No. L/E/9/999. Thus the demand for cement in India was approximately 390,000 tons per annum around 1925, whereas Indian factories were already producing 550,000 tons per annum, and this figure could rise to 600,000 tons.

[29]Lord Linlithgow, in *Capital*, 19, April 1928, p. 842.

> agriculture. Raise the purchasing power of the ryot, and in one stroke you will give to industry, to manufacture, and to commerce in general an extended field for service and so far legitimate gain.

But how to raise the real income of the *ryot* was the problem which to this day remains unsolved.

In addition to the difficulties as regards markets, technical knowledge and practical experience, the path of the native entrepreneurs was made more difficult by a policy of free trade which the Government of India followed till 1923, and from internal competition from other Indian provinces as was in the case of cotton and sugar. The late start that the natives made in industries further restricted the field of operation. In spite of all these shortcomings, the natives tried their best to involve themselves as much as possible in their country's industrial development.

PART II

In Part II, we shall study the supply of industrial entrepreneurship in the larger organized industries of Bengal with a view to bringing out the amount of native participation in them vis-a-vis other non-Indian communities, i.e., the British (and other foreigners).

The Jute Industry

Jute industry was one of those large-scale export industries in which the British had an early start. The pioneering effort in this line was undertaken by a group of British managing agents, who having the knowledge of world market could foresee the demand for this article. Nor did they lack in technical training and in organizational ability. No wonder till the end of our period of study, they were able to hold the virtual monopoly of this industry. The natives having only a brief span of industrial experience (to be precise from the Swadeshi Movement onwards) and having none of the advantages of technical knowledge and market, naturally could not undertake such huge industrial projects as jute industry, when in the smaller ventures they were having trouble. However, it did not deter the Indian entrepreneurs, especially some of the Marwaris from coming into this field. During the war many of them had been actively engaged in jute trade and had seen the high profitability of this industry. No sooner was the war over, many Indians ventured into this field.

Sir Sarupchand Hukumchand of Indore, Birla Brothers of Calcutta and the Maharaja of Durbhanga had established jute mills by the early part of the 1920's. In the second part of the 1920's, we find the establishment of such mills as the Adamjee Jute Mills by Adamjee Hajee Dawood and Company, Limited (1927); Agarpara Jute Mills Limited by B.N. Elias and Company, Limited (1927); Premchand Jute Mills Limited, by Raja Janoki Nath Roy and Brothers Limited (1928); and the Jute Manufacturing Company, Limited by Dayaram and sons (1929). Along with the establishment of jute companies by native entrepreneurs, the inter-war period also saw massive investment by the Indians in this industry. As a result of this, the management of the jute companies also underwent a change. Thus in 1911, all the 50 companies were controlled by European directors only.[30] The situation had improved by 1921 when out of 62 mills, there were six mills with mixed boards and one was purely an Indian concern.[31] The situation improved further in the late 1920's and there were a good many Indian directors on the board. Thus Sir Onkarmull Jatia was the director of no less than nine mills. Rai Bahadur Goenka Bahadur of at least four, and Rameshwar Nathany, Hazarimull, Doodwawalla, Chandmull Kanoria, Ram Kumar Bangur and Chhajuram of at least two concerns each.[32]

The entry of more Indian entrepreneurs into the jute industry was only restricted by the fact that by about the middle of the 1920's the industry was already possessed of a capacity (for production) far in excess of any demand that had arisen for the article it manufactured.[33] The price of jute products were only artificially kept high by a policy of restricting the output of mills in the membership of the IJMA.[34] But as new Indian mills were coming up almost every year and few were prepared to join the IJMA, there were protracted quarrels between the Association and the mills outside the Association. Ultimately, the Government of Bengal issued an Ordinance (Bengal Jute Ordinance, 1938) making

[30]*Census of India, 1921, Vol. V. Bengal, Part I, Report* (Calcutta, 1923), p. 404.

[31]*Ibid.*

[32]Pat Lovett, *The Mirror of Investment, 1927*, pp. 257-312.

[33]IOR: Vol. 12077, BFP (Commerce), March 1936, No. 24, p. 17.

[34]IOR: Vol. 12077, BFP (Commerce), March 1936, No. 24, p. 17.

it unlawful to increase the number of looms or to replace any existing looms in any jute mills.[35]

TABLE 5.3
CONTROL OF JOINT-STOCK JUTE COMPANIES IN BENGAL IN 1914 AND IN 1939

Name of the managing agent or secretary	*Number of mills controlled on 27 August, 1914*	*Number controlled on 1 June, 1939*
Andrew Yule and Co.	6	11
Begg, Dunlop & Co.	2	4
Duncan Brothers & Co.	1	1
Bird & Co.	8	8
George Henderson & Co.	1	2
James Finley & Co.	1	1
McLeod & Co.	3	4
Kettlewell, Bullen	2	2
Macneill & Co.	1	2
Gillanders & Co.	2	2
Barry & Co.	1	2
Ernsthansen Ld.	2	X
Mackinnon & Co.	1	2
Jardine, Skinner & Co.	2	4
Anderson Wright & Co.	1	1
F.W. Heilgers & Co.	2	2
Thomas Duff & Co.	3	3
A.H. Dawood & Co.	X	1
B.N. Elias & Co.	X	1
Birla Brothers Ltd.	X	1
Dayaram and Sons	X	1
Sir S. Hukumchand	X	1
Raja Janoki Nath Roy & Brothers	X	1
Babulal & Co.	X	1
Dass Brothers	X	1

SOURCE: *Capital*, 27 August, 1914, p. 557; and *Ibid.*, 1 June, 1939, p. 831.

Like jute manufacturing industry, jute pressing was also a great industry in Bengal, employing some 36,000 workers (seasonal and perennial) in 1937.[36] In 1911, out of 109 jute presses, more than 50

[35]*Star of India*, 10 September 1938, p. 4.

[36]Department of Commercial Intelligence and Statistics: *Large Industrial Establishments in India*, 1937 (Delhi, 1939), pp. iv & xii.

per cent (fifty-seven presses) were owned and controlled by the Europeans and Anglo-Indians.[37] The situation underwent a change during the World War I when large number of Indian entrepreneurs came into this field, especially the up-country Marwaris who were already engaged in jute trade. Thus according to 1921 Census, out of 188 jute presses, Indians owned 113[38] compared to 52 in 1911.[39] The entry of Indian entrepreneurs into this line was far easier than jute industry itself. It required no great technology as the presses could be worked by hand or steam power. Some of the big Indian enterprises (employing over 500 workers in 1937) included the Atlas and Union Jute Press (owned by Soorajmal Nagarmal), Hooghly Hydraulic Jute Press (Managing agent: P.E. Guzdar), and Chitpur Jute Press Ltd. (of Hursing Nehalchand and Surajmal Nagarmal). Here it may also be mentioned that many European managing agencies having jute mills under their control had also established large jute presses. In this group belonged such managing agency firms as Andrew Yule & Co; Bird and Co; George Henderson and Co; Jardine Skinner and Co; and James Finlay and Company. In this branch of the jute industry, the Ralli Brothers were also a great undertaker having their agencies at Cossipore, Narayanganj and Sarisabari.

Tea Industry

Like jute, tea industry also owed its origin to British commercial interests in the nineteenth century. When the East India Company lost its trading monopoly of China trade in 1833, it became anxious to obtain a source of tea supply entirely under its own control. Its anxiety was heightened in the 1830's by a suspicion that China like Japan might as well break off trading links with the West and thereby jeopardise its valuable tea trade.[40] This resulted in carrying out investigations and experimentations on tea culture in India and when it proved successful, large regions like that of Darjeeling and Jalpaiguri were brought under tea cultivation.

[37] *Census of India*, 1911, Vol. V, Bengal, Part II, Tables, p. 350.
[38] *Ibid., 1921*, Part II, Tables, p. 416.
[39] *Ibid., 1911*, Part II, Tables, p. 350.
[40] Harold H. Mann, 'The Early History of the Tea Industry in North-East India', *Bengal Economic Journal*, Vol. II, No. 1 (January, 1918), pp. 44-45.

The lead that the British took in the nineteenth century was maintained throughout the period under study. Thus, when we analyse the tea industry of Bengal in 1937-38, we find that the industry was still largely dominated by the British. Some 27 sterling tea companies had the lion's share of the industry. In that year, out of a total cultivated acreage of 201,680 some 86,856 acres or over 43 per cent belonged to them.[41] Not only that, among the companies operating in Bengal and having rupee capital, most were also found to be under the control of a group of British managing agencies like Kilburn and Co; Williamson, Magor and Co; Davenport and Co; Duncan Brothers and the like. Among the larger tea gardens in this category having 1,000 acres or more under tea cultivation in 1937-38, sixteen out of twenty were British controlled.[42] Among the Indian owned gardens, only four had 1,000 acres or more under tea cultivation in that year, and not many having more than 500 acres under tea cultivation.[43]

Why was it that the Indians lagged behind? There could be several probable explanations to this. But the two most important ones were, firstly, that the native entrepreneurs being late in entering this field found very little opportunity for further expansion in the twentieth century. By about the first decade of this century, the best available land for tea had already been taken up by the British for tea cultivation.[44] What was left were the jungles and less attractive places. Even then the Indian entrepreneurs made a gradual recovery from 1911 onwards. In 1911, for instance, Indians owned 36 gardens or 15 per cent of the total and by 1921 they had increas-

[41]The names of the sterling tea companies which had over 500 acres under tea cultivation in 1937-38 could be found in the *Thacker's Indian Directory*, 1937-38 (Calcutta, n. d.), Industries Section, pp. 156-167. For figures of the total cultivated acreage of Bengal, See, Department of Commercial Intelligence and Statistics: *Indian Tea Statistics*, 1938 (Delhi, 1940), p. 15.

[42]For detail see *Thacker's Indian Directory*, 1937-38 (Calcutta, n. d.), Industries Section, pp. 156-167, 178-79.

[43]*Ibid.* The four were the Ambari Tea Co. Ltd whose secretary was Bahupallabh Saha; the Anjuman Tea Company, Limited whose secretary was R.K. Moitra; Saroda Tea Co. Ltd whose secretary was S.N. Bose; and the Shikarpur Tea Estate of Raja Prasunna Deb Raikut Bahadur. All the four estates were located in the Dooars (Jalpaiguri).

[44]*Report of the Royal Commission on Lobour in India*, 1931 (PP XI of 1930-31), p. 971.

ed their share to 109 gardens or just over 32 per cent of the total number of gardens in existence.[45] Their aspirations were rather abruptly halted in the early 1930's due to over-production of this commodity in the world market with consequent fall in the prices of tea.[46] The Government of India in collaboration with Ceylon and the Netherlands East Indies restricted the export of tea and also the acreage under tea cultivation from April, 1933 onwards.[47] Secondly, the native entrepreneurs were at a disadvantageous position as regards knowledge of foreign markets compared to their British counterparts who possessed wider commercial contacts overseas. The cumulative outcome was that the Indian entrepreneurs were lagging behind in this industry compared to their foreign counterparts.

Coal Industry

Coal mining was another big industry in Bengal, producing some one-fourth of ths total production of India in 1924.[48] It was mainly required for the purpose of running railways, and large industrial establishments like jute, cotton and engineering industries; and for bunkers and inland steamers. The pioneering of this industry, like jute and tea, was undertaken by the European agency houses like Andrew Yule and Company; Macneill and Company; Balmer Lawrie and Company who established joint-stock coal companies soon after the East Indian Railways entered the Bengal coal fields in 1854. Thus the Bengal Coal Company was established in 1858; New Beerbhum Coal Company and Ranigunge Coal Association in 1873 and Equitable Coal Company in 1895.[49] The early ventures of these colliery companies were highly successful, and they were able to dispose of their increasing output without any difficulty and

[45]There were also 11 companies with mixed boards in 1921. *Census of India*, 1921, Vol. V, Bengal, Part I, Report, p. 389.

[46]See, Economic and Overseas Department Collections, File No. L/E/9/1294; and also, Memorandum by the Secretary, Indian Tea Association, Calcutta to the Secretary to the Government of India, Department of Commerce, in Economic and Overseas Department Collections, File No. L/E/9/1296.

[47]See, *Report of the International Tea Committee*, 1st July, 1933, to 31st March, 1934 (London, n. d.). The Report could be found in Eco. & Overseas Deptt. Collections. File L/E/9/1296.

[48]Economic and Overseas Department Collections, File No. L/E/9/1004.

[49]Department of Commercial Intelligence and Statistics: *Indian Coal Statistics*, 1938 (Delhi, 1940), pp. 65, 67-69.

at a fair profit. This encouraged others into the field and by 1921 no less than 202 private and public colliery companies were in operation in Bengal (see Table 5.4).

TABLE 5.4

PARTICULARS OF COLLIERY OWNERSHIP IN BENGAL, 1911 AND 1921

	Number owned by				
	Companies of which the directors are			*Private persons who are*	
	Europeans or Anglo-Indians	*Indians*	*Mixed*	*Europeans or Anglo-Indians*	*Indians*
1911	53	6	21	7	43
1921	65	19	18	8	64

SOURCES: *Census of India*, 1911, Vol. V, Bengal, Part II, Tables (Calcutta, 1913), p. 350; and *Ibid.*, *1921* (Calcutta, 1923), p. 416.
Note: In 1911, one private concern returned two owners of different castes. In 1921, the classification of owners of 30 collieries was not available while another two concerns returned, one three owners and the other two owners of different class. One colliery was also owned by a Russian in 1921.

An analysis of the Bengal coal industry in 1938 shows that only a few large British controlled colliery companies still dominated the industry so far as annual coal production was concerned.[50] In that year, out of a total production of 7,745,372 tons[51] no less than 4,186,572 tons or 54.05 per cent were produced by the larger eleven British controlled colliery companies from their 18 bigger ventures alone (the production of their smaller collieries producing less than 100,000 tons have not been taken into account.[52] Of these, the

[50]See, *Indian Coal Statistics*, 1938 (Delhi, 1940), pp. 38-41; and *Capital*, April, 5, 1928, pp. 776-77.

[51]*Indian Coal Statistics*, 1938, p. 18.

[52]The 18 collieries were Banksimula, Bejdih, Dhemo Main, Dishergarh (west), Jamuria, Jamuria (west), Methani, Sitalpore, Sripore, Sripore (pits 1&3), Banksimula (7&8 pits), Barmondia, Kajora (khas), Patmohna, Pretoria, Seebpore, Sodepore (Nos. 9 & 10 pits), Victoria and Victoria (west). See, *Indian Coal Statistics*, 1938, pp. 38-41; and *Capital*, 5 April, 1928, pp. 776-77.

Equitable Coal Company of Macneill and Co., produced 1,029,173 tons or 13.29 per cent of the entire production of that year from their three collieries of Bejdih, Dishergarh (west) and Jamuria.[53] This production was more than the total output from Bengal's 21 largest private collieries producing over 25,000 tons of coal each and whose total production in 1938 amounted to 898,030 tons or 11.59 per cent.[54] Indians owned, however, none of the larger joint-stock companies. Their ownership was mainly restricted to small private collieries, and among these there were only three which were producing 50,000 tons or over in 1938.[55]

The relative smallness of the Indian owned collieries, however, does not prove that the Indians were less enterprising than their European colleagues. Unable to attract sufficient capital resources[56] Indian entrepreneurs went to float private collieries or small joint-stock ventures. This in turn necessarily prevented the installation of modern mining equipment and the employment of essential technical expertise to run the mines in an efficient manner. As a result most of these small collieries worked only at or near the surface which made it quite impossible to work the coal satisfactorily. Consequently, output of each of these collieries were small and return less profitable than the larger colliery companies under established groups of managing agents. The manner of leasing out (by the landlords who under the Permanent Settlement were the sole proprietors of colliery lands in Bengal and Bihar) small patches of land to diverse persons with the object of receiving as much money as possible without due regard to the economical working of the estate was no less responsible for creating small uneconomic collieries to which inexperienced Indian entrepreneurs increasingly sunk their capital.

[53]*Ibid.*

[54]See, *Indian Coal Statistics*, 1938, pp. 41-45.

[55]*Ibid.* These three private collieries were Baraboni Khas (South East), owned by Maharaja S.C. Nandi; Kajora by Roy, Dutt and Co; and Nimcha by R.S. Chandan Mull Indra Kumar.

[56]A.C. Banerjee, Honorary Secretary, Indian Mining Federation, representing the Bengal National Chamber of Commerce, Calcutta, in his evidence before the IIC. See, IIC, Vol. II (PP XVIII of 1919), p. 286. Also see, I. Treharne Rees, Report on the Methods of Coal Mining in India, IOR. L/E/7/938, File No. 2874.

General Engineering Industry[57]

Till the beginning of the World War I, the flow of entrepreneurs into this industry was extremely limited. A few foreign companies like Burn and Company and Jessop and Company existed for about a century or more, but these were engaged in making various sorts of water transport like steamers, flats, barges and in the construction of buildings and bridges and other structurals for mills and workshops.[58] It was the First World War which by virtually stopping the import of machinery, railway wagons and appliances gave a real chance to its development. During this time several large engineering firms were established like that of Jas. Alexander and Company's Engineering Works at Kidderpore (1915); Britannia Engineering Works, Titaghur (1917); Angus Engineering Works, Hooghly (1917); Hukumchand Electric Steel Works at Ballygunge (1918); Indian Standard Wagon Company, Burnpur (1918); and immediately after the war, the Bridge and Roof Company's Structural Works at Howrah (1920). This tempo of development, however, seems to have suffered when normal conditions returned in the 1920's and due to the depression in the 1930's.[59] In 1937, there were only 152 general engineering firms in Bengal, employing some 23,700 workers.[60]

[57]By 'general engineering' is meant those workshops other than electrical engineering, electricity generating and transforming stations, foundaries, iron and steel smelting and steel rolling mills, copper smelting and copper rolling mills and lead smelting and lead rolling mills.

[58]Jessop and Company was started under that name in 1820 and was carried on before that under another name. See, Indian Tariff Board: *Evidence recorded during enquiry into the Steel Industry*, Vol II (Calcutta, 1924), p. 446. Burn and Company, on the other hand, was originally started in 1781 by Colonel Archibald Swinton. It gradually gained a great reputation in connection with building and construction work. Arnold Wright (ed.) and Somerset Playne (compiler), *Bengal and Assam, Bihar and Orissa* (London, 1919), p. 91.

[59]This is evident from the aggregate paid-up capital of the engineering companies in Bengal. In 1920-21, the paid-up capital of the engineering companies stood at Rs. 319 lakhs and in 1935-36 it had increased only to Rs. 441 lakhs. See, DOIB: *Bulletin No. 83, Report on the Growth of Joint-Stock Companies in Bengal* (Alipore, 1939), p. 11.

[60]Commercial Intelligence and Statistics Department: *Large Industrial Establishments in India*, 1937 (Delhi, 1939), p. 20. It included all factories which came under the operation of the Factories Act (XXV of 1934), as amended by Act XI of 1935. See, 'Introductory Note', *Ibid.*, p. iii.

An analysis of the general engineering firms operating in Bengal and employing over 250 workers in 1937 shows that most of these industries belonged to the British owners.[61] It does not need any elaborate explanation as to the reasons why this should have been so. Having the required technical background, and the possible advantages of securing better marketing facilities (due to British domination of large purchasing bodies like the railways), they could take a lead in establishing engineering firms. On the other hand, the Indian entrepreneurs had none of these advantages. Lacking in the required technical know-how and in the absence of all round trade knowledge they could not possibly venture into engineering establishments. A few who went and established big firms like that of Sarupchand Hukumchand had to employ foreign technicians and management. Moreover, the depression of the 1930's had a generally discouraging effect on the entry of new entrepreneurs into this field.

Cotton Mill Industry

In spite of having a large demand for cotton products, we do not find the establishment of very many cotton mills in Bengal till the end of the period under study. In 1921, there were only 18 spinning and weaving mills in operation employing some 13,735 workers,[62] However, at attempt was made to float a number of cotton mills after the granting of protection to this industry in 1926-27; that too did not make any significant headway. A question at once looms large: why was it that the cotton mill industry could not make sufficient progress in Bengal? The answer to this question is not, however, unaccountable. In the first place, Bengal produced only a small amount of raw cotton.[63] Therefore, to establish cotton mills, cotton had to be imported from outside the province, i.e., Bombay

[61]See, *Large Industrial Establishments in India,* (Delhi, 1939), pp. 18-20 and *Thacker's Indian Directory*, 1937-38. Industries Section, pp. 41-44.

[62]*Census of India*, 1921, Vol. V, Bengal, Part II, Tables. p. 402.

[63]This could be seen from the following figures of cotton production of Bengal:

Year	*Yield in bales of 400 Ibs.*
1915-16	30,000
1916-17	20,000
1917-18	19,000
1918-19	32,000
1919-20	24,600

See, IOR: Vol. 10971, BFP (Commerce), March 1921, No. 20, p. 17.

area or from abroad. This entailed additional costs of transport, securing a constant flow of right kinds of cotton, costs as regards additional men employed to survey and despatch goods and so on. On the top of it, there was the perennial problem of wagon shortages.[64] Secondly, Bengal cotton mills had to face fierce competition from established and mature foreign and internal mills of other provinces. The foreign competition mainly came from Lancashire and later on from Japan as well. Even when partial protection was granted to this industry, it did not benefit Bengal much. Bombay having the advantages of raw materials and considerable experience in the field, easily dominated the industry. Thirdly, the native entrepreneurs failed to attract sufficient capital resources into this inddustry. This was due to their failure in creating confidence in the minds of the Bengali investors rather than due to the shortage of capital.[65]

As late as 1937, there were only 26 mills in operation in Bengal. Out of these only 9 could be said to be big enough to employ 1,000 workers or more a day.[66] An analysis of these mills show that excepting two, Dunbar Cotton Mills Limited, No. 4 and Bowreah Cotton Mills, the rest of the mills were owned by the Indians themselves.[67] The biggest of these, Kesoram Cotton Mills was owned by Messrs. Birla Brothers Limited and had a paid-up capital of Rs. 35,00,000.[68] This mill was so big that it alone employed over one-fifth of

[64]See, for instance, *Report of the Committee appointed by the Secretary of State for India to enquire into the administration and working of Indian Railways, Report* (PP X of 1929), p. 931.

[65]This lack of confidence among the capitalists was because of the registration of large number of bogus concerns intended to cheat the public from their very inception, want of experienced entrepreneurs, the ignorance of the investors as to the nature and condition of the business in which they were supposed to invest their capital, and almost passive economic attitude of the government. *IIC*, Vol, II (PP XVIII of 1919), p. 130.

[66]These mills were the Kesoram Cotton Mills and Dunbar Cotton Mills. Limited, No. 4 (Ring) of 24 Parganas; Mohini Cotton Mills of Nadia; Bowreah Cotton Mills (Ring Mill) and Sree Radha Krishna Cotton Mills, No. 1 and No. 2 of Howrah; the Bengal Luxmi Cotton Mill and the Rampooria Cotton Mill of Hooghly; and the Dhakeswari Cotton Mills Limited, Dacca. See, *Large Industrial Establishments in India*, 1937 (Delhi, 1938), p. 4.

[67]See, DOIB: Bulletin Mo. 75, *Bulletin No. 75, Cotton Mill Industry in Bengal* (Alipore, 1937), pp. 12-19.

[68]*Ibid*,.

the total labour-force engaged in cotton mills in Bengal.[69] The next two bigger ones, the Bengal Luxmi Cotton Mills and the Dhakeswari Cotton Mills, both of which employed over 2,500 workers, also belonged to Indian owners.[70] Why was it that the European managing agency firms did not come forward to establish large numbers of cotton mills? The answer to this is very difficult to find, especially in view of the fact that having wide experience and technical know-how they could possibly make a significant contribution in this line. The failure to come forward may be attributable perhaps to their conservatism and fondness for stereotyped businesses in which it was easier to make money.

Sugar Mill Industry

Like cotton mill industry, the growth and development of sugar factories was limited. This was because of two factors. Firstly Bengal was not a major sugar producing area in India. For example, in 1936-37, Bengal's total area under sugar-cane cultivation was only 354,800 acres in comparison with U.P.'s 2.5 million acres during the same time.[71] This supply of sugar-cane was not sufficient to run an unlimited number of mills. Moreover, the cost of sugar-cane cultivation in Bengal was also more than in the upper Indian provinces. Thus the cost of cultivating one maund of sugar-cane in the United Province and Bihar was 4 to 5 annas, in the Punjab—5½ annas while in Bengal it amounted to no less than 7 annas.[72] As such from the point of view of raw material supply, Bengal was not happily placed against the upper Indian provinces. Secondly, till 1932 there was hardly any scope for its development due to foreign competition. With the granting of protection to this industry in that year, however, many entrepreneurs showed great eagerness to establish sugar industries.[73] But unfortunately Bengal could not make any satisfactory headway in this industry as comparative advantages lay with

[69]*Large Industrial Establishments*, 1937, p. 4.

[70]*Large Industrial Establishments*, 1937, p. 4; and DOIB: *Bulletin No. 75, Cotton Mill Industry*, pp. 12-19.

[71]*Report of the Indian Tariff Board on the Sugar Industry* (Delhi, 1938), pp. 21&24. The total acreage under sugar-cane cultivation in India in 1936-37 was 4.4 million acres. Durgapurasad Khaitan, 'Survey of Indian Sugar Industry', Supplement to '*Capital*', 14 December, 1939, p. 17.

[72]*Report of the Indian Tariff Board on the Sugar Industry* (Delhi, 1938), p. 36.

[73]This is evident from the large number of flotations of new sugar industries. See, DOIB: *Annual Administration Report*, 1933-34, p. 3.

upper Indian provinces. The sugar industry in Bengal was also handicapped from transport difficulties due to "practically no communication by any cartable roads or railway system."[74]

An analysis of the sugar-mill industry shows that there were only ten mills in existence in 1938-39.[75] Out of these, no less than eight were owned by the Indians themselves.[76] The firm of Messrs. Surajmal Nagarmal owning two, the Setabganj Sugar Mills and the North Bengal Sugar Mills Limited, both of which were started after the granting of protection to this industry in 1933.[77] These two factories had a total crushing capacity of over 1,500 tons.[78] The rest of the Indian owned mills were comparatively small and the six together had a crushing capacity of 1, 325 tons or less than that of Carew Co., Limited of Nadia owned by Messrs. Lyall Marshall & Co.[79] Whatever the case may be, at least it shows that the Indian entrepreneurs were far from shy and were much more willing to experiment with new-found opportunities than traditional opinion projected them to be.

The Chemical Industry

The chemical industry in Bengal was one of those few fields in which Indian enterprise predominated. Out of some 69 Bengal chemical and pharmaceutical works mentioned in *Thackers Indian Directory*, 1938-39, the majority were owned by the Indian entrepreneurs.[80] Of the four perennial factories employing over 250 work-force in

[74]Indian Tariff Board: *Written Evidence recorded during enquiry on the Sugar Industry* (Delhi, 1938), Vol. II, p. 277.

[75]These were the Setabganj Sugar Mills, Dinajpur; North Bengal Sugar Mills Co., Rajshahi; Sree Radha Krishna Sugar Mills, Ltd, of Murshidabad; Ramnagar Cane and Sugar Co., Ltd of Nadia; the East Bengal Sugar Mills Limited and the Deshbandu Sugar Mills Limited of Dacca; Shikarpur Sugar Mills of Jalpaiguri; the Dayamoyee Jayanti Sugar Mills of Mymensingh and the Rajlakshmi Sugar Mills of 24 Parganas. See, *The Sugar Technologists' Association of India, Cawnpur, Year-Book*, 1939-40 (Cawnpur, n. d.), Appendix, List A, List of Modern Sugar Factories and Refineries existing in India in the year 1938-39, pp. 14-15.

[76]*Ibid.*

[77]See, *Written Evidence recorded during enquiry on the Sugar Industry*, Vol. I, (Delhi, 1938), p. 2.

[78]*The Sugar Technologists' Association of India, Cawnpur, Year-Book*, 1939-40. pp. 14-15.

[79]*Ibid.*

[80]See, *Thackers Indian Directory*, 1938-39 (Calcutta, n. d.), Industries Section, pp. 9-12.

1937[81] three belonged to the Indians. The biggest of these was the Bengal Chemical and pharmaceutical Works, Limited, which owed its origin (in 1892) to the vision and enterprise of Dr. Profullah Chandra Roy (later Sir) who was then a professor of chemistry at the Presidency College, Calcutta.[82] In 1901, he incorporated this as a Public Limited company[83] and since then it grew in size.[84] The principal articles manufactured by this company were acids, chemicals, pharmaceutical preparations, scientific intruments, disinfections, surgical dressings, laboratory furniture, vaccines, serum, biological products, toilet preparations and toilet and household soaps.[85] Its manufactures were regularly supplied to several railways, municipalities, provincial government stores, Indian Stores Department, colleges, schools, hospitals, and various other bodies and to the public in all parts of India.[86] In 1937, it had two factories, one at 164, Maniktolla Main Road, 24-Parganas employing some 1,481 men and the other at Panihati, also in 24 Parganas.[87] The remaining two companies were the Bengal Immunity Company Limited, whose managing director was Capt. N.N. Dutt and the D. Waldie and Company's Chemical Works at Konnagar in Hooghly. The latter company was also the pioneer in the field of chemical industry in Bengal. It was established in 1853 by a Scottish doctor named, David Waldie.[88]

Pottery, Brick and Tile Industry

The Indians showed considerable enterprise in the field of pottery. In 1907, the Calcutta Pottery Works was started by Maharaja Maninder Chander Nundy of Cassimbazar and Babu Boykonto Nath Sen of Berhampur, with the aid of an able ceramist, Satyasun-

[81]*Large Industrial Establishments in India*, 1937, p. 75.

[82]Bulletins of Indian Industrial Research: *Bulletin No. 8, Development of the Heavy Chemical Industries in India* (by N.N. Sen Gupta) (Delhi, 1937), p. 4.

[83]*Ibid.*

[84]The sales of the company increased from Rs. 25,000 in the first year to nearly Rs. 44 lakhs in the Bengali year ending in 1339 i.e., year ending on 13 April, 1933. See, the humble petition of the Bengal Chemical and Pharmaceutical Works, Ltd, to the Land Acquisition Collector, Calcutta, dated the 9th March, 1934 in BSR: Bundle No. 1, PAI (Industries), B Proceedings, File No. 4L/4 of 1934.

[85]*Ibid.*

[86]*Ibid.*

[87]*Large Industrial Establishments in India*, 1937, p. 75.

[88]Bulletins of Indian Industrial Research: *Bulletin No. 8, Development of the Heavy Chemical Industries in India*, p. 3.

dara Deb, who had studied his art at the Higher Technological Institute, Tokyo. This was the first factory in India for the manufacture of glazed pottery of the superior grade, and could turn out glazed ware consisting of cups, saucers, insulators, ink-pots, dolls and figures.[89] Another factory was that of P.N. Dutt and Co.'s Bengal Potteries, whose shares were quoted at the Calcutta Stock Exchange.[90]

In the field of brick and tile making, the natives owned the majority of the concerns. According to the Census Report of 1921, out of some 412 brick, tile and firebrick factories, Indian entrepreneurs owned 387.[91] In this field, Messrs. Keshoob Chandra Paul and Co. was very prosperous. The Company had factories at five different places, and their monthly production was over two lakh tiles.[92] However, in this field Burn and Company was far ahead of all others. They perfected the methods of production and turned out the best varieties of bricks, pipes, tiles and sanitary wares. The value of their articles produced at the Pottery Works at Ranigunge was estimated at over three lakhs of rupees in the year 1908-09 compared to over six lakhs of rupees in the previous year and that of their Durgapur Brick and Tile Works at half a lakh rupees.[93]

Conclusion

From our study of the major organized industries in Bengal, it is clear that Indians did not lack in industrial enterprise. Wanting in technical and commercial education, business knowledge and "discouraged by the political, administrative and financial arrangements maintained by the British rulers"[94] Indians had to struggle against

[89]Henry Hemantakumar Ghosh, *The Advancement of Industry* (Calcutta, 1910), p. 91.

[90]See, *Capital*, August 28, 1920. The Company had a capital of Rs. 7,62,212.

[91]Out of the other 25 factories, 3 were owned by the Government or local authority, and in the case of another 5 companies, the directors came from both the communities. *Census of India*, Vol. V, Bengal, Part II, p. 417.

[92]*BISC*, p. 133.

[93]*Miscellaneous Annual Report of the Burdwan Division for the year 1908-09*, IOR: Vol. 8136, BRP (Miscellaneous), October 1909, Nos. 4-5 p. 150. Ranigunge Pottery Works was originally established by a retired engineer by the name of George Macdonald in 1866. But due to financial trouble, the works was sold to Messrs. Burn and Co. in 1870. In 1894, a Government test found their products superior to many imported wares and since then their manufactures had flourished. Henry Hemantakumar Ghosh, *op. cit.*, pp. 89-90.

[94]Amiya Kumar Bagchi, *Private Investment*, p. 423.

heavy odds. In spite of such obstacles, they attempted to float large numbers of industrial establishments and in new lines quite in contrast to the Europeans who were mostly content by their success in certain directions only and devoted their time and attention to foreign trade at the expense of indigenous industries.[95] If the Indians had failed in most of their attempts that was another matter and must not be confused with the factor of industrial enterprise. On the contrary, it only showed their urge for industrial ventures. By the end of our period of study, other than jute, tea and coal engineering concerns in which the Europeans had either an early start or were better fitted by virtue of their superior knowledge and contacts, most others were dominated by Indian entrepreneurs. Examples may be cited in the case of sugar factories; chemical and pharmaceutical works; pottery, brick and tile making factories; and also probably rice, soap and match factories. Even in the export oriented industries where the Indians were handicapped as regards the knowledge of foreign markets and their late start, they gradually made significant recovery in the 1920's. Further entry into these fields (i.e., jute and tea industry) frem the early 1930's was only restricted due to over-production of the articles in the world market.

[95]Chatterton, however, states that the European merchants and manufacturers did try for nearly a century to create an industrial system but failed due to lack of central markets, to the absence of skilled labour, to the intensity of foreign competition, to the poverty of the local resources, to the cost of internal transport, to the inability to obtain a monopoly and finally to an imperfect study of local problems. Having tried and failed "they are not altogether to be blamed if they have in recent years devoted their time and attention and employed their capital in creating a big foreign trade at the expense, more or less, of the indigenous industries." Alfred Chatterton, *Industrial Evolution in India* (Madras, n. d.), pp. 97-98.

6 The Growth of the Jute Manufacturing Industry

At the turn of the twentieth century, Bengal had only one notable manufacturing industry—that of jute. It occupied a vital position from the point of view of Bengal's industrial economy employing no less than half the total factory labour of Bengal. The export value of jute manufactures accounted for nearly 33 per cent of the entire export trade of Bengal in 1900-01 and if account was taken of the great quantity of jute manufactures exported from Calcutta by rail and coastwise for the packing of Indian produce and the quantity used in the local markets for the same purpose it is probably no exaggeration to say that quite half of the trade of Calcutta was dependent on the jute fields of Eastern Bengal and the jute mills established along the banks of the Hooghly.[1]

Despite its pre-eminence in Bengal's economy, the growth of the industry was fairly recent. Indeed the first jute mill was established only in 1855. Prior to that date the fibre was used locally by the handloom jute weavers of Bengal to make twines, ropes, coarse fabrics for the poor, and also in the fishing industry and for mooring smail vessels. By the end of the eighteenth century, however, it had definitely attracted the attention of the Board of Trade of the East India Company which sent a consignment of jute samples to England in 1791. Since that data until 1832 when the fibre was first successfully spun mechanically by Messrs. Balfour and Melvelle at their Chapelshade works in Scotland, raw jute of various quantities was being regularly sent for experimentations. Once the pioneers were successful in spinning yarn by flax machinery, they soon found out means to soften the hard and brittle nature of the fibre by adding oil and water in the preliminary processes which made the fibre more pliable and more easily separable, and resulted in the production of a more usable

[1] *RAB*, 1900-01, p. 118.

thread. The alteration of the existing machinery and the construction of the newer forms particularly suitable to the treatment of a coarse fibre helped considerably in the production of a good yarn. But it was not till 1835 that the desired sizes of spun yarn made solely from jute were regularly sold in the market. Three years later, the Dutch Government specified bags made of jute instead of flax for moving their East India coffee. This helped to establish jute in the eyes of the cloth and bag manufacturers and gave a fresh impetus to the industry.[2] However, it was the Crimean War of 1854-56 which really set the Dundee jute industry on its feet. The occasion was caused by the stoppage of flax from Russia which forced the military authorities to look for substitutes. The American Civil War (1861-65) gave further impetus to the jute trade, for the supplies of American cotton was much restricted and consumers had to make use of jute. In both these cases, the industry acquired new users who did not return to flax or cotton when it was again possible to get supplies of the fibres.[3] The main reason for this permanent change over to jute seems to have been its comparative cheapness as a wrapper to other fibres in use.

Thus when Bengal had the first jute mill in 1855, Dundee was already well established and was busy in opening up more markets for its products. In spite of early vicissitudes, the Bengal mills were able to capture the local markets and by the end of the 1860's one company—the Borneo Jute Company in fact tried its hand at exports abroad. Though the first attempt was not much of a success due to variations in weight and counts, then onwards Bengal became a regular exporter of sacking bags. But when Bengal began to invade Dundee's valuable Hessain market in America, open hostilities broke out. In the ensuing struggle that followed Dundee lost to Calcutta but not without much bitterness on both sides. The point which ultimately settled the score in favour of Calcutta was that of comparative costs of production. Calcutta was situated in close proximity to jute-growing districts of Eastern Bengal and Assam; she had cheap labour, estimated at one-third cheaper than British labour; the mills had long working hours, said to be from 15 to 16 hours daily and in some cases, 22

[2]See, *Star of India*, 20 July, 1934, p. 6.
[3]*Capital*, 17 October, 1935, p. 612.

to 24 hours daily on two and three shift system, respectively; and not the least the lax working and factory conditions were also attributed to be one of the advantages of Calcutta compared to Great Britain. Thus the clear advantage of Calcutta manufacturers in monetary terms was at least £3 per ton, besides having a finer quality of jute.[4]

The result was that by the end of the nineteenth century, Calcutta had become the world's largest jute manufacturing place supplying not only the Near Eastern markets but also the United States, Argentine and Australasia. Dundee, as the Times correspondent observed:[5]

> ...only gets a look in when there is a failure in the Calcutta supply to foreign markets, and particularly when the Argentine, finding suddenly that there is a very good wheat harvest, require sackings and baggings delivered in a hurry, as shipments from Calcutta to the Argentine take three or four months and from Dundee to the Argentine only three or four weeks. The Argentine in those circumstances is compelled to buy in Dundee; but even then Germany competes with Dundee and sometimes outstrips her altogether.

Location

While Bengal's supremacy as a major jute manufacturing centre was quite understandable, one could not but wonder as to why all the jute mills of Bengal should have been located in one particular area—extending along a 60 mile stretch on both banks of the river Hooghly, from Bansberia Jute Mills (35 miles above the city) to Uluberia (20 miles below on the Howrah) on the North bank of the river, and from Hukumchand Mills at Halisahar (28 miles above the city) to Birla Mills at Birlapur (22 miles below Calcutta) on the South bank. Within that narrow belt lay more than 100 jute mills with a total loomage of over 65,000 and an industrial labour force of over quarter of a million. This apparently perplexing locational factor of this industry needs some explanation before we proceed

[4] *The Friend of India and Statesman* (weekly edition), 8 February, 1906, p. 22.
[5] *The Times*, 8 May, 1908, p. 16.

MAP SHOWING THE LOCATION OF JUTE MILLS IN BENGAL

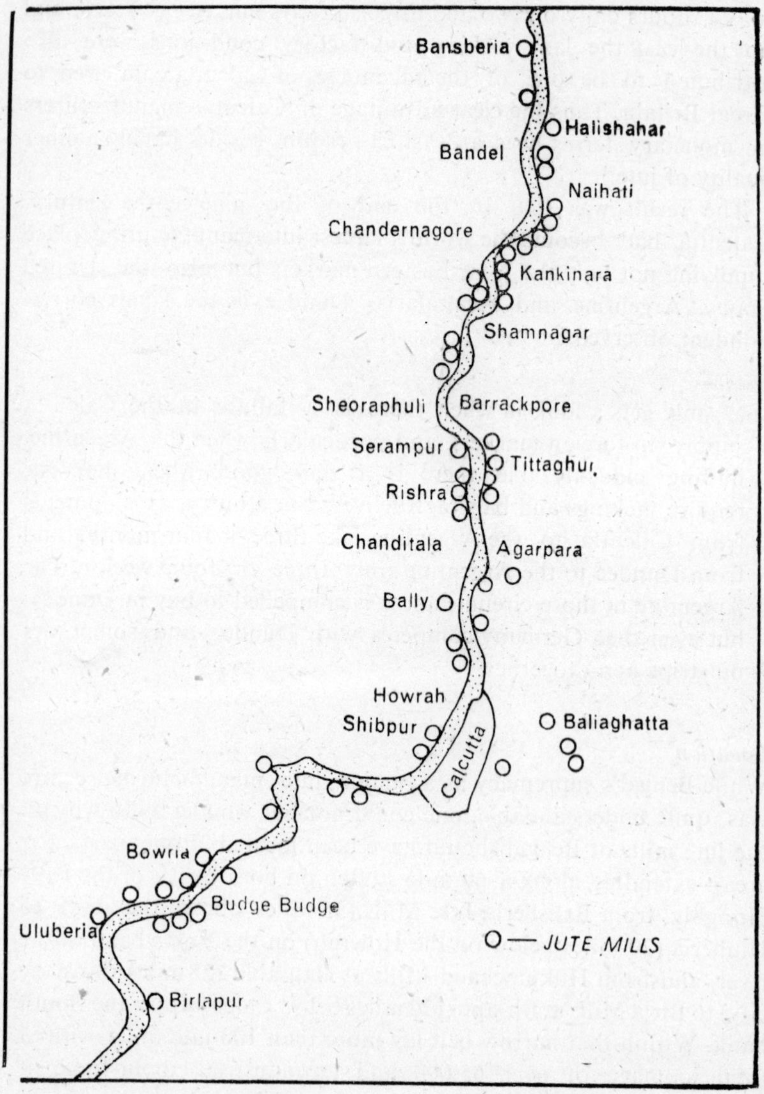

SOURCE: *Report on the Marketing of Jute and Jute-products, Second Report* (Calcutta, 1941).

to analyse the record of its further growth and development in the twentieth century.

At first glance even though it looks perplexing, there was much calculated enterprise in their location. No doubt from the point of view of raw material supply only, a jute mill situated in Eastern Bengal would have escaped the heavy freight charges that was entailed in the transportation of raw jute from Eastern Bengal (where most of the jute was produced) to the West; it must not be forgotten then that jute industry was an export-oriented industry and therefore needed an outlet. But such an outlet was not present in Eastern Bengal except through that of Chittagong which was just then developing as a port.[6] Hence, even if a mill was located in Eastern Bengal it would have necessitated the transportation of its finished products to the port of Calcutta for quick and speedy delivery. In other words, whatever gain the mills would have made by consuming raw materials locally, they had to incur almost the same amount in transporting their finished products to Calcutta for export purposes.[7]

But there was much more to it than just the question of the supply of raw material and its transportation. Jute mills required heavy machinery and stores and the freight for sending the same from Calcutta to any Eastern Bengal district would have to be incurred. On the other hand, a mill situated on the Hooghly escaped from such a burden. Moreover, when one looked at the difficulties of transport which involved such long distances including transhipments in the case of Mymensingh, Dacca, Tipperah and other districts on the eastern side of the river Brahmaputra, one would wonder twice before setting foot on such adventures.

Another great problem for an Eastern Bengal mill would have been regarding its power supply and fuel. In this regard, the mills

[6]This is obvious from the following figures of the value of trade of Bengal that passed through Calcutta in 1900-01 (000's omitted)

Merchandise	*The province*	*Calcutta*
Imports	31,86,91	31,79,44
Exports	55,14,44	54,22,40

See, *RAB*, 1900-01, p 115.

[7]However, in the process a saving of 5 per cent in the freight charge would have been made by an Eastern Bengal mill as the processed jute would have been lighter by that weight. See, G.N. Gupta, *A Survey of the Industries and Resources of Eastern Bengal and Assam for 1907-08* (Shillong, 1908). p. 63.

at the Hooghly had the special advantage of being situated near the coal fields of Ranigunge which had good railway connections with that of Howrah. Indeed it was the railway link between Ranigunge and Howrah established around 1855 (by the East India Railway Company) which finally set the ground for erection of power-driven machinery in that area. As there were no coal mines in Eastern Bengal, it would have meant large-scale movements of coal from western Bengal with consequent addition to the cost of production. Moreover, the rates of electricity also differed greatly between 'Greater Calcutta' area and the various other *mufassal* towns of Eastern Bengal. This was mainly because of the fact that the 'Greater Calcutta' area could afford the load which was most desirable from the point of view of power generation, and also because it had cheaper coal and had an efficient administration. The cumulative result was that it could supply power at a cheaper rate than any other place in Eastern Bengal. For example, the average rate per unit charged for industrial purposes by the Calcutta Electric Supply Corporation in 1923 was 1.288 annas which was further reduced to 0.896 annas in 1927 with the continued cheapness of coal (due to the expensive and modern appliances which had been provided at considerable costs).[8] On the other hand, in no place in Eastern Bengal had the rates been lower than this. Thus in Narayangunj it was 3.3 annas per unit, in Dacca 3.68 annas, in Chittagong 3.78 annas and in Chandpur it was as high as 5.96 annas per unit.[9] Furthermore, a mill situated in Eastern Bengal would have suffered disadvantages arising from the absence of large engineering firms capable at a short notice of carrying out expensive repairs and alterations of machinery.

From the factors discussed it is clear that it would have been most unwise to establish large-scale jute manufacturing mills in Eastern Bengal. Indeed, one of the early mills—Serajganj was established there but was found unworkable and when it was damaged in 1897 in an earthquake, its machinery was brought to Hooghly to be installed in Delta Jute Mill. In the twentieth century also, from time to time rumours had been rife of the establishment of

[8]*Capital*, 31, May 1928, p. 1192.

[9]*Annual Report on the Administration of the Indian Electricity Act, 1910, in Bengal for the year 1938* (Alipore, 1939), Appendix II, p. 32.

jute mills at various places in Eastern Bengal. One such rumour was regarding Narayanganj.[10] The idea behind the establishment of such a mill was probably to supply local needs by manufacturing on the spot and thus eliminating the cost of bringing back the manufactured jute products from Calcutta. The place also offered probably more attractions to an entrepreneur than any other due to ample supplies of labour and raw material. But nothing was heard of the project till later Pakistan came into existence in 1947 and the first mill was established at Narayanganj.

THE GROWTH OF THE JUTE INDUSTRY

The twentieth century was an extraordinary leap forward in the fortunes of the jute manufacturing industry in Bengal. The history of this expansion can be studied in three distinct phases (1) from 1900 to World War I, (2) World War I to 1929 and (3) the period of the depression from 1929-30 to 1939.

The Jute Mill Industry, 1900-1914

Having extended their markets in both the hemispheres by the close of the nineteenth century, the jute mills of Bengal were confident of success. Their confidence was further strengthened by the fact that still a large percentage of raw jute was being exported from India every year to be manufactured into jute goods abroad. As a result not only did they extend their mills but several new ones also came into existence, increasing their total loomage from 9,481 in 1895 to no less than 37,316 by 1912.[11] The mills in this regard were greatly helped by a continued and rising world demand of their products which increased by over 300 per cent between 1895 and 1912.[12] This extraordinary growth of the jute trade attracted the attention of a contemporary who wrote:[13]

> In the sphere of commerce it would be difficult to find anything more remarkable than the recent expansion of the jute trade. Prices have risen to an unprecedented height, and yet the demand

[10] *Capital*, 22 November, 1934, p. 864.
[11] *The Statesman* (weekly overseas edition), 13 February, 1913, p. 20.
[12] *Ibid.*
[13] *The Times* (Financial and Commercial Supplement), 10 September, 1906, p. 309.

> has continued. Jute has not been made dearer by any diminution in the supply, for on the contrary, the production of fibre has increased; it is solely the other great factor in price, an enhanced demand, that has sent up this cheapest of raw materials to a figure which almost suggests dearness. . .in spite of everything the producers of raw materials throughout the world clamour for sacks and sack cloth. Everywhere stocks seem to be bare.

This strong world demand for Indian jute goods was, however, subject to external limitations. Its growth or indeed its very prosperity depended upon the prosperity of world agriculture. A good harvest the world over would result in soaring demand, conversely, a bad one would glut the market. In addition to world agricultural condition which itself was subject to fluctuating weather conditions, the demand for jute goods depended upon the volume of world trade and growth of protectionism. Since the demand for jute goods depended upon such a wide variety of factors, the early poineers found it almost impossible for any single mill to regulate its supply to demand without taking unnecessary risks. Moreover, since the profit margins of mills also to a great extend depended upon such internal factors as the price level of raw materials, transport charges, etc it was thought that some sort of a central organization which could speak as a body was essential. This resulted in the foundation of the Indian Jute Mills Association (till 1902 called Indian Jute Manufacturers Association) in 1884. Although it looked after all matters relating to the jute industry, i.e. collection and classifying facts and statistics, opening markets, obtaining the removal of grievances, communicating with public bodies and kindred associations; its main function was to restrict output either by short-time working or by sealing of looms. Another method of maximising profits was by fixing the minimum rates for different jute products. Since 1886 when short-time agreement was first introduced, it had been a regular feature in the life of the Bengal jute industry. In 1906, the method was resorted to from 1st January to 30th June when raw jute prices soared to a level which threatened to make manufacturing profits vanish. In 1908, when trade depression set in due to the extreme lightness of the money market and which continued till 1911-12 as a result of the financial crisis in America, IJMA prescribed the same course, i.e. five days a week for most of the time. Had not the mills followed (with one or two exceptions) the IJMA directives and acted in unison, it is difficult to imagine how they would have braved the storm. The IJMA also from time to time fixed the scale of minimum rates, thereby acting as a sort of quasi-monopolistic body. Such perscriptions almost amounted to guaranteed profits for the member mills. However, it could do little as regards the unbridled expansion of mills, partly caused by trade jealousy and partly after windfall profits. Indeed one of the additional reasons for the jute mill crisis of 1909-12 was caused by the augmantation of jute mills after a very successful year in 1906-07. New machinery was ordered and existing mills extended which actually brought about and further deepened the crisis.

Not only did extensions and erection of new mills take place in Bengal but as soon as foreign countries realized that the jute industry was important and remunerative, they imposed high import duties on the jute manufactures sent to them from India. Thus the duty on jute yarns in Germany was from £2 to £6 10s per ton; in France from £2 15s to 8 15s; in Austria from £1 10s to £5; in Italy from £4 to £21 10s; and in Russia it was as high as £65 per ton.[14] Under such high protective tariffs large jute manufacturing industries sprang up in Europe and America (and one or two elsewhere); the number of factories were said to have been no less than 202 towards the beginning of the First World War.[15] The outcome of such hasty expansions brought about a problem. Raw jute which had so far been cheap and plentiful, began to rise in prices. This happened not because there was a shrinkage in the total area under jute cultivation or because the output had decreased due to low yield or actual deterioration of the plant but because the demand for this article had been so insistant that supply could not keep pace with demand. Consequently, prices of raw jute continued to exhibit sudden rises as could be seen from Table 6.1. It will be seen that for the ten years ending 1903 the average price was about Rs 30 per bale. Then prices advanced and the average price for the last eleven years rose to nearly Rs. 47.

[14]*The Times*, 8 May, 1908, p. 16.

[15]The mills were located in the following countries : United Kingdom 30; Germany 36; Austria-Hungary 17; France 32; Italy 25; Belgium 23; America 16; Russia 7; Sweden 5; Denmark 2; Switzerland 2; Holland 2; Brazil 2; Norway 1; Rio 1; Argentine 1. See, *BLCP*, 19th December, 1917, Vol. XLIX, p. 1004.

TABLE 6.1

PRICE OF RAW JUTE (M QUALITY) PER BALE, 1894-1914

Year	*October 1*		*November 1*	
	Rs.	An.	Rs.	An.
1894	29	0	27	8
1895	30	8	31	8
1896	39	0	35	8
1897	23	0	22	8
1898	29	0	30	8
1899	33	0	35	8
1900	31	8	32	0
1901	27	12	25	0
1902	31	8	31	0
1903	30	4	28	0
1904	30	8	33	0
1905	43	0	45	0
1906	59	0	57	8
1907	43	0	41	8
1908	42	8	40	0
1909	33	8	34	0
1910	40	0	45	8
1911	50	0	48	0
1912	57	0	63	0
1913	82	8	77	8
1914	34	8	—	—

SOURCE: *Capital*, October 29, 1914, p. 975.

The manufacturing industry would probably have been only too glad to buy at such extraordinary prices had it been possible for them to pass these on to the customers and thus ensuring a relatively good margin of profits for the industry. But this was far from so. The fear of encouraging jute substitutes through such a pricing policy had always been a major deterrent to the industry. They had earlier seen such monopolies as indigo and raw silk vanish from Calcutta's export list and were thus naturally anxious not to push the prices of its manufactures too high.[16] The result was that excep-

[16]The cautiousness of the IJMA could be understood from the fact that while the average quinquennial price of raw jute had doubled in 30 years ending 1913-14; the price of its hessian products (10^4 Oz. 40^{11}) had only risen by about 20 per cent during the same period. *Capital*, 5 April, 1918, p. 795.

ting those mills which where fortunate in their purchases, manufacture became unprofitable, heavy losses had to be incurred, and restricted production became unavoidable in many cases. That the position of the industry was not always promising could partly be gauged from its depressed share values;[17] and partly from the average dividends declared by ten jute mills (selected at random) prior to a period of seven years previous to 1915 as given below.[18]

Company	*Average dividends*
Alexandra	Nil
Alliance	8 per cent
Anglo-India	4½ ,, ,,
Baranagore	6⅓ ,, ,,
Belvedere	4 ,, ,,
Delta	6⅓ ,, ,,
Fort William	Nil
Gondolpara	1½ ,, ,,
Kelvin	5 ,, ,,
Soorah	5½ ,, ,,

The IJMA had also a second ground for concern. The rise in prices of jute had also aggravated the practice of adulterating raw jute with sand and water. This practice, to which was due much deterioration as regards both colour and strength (called "heart disease") was generally attributed to a certain class of middlemen who bought jute more or less in dry condition and then saturated it with sand and water to such an extent as to give them a profit due to its increased weight.[19]

[17]The average share value of Rs. 100 invested in jute mills were as follows:

1907-08	Rs. 131
1908-09	Rs. 129
1909-10	Rs. 116
1910-11	Rs. 114
1911-12	Rs. 119 8 annas
1912-13	Rs. 136 13 annas
1913-14	Rs. 126

See, *Review of the Trade of India*, 1910-11, p. 72; *Ibid.*, *1911-12*, p. 74; *Ibid.*, *1912-13*, p., 59; *Ibid.*, *1915-16*, p. 47.

[18]*Capital*, 15, March 1918, p. 616.

[19]The phenomenon of "heart disease" was restricted only to damp jute, and was so called because it appeared first in the centre of the bundle. When damp jute was baled, it caused a rise in temperature, sometimes upto 40° C (104° F) in the interior of the bale. This was due to the action of thermoplilic bacteria which

Therefore, with a view to removing their grievances, the industry approached the Government on several occasions. In 1912, the IJMA urged the creation of a special department for the pupose of supervising thc extension of jute cultivation in Bengal.[20] In a lengthy document published in 1913, the IJMA appealed to the Government to take positive steps to increase the cultivation of jute crops in India and if this was not done, it pointed out " no efforts will be spared to provide substitutes or to discover other means of handling the produce of the world". It rejected the idea that any increase in the cultivation of jute would be at the expense of rice, which was the principal crop and chief article of food in the province.[21] In 1914, it was the Dundee of Commerce which was urging the government to encourage the extension of jute cultivation. On all these occasions the government refused to take direct action for the extension of area under jute. This was because of two reasons, firstly, the government was of the view that the area under any particular crop must depend on the profit which the cultivator expected to derive from any other crop; and secondly, that the government would be exceeding its legitimate functions if it brought any pressure to bear on the cultivators in this matter.[22] Likewise, pressure was also brought upon the government to legislate and put an end to the practice of adulteration of jute by mixing sand and water.[23] The government while admitting to the prevalence of the practice, refused to legislate on the ground that the purchasers in this country protected themselves to a great extent by rebates in the case of excessive moisture; and secondly, legislation would cause disturbance in the trade as damaged jute would be driven out of the market and hence there would be a rise in the nominal price. Moreover, it might alarm the cultivators, as was probable, misleading reports

---

attracted the cellulose constituent of the fibre and apparently hydrolized it. The result was that a large proportion sometimes approaching 60 per cent of such damaged fibre became soluble in water, or in dilute acid, or alkali, causing loss of all tensile strength. The fibre would then become useless for spinning purposes. *Capital*, 6 September, 1918, p. 552.

[20]*BLCP*, 22 February, 1921, Vol. I, No. 3, p. 71.

[21]*Captial*, 24 December, 1913, pp. 1595-98.

[22]*BLCP*, 22 February, 1921, Vol. I, No. 3, p. 71.

[23]The proceedings relating to the jute adultration are available in government files. See, IOR: Vol. 7574, BRP (Agriculture), August 1907, Nos. 1-46, pp. 205-296.

of the intentions of government could cause diminution of production and would thus intensify the danger which was under contemplation. A special danger was that if legislation was resorted to, it would be necessary to fix a limit of permissible saturation of jute, and that if this was done the tendency would be strong for all jute to be saturated upto that limit. If this was to happen: the result would be that, while exceptionally bad jute might disappear from the market the general quality of jute supplied would deteriorate, and this would, perhaps, be the greater evil of the two, and that it would necessitate appointing inspectors of unimpeachable integrity and judgement otherwise there would be a danger of making mistakes through acting on corrupt evidence or misleading information.[24]

The action of the government in refusing to bring pressure on the cultivators to extend the area under jute cultivation was correct. The ordinary laws of supply and demand was enough to look after itself. If the prices of raw jute had increased, it was mainly due to the enormous pressure of the sudden expansion of mills, both in India and abroad. It was not unnatural that illiterate and proverbially conservative ryots should take some time to adjust to the newly-created situation. Likewise, by refusing to enact legislation for adulterating jute, the government had taken the right step. The solution to this meance did not lie in legieslative interference which would have brought ryots within the act but in the hands of the jute trade itself which could always refuse to buy adulterated jute.

The jute industry was also concerned about the correctness of the jute forecasts, issued annually by the Department of Agriculture. It was of the gravest importance to the jute industry that the forecasts should be correct as upon them prices were calculated, both of the raw and manufactured articles. It was largely on the basis of government jute forecasts that different mills decided when to purchase their seasonal requirements and when to sell their cloth and bags which they would manufacture during the same period; and mistakes in the forecasts necessarily meant widespread loss, confusion and disaster. The government jute forecasts during this period show much discrepency between the final forecasts and the actual outturn of jute at the end of the season. Thus in 1901-02, thers was

[24]*The Friend of India and Statesman* (weekly edition); 24 January, 1907, p. 19.

a difference of 10 per cent and next year it was 7 per cent.[25] Although, we have the full statistics for the intervening period, we know that in 1908-09, the crop exceeded the government forecast by 23.8 lakhs, the government forecast being 64,01,700 bales while the actual outturn was 87,80,500 bales. Since then such erroneous figures were common.[26]

The reasons for such inaccurate jute forceasts are not far to seek. Firstly, there was no statistical basis for a forecast in Bengal except where a cadastral survey had been made. The result was that the area under jute was reported by the police, who got the information from the village chaukidars. This, in the words of a former director of agriculture, Mr. Gourlay, amounted more or less to mere guess work.[27] Secondly, the yield per acre also differed greatly from district to district. But the agricultural department in calculating the outturn multiplied the total area by a fixed standard of three bales per acre.[28] Thirdly, in compiling the estimated yield due considerations were not taken of the weather and crop reports sent periodically by district officers to the agricultural department. This was further complicated by the vague terms used by district officers such as "Good", "Fair", "not Good", "Poor" etc., which the agricultural department interpreted as it liked. Thus the word "Not Favourable" was actually interpreted to mean anything from 40 per cent to 70 per cent; "Fair" from 72 per cent to 92 per cent; "Poor" from 45 per cent to 80 per cent of the normal outturn in the year 1913.[29] The net result of such compilations was more or less a gamble which unfortunately for the industry meant financial loss.

It was during this period that the foundation was laid for the speculative market in jute, what later on came to be known as the *Bhitar Bazaar* or *Fatka* market. Jewanmal Bengani started this speculative business in 1905-06 when prices of jute suddenly rose.[30]

[25]*The Friend of India and Statesman* (weekly edition), 24 September, 1903, p. 20.

[26]See, for example, the tables relating to jute forecasts in the *Statesman* (weekly overseas edition), 6 September, 1923, p. 5; *Ibid.*, 30 September, 1926, p. 16; and *Ibld.*, 30 September, 1937, p. 6.

[27]*Capital*, 26 February, 1914, p. 502.

[28]*The Statesman* (weekly overseas edition), July 18, 1912, p. 5.

[29]*Capital*, 24 December, 1913, p. 1596.

[30]H. Sinha 'The Jute Mill Industry Today: jute futures in Calcutta', *Capital*, 16 January, 1930, p. 139.

But the movement soon cought on; so much so that regular contracts, known as "pink" and "white" contract had to be provided for the purpose when the speculative fever was at its height. Under such contracts no delivery of jute took place, and indeed none was intended for. Provision was made in the concluding paragraph of the contract form for the payment of differences being arrived at upon a comparison of certificates to be obtained from several Marwari firms whose names were mentioned. To keep up the farce of the contract being a genuine one in respect of jute bought and sold, the usual practice was for the buyers to write a letter to the sellers for a declaration of the marks to be delivered. Indeed all the formalities in connection with a genuine contract were gone through in respect of such contracts.

The effect of such contracts was detrimental to the jute industry as a whole. It turned legitimate trade into a huge gamble. In 1913, for example, when abnormal rainfall threatened great loss of crop and the world demand for bags was so insistant that it was believed manufacturers would buy at any price, *Bhitar Bazaar* took good care to inflate the prices long before the actual deficiency was estimated.[31] To be on guard, therefore, jute manufacturers had to buy their raw material supplies at least eight months ahead. This meant the locking up of a large amount of working capital for which they had to pay bank interests. Similarly, it also meant the erection of large warehouses and the payment of insurance for the goods therein.

The Jute Industry, 1914-1929

With the start of the First World War, the jute industry also entered into a new phase—a phase which was to place the mills then in existence into an unassailable position economically. The war by generating a tremendous demand for gunny bags and cloth kept the mills busy till the end of the war. So insistant was the demand for jute goods that the Hon'ble Commerce Member discussed with the trade in Calcutta as to how immediate the goods could be produced and despatched. The result of this conference was the placing of huge orders with the mills in Bengal. Not only did the British Government buy for itself, but under its orders substantial quantity of bags and cloth had also been sent to Russia and France. The magnitude of the Government orders since 1915 can be measu-

[31] *Capital*, 11 September, 1913, p. 670.

TABLE 6.2

NUMBER OF MILLS, LOOMS, SPINDLES AND PERSONS EMPLOYED IN THE JUTE TEXTILE INDUSTRY IN INDIA, 1900-01 TO 1938-39

Year	*No. of mills*	*Looms*	*Spindles*	*Persons employed*
1900-01	36	15,340	317,348	111,272
1901-02	36	16,119	331,382	114,795
1902-03	38	17,189	352,214	118,904
1903-04	38	18,400	376,718	123,869
1904-05	38	19,991	409,170	133,162
1905-06	39	21,986	453,168	144,879
1906-07	44	25,284	520,504	166,895
1907-08	54	27,244	562,274	187,771
1908-09	56	29,525	607,358	192,181
1909-10	60	31,418	645,862	204,104
1910-11	58	33,169	682,527	216,390
1911-12	59	32,927	677,519	201,324
1912-13	61	34,033	708,716	204,092
1913-14	64	36,050	744,289	216,288
1914-15	70	38,379	795,528	238,274
1915-16	70	39,890	812,421	254,143
1916-17	74	39,697	824,315	262,552
1917-18	76	40,639	834,055	266,038
1918-19	76	40,043	839,919	275,500
1919-20	76	41,045	856,307	280,131
1920-21	77	41,588	869,879	288,401
1921-22	81	43,025	908,359	288,450
1922-23	86	47,528	1,003,179	321,296
1923-24	89	49,038	1,043,417	330,408
1924-25	90	50,359	1,067,633	341,723
1925-26	90	50,503	1,063,700	331,326
1926-27	93	51,061	1,083,816	333,659
1927-28	93	52,221	1,105,634	335,804
1928-29	95	52,409	1,108,147	343,868
1929-30	98	53,900	1,140,435	343,257
1930-31	100	61,834	1,224,982	307,676

Year	No. of mills	Looms	Spindles	Persons employed
1931-32	103	61,426	1,220,586	276,810
1932-33	99	60,506	1,202,183	263,442*
1933-34	99	59,501	1,194,405	257,175
1934-35	100	61,387	1,221,786	263,739
1935-36	104	63,724	1,279,416	277,986
1936-37	104	65,273	1,300,077	289,136
1937-38	105	66,705	1,337,958	295,162
1938-39	107	67,939	1,350,465	298,967

SOURCES: *Statistical Abstract relating to British India from 1900-01 to 1909-10* (Forty-fifth number) (London, 1911), p. 263 and subsequent issues.

*From 1932-33 to 1938-39, the average daily number of workers are for calender years from 1932 to 1938.

red from Table 6.3. Along with large government orders, Bengal had her traditional markets like that of the United States and the Argentine Republic also open. Therefore, contrary to falling demands due to transport and exchange difficulties as was expected, jute goods had a steady and rising market during the war. "Never in the history of the trade has there been such a demand for all classes of jute fabrics and even with the resumption of full time working it had been difficult to deal adequately with it. Practically all markets maintain a firm tone and goods continue to be readily

TABLE 6.3

SHIPMENTS ON GOVERNMENT ACCOUNT, 1915-16 TO 1918-19

Year	Bags (millions)	Cloth (million yards)
1915-16	297	35
1916-17	385	135
1917-18	391	205
1918-19	221	269
Total	1,294	644

SOURCE: *Review of the Trade of India in 1918-19* (Calcutta, 1919), p. 15.

absorbed at full prices"—wrote Kanknarrah Company in their half-yearly report in 1918.[32] If the Kanknarrah expectations had been more than fulfilled, so was the case with the rest of the mills in Bengal.

But the story of its prosperity did not lie in the demand factor alone. During the war, due to restrictions placed by the Government of India on the import of machinery and mill stores, jute mills could not be expanded as was desirable. In fact, there had been an increase of some 4,000 looms during the period of five years between 1913-14 and 1918-19. The outcome was that increased demand for jute goods had to be met by the existing mills in Bengal which naturally placed them in a strong position to bargain for higher prices. Moreover, as government orders arrived without much previous notice, it had the effect of acute competition which sent the prices still higher. During the war years, the raw jute market also underwent a radical change. Foreign Europe which consumed about a quarter of raw jute export was shut off with the consequent result that the prices of raw jute took a sharp downward turn. This, was however, a boon to the jute manufacturing industry which could now buy raw materials at prices highly favourable to them. Cheap jute and increased demand thus brought about a prosperity which the jute industry could not even think of, a few years earlier. The industry had also the additional advantage of not paying ony excess profits tax which, for example, Dundee had to. This, indeed made a very big difference on the profitability of mills so much so that out of nine sterling companies (including one at Chandernagore) existing from 1914 to 1916, three had transformed themselves into rupee companies in 1917 under the Indian Companies Act.[33]

Thus a combination of favourable circumstances placed the jute mill industry in an enviable position. The index of the net profits of the mills rose from 100 in 1914 to 566 in 1915, 748 in 1916 and 570 in 1917 which amounted to 10, 58, 75 and 54 per cent of the total paid up capital of the companies respectively.[34] The net profits of the mills for the first half of 1918 was almost as high as

[32]*Capital*, 2 August, 1918, p. 270.
[33]*Capital*, 24 January, 1919, p. 190.
[34]*The Times*, 10 August, 1918, p. 10. The full details are as follows :

that of 1916.[35] This high profitability of the mills resulted in the declaration of large dividends-sometimes of over 200 per cent.[36] It also enabled the mills to accumulate substantial sums of capital in the reserve and depreciation funds. After the war, Samnuggar, Tittaghur and Victoria were in the field as large bonus distributors also. This resulted in the distribution of shares at the rate of 50 per cent of their holdings. Preference shareholders, who had as a rule no claim to any such increases, were also encouraged by being given an increased rate of dividends.[37] How well the jute mill industry did compared to other industries in India during the war could be understood by looking at Table 6.4.

TABLE 6.4

INDEX TABLE OF PRICES OF SECURITIES AND SHARES OF CERTAIN SELECTED INDUSTRIES IN INDIA, 1914, 1917 AND 1918

	July 1914	*July 1917*	*March 1918*
66 cotton mills	100	132	161
90 coal companies	100	141	137
88 tea companies	100	127	125
32 jute mills	100	311	467
7 flour mills	100	120	162
1 iron and steel company (Tata)	100	332	295

SOURCE: *The Times Trade Supplement,* 29 March, 1919, p. 34.

	1914 £	1915 £	1916 £	1917 £
1. Total profits	982,000	4,820,000	6,309,000	4,831,000
Do; Index Nos.	(100)	(491)	(643)	(492)
2. Debenture int.	159,000	159,000	154,000	142,000
3. Net profits (subject to depreciation)	823,000	4,661,000	6,155,000	4,689,000
Do; Index Nos.	(100)	(566)	(748)	(570)
4. Ratio of net profits to paid up capital	10	58	75	53

[35]*Capital,* 24 January, 1919, pp. 190 & 192. The ratio of net profits to total paid up capital for the first half of 1918 was 73.

[36]*Capital,* 15 Ferbuary, 1918, p. 387. For the year 1916-17 Kinnison, for example, declared a dividend of 225 per cent.

[37]*Capital,* 14 November, 1919, p. 1292.

The prosperity that war brought to the jute industry continued even after its end, right till 1929. This was made possible by means of a series of short-time agreements entered into by the mills in the membership of the Association. This working agreements had been in force in one form or other since shortly after the cessation of hostilities. From early 1921 to the 30th June 1929 short-time working agreements provided for a restriction of the mills' working hours to 54 per week while in February 1924 a supplementary agreement was entered into providing that during the currency of the original working time agreement extra productive machinery or relative buildings would not be installed or ordered.[38] How effective the IJMA policy of restriction was could be understood from the fact that even during the post-war depression which lasted from 1920-21 to 1923-24, the IJMA was able, more or less, to maintain its wholesale price level by reducing production to world demand.[39]

The prosperity of the war years brought about large extensions and additions in the number of mills. No sooner the war was over jute mill machinery and stores began to arrive and within a period of three years no less than ten jute mills came into existence and by 1929 the total number of looms of India had increased to over 52,000.[40] An estimate of their gross investment of capital is, however, almost impossible to make. The limitations of such estimates are numerous. Firstly, we do not have the full statistics as regards the block capital and other particulars like the total paid-up capi-

[38]IOR: Vol. 12077, BFP (commerce), March 1936, No. 24, p. 17.

[39]The world demand for jute products during the three years ending 1923-24 was less due to several factors. The primary factor was, of course, the lack of purchasing power of the Central European countries. South America also reduced its demand owing to serious restrictions placed on bank credits. In Russia, not only were the railways dislocated but also due to decimation of horses, cultivators could not market their produce and in Rumania it was the change in the system of land tenure, particularly the splitting up of large estates into small holdings which reduced exportable surplus (*Review of the Trade of India in 1921-22*, p. 18). It was also said to have been due to the enormous stock accumulated over the last three years in the United States and the United Kingdom which brought about a decreased demand. *The Statesman*, 15 June, 1922; p. 6. See, Letter to the Editor by "G.O."

[40]The ten jute mills were the Orient (1920), Ludlow (1920), Cheviot (1920), Nuddea (1921), Birla (1921), Craig (1921), Presidency (1921), Waverley (1921) Meghna (1922), and Hukumchand (1922).

tal, depreciation funds and reserves etc., in the case of the privately-owned mills and in the concerns under the American management. Secondly, mills always carried large stocks of raw material and other stores, the value of which is almost impossible to estimate. In spite of such limitations, in Table 6.5 we have attempted an estimate of the amounts invested in the jute mills of Bengal which were listed in the issues of "Capital" dated 28 August, 1920 and 5 April, 1928.

TABLE 6.5

INVESTMENT OF CAPITAL IN BENGAL JUTE INDUSTRY, 1920 & 1928

1920		*1928*	
Gross Block Account			
Rs (lakhs)	21,65	Rs (lakhs)	38,00
+		+	
£3 million		£3.45 million	
Ordinary Capital			
Paid-up Rs (lakhs)	10,21	Rs (lakhs)	11,16
+		+	
£1.6 million		£1.88 million	
Preference capital			
Rs (lakhs)	5,08	Rs (lakhs)	5,31
+		+	
£650,000		£650,000	
Debenture Rs (lakhs)	3,05	Rs (lakhs)	3,44
+			
£38,052			
Reserve and other Funds, including depreciation			
Rs (lakhs)	21,69	Rs (lakhs)	32,40
+		+	
£2.17 million		£2.65 million	
Profits and Loss			
Balances Rs (lakhs)	1,32	Rs (lakhs)	68
+		+	
£282,037		£266,356	

SOURCES: *Capital*, 28 August, 1920; and *Ibid.*, 5 April, 1928.

From the above table (Table 6.5) it will be seen that the gross block account had almost doubled within a period of about eight years. This was due mainly to the increased cost of installing new looms which previous to the war was about Rs. 6,000 per loom and had increased to around Rs. 16,000 after it.[41] The sustained increase in the reserves and depreciation funds enabled the mills to carry out the extensions necessary without greatly increasing the total paid-up capital of the companies.

Of the capital invested in the jute mills, it is believed that over 60 per cent of it was owned by the Indians themselves which was quite in contrast to the situation prior to 1914 when hardly any Indian had any share in the industry. The changed attitude of the Indian capitalists towards this industry was perhaps brought about by war profits. The European shareholders finding their shares considerably appreciated in value perhaps also took the opportunity of unloading these during the war which made it easier for the speculative Marwari investors to increase their shareholdings substantially. The period also marked the entry of Indians as jute mill entrepreneurs. In 1921 Birla Brothers established a mill with 450 looms. But the finest example of Indian entrepreneurship was the flotation of the Hukumchand Jute Company, Limited in May, 1922. Not only was this an Indian concern—much of the equipment was also for the first time manufactured in India. For instance, the looms, of which there were 425, and the softners, six in number, were the work of the Britannia Engineering Company, while the spindles, numbering approximately 12,000 were manufactured by the Angus Engineering Works.[42]

The prosperity of the period, however, did not mean prosperity to the jute ryots. The war meant the closing down of raw jute markets of Germany and Austria, which consumed more than a quarter of Bengal's exports of raw jute.[43] Subsequently, more markets were closed either as a result of shortage of freight or being declared a prohibited zone. Thus the total exports of raw jute in 1916 showed a decrease of 19 per cent as compared with 1915, and 35 per cent as compared with the pre-war year 1913.[44]

[41]A.K. Bagchi, *Private Investment in India* (Cambridge, 1972), pp. 273-274.
[42]*The Statesman* (weekly overseas edition), 25 May, 1922, p. 19.
[43]*Capital*, 27 August, 1914, p. 535.
[44]*Ibid.*, 16 February, 1917, p. 416. See. "Official Papers".

With the fall in exports, prices of raw jute also fell considerably.[45] The situation was worsened by the monopolistic hold of the jute manufacturers who would only buy at dictated prices. The result was widespread distress among the ryots, sometimes leading to looting of hats and bazaars.[46] The Government of Bengal, however, could do little, as it felt that it was extremely difficult, if not impossible, to enforce any provision of minimum prices due to the presence of innumerable number of middlemen and the different grades and qualities of jute that was involved.[47]

However, it would be too much to say that the jute industry itself had no problem to contend with during this period. The first was as regards the supply of coal of which the jute industry required annually 1,052,000 tons.[48] This supply had been severely interrupted by the shortage of waggons in the early 1920's and in spite of the Coal Transportation Officer's earnest efforts the stocks at the mills were insufficient to run all the mills and consequently several mills had to be closed down.[49] The position would have been much more severe had not the post-war depression coincided with the scarcity of coal.

The problem of jute forecasts also arose again during this period. So pitifully inaccurate were the government estimates with the actual outturn that the whole exercise of issuing forecasts had been reduced to a farce. Thus the figures were incorrect to the extent of 28 per cent, 76 per cent and 43 per cent in the years 1920-21, 1921-22, and 1922-23 respectively. Such estimates upset mill calcultions very gravely. For example, in 1925-26 when the forecast figure put the estimated outturn to 79 lakh bales, apparently insufficient for the world consumption, jute prices rose

[45]Prices of raw jute (M. Group) in Calcutta at the end of March were as follows (per bale of 400 Ibs.):

1915	Rs. 40
1916	Rs. 59
1917	Rs. 49
1918	Rs. 40
1919	Rs. 64

See, *Review of Trade of India*, 1920-21, p. 14. For pre-war prices of raw jute, see, p. 246 of this chapter.

[46]*Capital*, 18 January, 1918, p. 142,

[47]*BLCP*, 4 July, 1918. Vol. L. p. 744.

[48]*Capital*, 23 March, 1917, p. 677.

[49]*The Statesman* (weekly overseas edition), 9 February, 1921, p. 19.

to the unprecedented level of Rs. 140 per bale for First Marks. But later on it was found that the outturn was actually much in excess of government forecasts and prices came down sharply to Rs. 80. But unfortunately for the manufacturers the gunny prices could not keep pace with the jute price.

The Jute Industry in Depression, 1929-30 to 1939

Since 1921 when the mills within the membership of the IJMA adopted short-time working agreement of 54 hours per week, Calcutta mills had enjoyed a good measure of prosperity. The output of the mills had always commanded a ready market at rates which left a handsome manufacturing profit. The managing agents, while declaring large dividends to the shareholders, had been able to consolidate and strengthen the financial position of the companies under their management. But all this was to change radically with the coming of the world-wide depression which was particularly severe in the case of primary products. This meant a greatly-reduced demand for jute manufactures. Further, as there was little demand from other industries and less movement of goods in the international market, the demand for jute manufactures slumped very low.

However, since the IJMA was a closely-knit body and acted as a quasi-monopolistic group, it could probably have reduced its production to world demand as it did previously; but the situation was quite altered against it by the erection of new mills not within the membership of the Association. The erection of these mills had seriously upset the effects of regulated production upon which the profitability of the member mills depended. Therefore, with the incoming of the depression the first task of the IJMA was to bring those mills within the membership of the Association so that it could regulate supply to demand as before. In its effort, the IJMA was able in 1930 to bring Adamjee, Gagalbhai, Shree Hanuman and Premchand—four of the six of the principal non-Association mills (the other two were Agarpara and Ludlow) to become signatories to the working time agreement then in force. However, in March 1931, when the Association mills reduced their hours of work to 40 per week, sealed up 15 per cent of their looms and continued to observe the principle that no extension of productive machinery would be made, the recently joined new mills seceded from the Association.

Nor was it a surprise move on the part of the recently erected mills to take such a step. If the older establishments within the IJMA were acting with the instinct of self-preservation, so were the new mills. The IJMA mills had behind them large reserves and depreciation funds which enabled them to restrict production or to seal looms or even to pay dividends out of these if need be; but the case was not the same with the newly-erected mills. Already the 54 hour-a-week working scheme was hurting them (realizing which, Agarpara and Ludlow did not even become signatories to the IJMA working agreement in the first place) which led to complaints, off and on, but the Association paid no heed to their expression of grievances[50] and when the 40 hour-a-week prescription with a uniform closing of 15 per cent of the total looms came, they naturally resigned one by one from the IJMA.

But the trading conditions had already touched the bottom by 1932 and so did the profits of the mills. The prescribed policy had failed miserably to improve the situation, and over and above that if the outside mills were allowed to continue to work for 108 hours weekly on the double shift system as some of these were doing, the future of the jute industry was indeed very bleak. Moreover, certain of the Association mills were under the strong temptation to increase their production by nearly two-thirds and thereby reduce substantially their overhead costs. It was feared that these might break away from the 40-hour-agreement unless some effective action was taken against them. Under the circumstances, the IJMA had but only three options open. The first was to suspend temporarily the working agreement, come out into the open market and fight the non-Association mills. But the financial consequences of such a move were likely to be disastrous. It would have meant the collapse of gunny prices and banks would have been obliged to call in their money which they advanced against stocks of goods and shares. The seoond alternative was to persuade the non-Association mills to adopt some form of restriction in production. But this implied the giving of certain advantages to the non-Association mills, possibly longer working hours and the employment of all looms which it was quite unwilling to do. The third alternative was to seek government intervention and which it did when Sir John Anderson was

[50]*Capital*, 31 March, 1932, p. 482. Letter to the Editor by R.N. Roy.

appointed as the new Governor of Bengal in May, 1932 and ultimately an agreement was signed which was to run for a period from 1 August, 1932 to the 30 June, 1933. The main features of the agreement were as follows:

(*a*) that the Association mills would work 40 hours a week with 15 per cent of their looms sealed;

(*b*) that outside mills would work 54 hours a week with a full complement of machinery;

(*c*) that the Agarpara mill would be permitted to increase its loomage by 64;

(*d*) that during the period of the agreement there should be no increase in productive machinery in any other mill; and

(*e*) that the Premchand Jute Mills and the Shree Hanuman Jute Mills would continue to be members of the Association, and would be given the privilege of working with their full complement of machinery for 54 hours per week during the currency of the agreement and that the IJMA would be at liberty to consider the claims of certain other mills within the Association to similar treatment subject to the condition that the privilege of working 54 hours a week would not be accorded to more than 4 per cent of the total number of looms of the mills within the Association including the Premchand and the Shree Hanuman Jute Mills.[51]

Although the new arrangement between the IJMA mills and certain other non-Association mills improved the position of the industry financially and stocks fell to a certain extent, it could not stop other mills from being erected, both in Bengal and in other provinces of India.[52] Unrestricted by any form of control, these mills were working by double and triple shifts anything from 108 to 120 hours per week and thereby could produce three times what an Association mills could do with the same complement of machinery. Their profits were consequently much more than those of the mills whose output was regulated. It was this special advantage of not being subject to any control regarding output which was providing the greatest attraction for those who wanted to start new

[51]*Review of the Trade of India in 1931-32* (Calcutta, 1932), pp. 83-84. It could be seen from the above arrangement that in spite of government intervention, the IJMA had to concede certain important advantages to the non-Association mills.

[52]Stocks of Calcutta mills fell from 305 million yards in 1931 to 143 million yards by 1935. *Capital*, 4 February, 1937, p. 185

mills.[53] Moreover, although there was only about 500 such outside looms in July 1934, there was definite proof that further expansion, by way of extension of existing mills, was contemplated, which would give to this group of mills an aggregate of approximately 1,800 looms, which would be equivalent to about 7,000 to 7,500 Association looms under the present conditions of working hours adopted by the outside mills.[54] This serious situation led the IJMA to ask the Government of Bengal for legislative intervention which, however, the government declined unless the mills themselves adopted a scheme of rationalization.[55]

Having failed to persuade the government to legislate and having been confronted with the dangerous expansion of outside mills who were unwilling to restrictive production, the IJMA decided to employ the only means in its power, which was to increase production and accordingly it unsealed all its looms by February 1936. It also decided to terminate its working agreement with the non-Association mills with effect from 31 March, 1936. Since then there was no restriction on the working hours of mills in India and stocks grew to alarming proportions, far outstripping the needs of the market.[56] Prices of manufactured goods fell to its lowest point

[53]It was estimated that a membership mill of 600 looms (400 hessian plus 200 sacking) working 40 hours a week would manufacture at least 7,200 tons (3,200 hessian plus 4,000 sacking) per annum whereas the outside mills with the same complement of looms but at 62 hours per week would manufacture 10,800 tons (4,800 hessians plus 6,000 sackings). Therefore, the productive capacity of the outside mills were 50 per cent higher. Its cost of manufacture was also thought to be Rs. 20 per ton cheaper than that of the membership mill. If the margin of jute manufacture was Rs. 40 per ton, the membership mill would earn a yearly profit of Rs. 2,88,000 or Rs. 480 per loom (in effect the actual profits per loom was even less than this in 1936, *Capital*, 3 June, 1937, p. 895) whereas the outside mill with its extra production and redueed cost of manufacture would earn Rs. 60 per ton or Rs. 6,48,000 per year, i.e., Rs. 1,080 per loom or in other words an extra profit of Rs. 600 per loom. *The Statesman* (weekly overseas edition), 3 October, 1935, p. 6. See, Letter to the Editor by "Anti Speculation".

[54]Letter from the Secretary, IJMA to the Secretary to the Government of Bengal, Commerce Department. IOR: Vol. 12077, BFP (commerce), March 1936, No. 24, p. 20.

[55]See, the text of the letter adressed to the Secretary, IJMA by the Government of Bengal, Commerce Department, *Capital*, 5 September, 1935, p. 399.

[56]Stocks of manufactured goods in India held by the major portion of the industry had increased from around 161 million yards on 31 March, 1936 to 531 million yards by 30, April 1938. *The Statesman* (weekly overseas edition), 12 May, 1938, p. 9.

TABLE 6.6

PROFITS OF JUTE MILL INDUSTRY, 1928 TO 1937

Year	*No. of companies*	*Profits (Rs. '000)*	*Profits, same companies, previous year (Rs. '000)*	*Chain index (Base, 1928-100)*
1928	47	7,69,30	N.A.	100.0
1929	47	6,58,17	7,69,30	85.9
1930	47	2,91,50	6,58,17	37.9
1931	49	68,60	2,99,90	8.7
1932	50	1,02,84	70,49	12.6
1933	52	1,61,92	1,03,66	19.8
1934	53	2,86,70	1,64,71	34.4
1935	53	3,33,29	2,86,70	40.0
1936	53	2,16,33	3,33,29	25.9
1937	54	1,00,75	2,18,41	12.0

SOURCE: *Capital*, 8 December, 1938, p. 823.

ever since the war and manufacturing profits almost vanished. Many mills which did not have sufficient reserves to enable them to continue paying losses or did not think it advisable to manufacture any longer, closed down. When faced with such a situation, the Bengal Government had no alternative but to promulgate an Ordinance (Bengal Jute Ordinance, 1938) whereby it made it unlawfull except with the previous sanction of the Chief Inspector of Factories to increase the number of looms or to replace any existing looms in any jute mill.[57] The maximum working period was also fixed at 45 hours per week for all mills, excepting 72 hours a week for the five small mills having 175 looms or less.[58] Under the threat of this Ordinance, the mills had no option but to join the IJMA and sign a working agreement.[59] The Bengal Jute Ordinance also,

[57]*Star of India*, 10 September, 1938, p. 4.

[58]*Capital*, 15 September, 1938, p. 397. The decision was made by the Advisory Committee appointed by the Government of Bengal in accordance with the provisions of the Jute Ordinance.

[59]The only mills of Bengal which did not become members of the IJMA were Ludlow and Gagalbhai which represented approximately 2 per cent of the loomage in Bengal. *The Statesman* (weekly overseas edition), 9 March, 1939, p. 13.

having served its purpose was withdrawn by the government and the manufacturing industry was once again a united Association. The successful completion of the negotiations was followed by large government orders for sandbags which moved the prices of manufactured goods sharply on the markets.

The threat to the Bengal jute industry did not come only from expanding mills within India but also from foreign countries. Thus ever since the close of the war, Bengal had been exporting increasing quantity of raw material abroad to be manufactured there into finished products. Thereby those countries were not only able to supply their home requirements adequately but also gradually invaded overseas markets (as could be seen in Table 6.7). So far as the supply of their respective home market was concerned, Calcutta could do but little. This was mainly because most of these countries had high tariff duty which protected their home industry against foreign competition. But it is a sad commentary to note that Calcutta itself was no less responsible for the increasing growth of overseas mills. By securing an artificially high price for its products it encouraged foreign countries to set up their own mills. Moreover, since those foreign countries had no restriction in pro-

TABLE 6.7

EXPORTS OF JUTE YARN, JUTE CLOTHS AND JUTE BAGS FROM THE MAJOR EUROPEAN JUTE MANUFACTURING COUNTRIES IN 1922 AND 1927

Country	*1922 Tons*	*1927 Tons*
France	7,852	19,171
Germany	13,519	17,228
Belgium	1,372	14,299
Austria and Czechoslovakia	7,515	17,887
Italy	5,027	11,589
Poland	138	3,622
Great Britain (Home made goods)	68,536	81,435
Total	103,959	165,231

SOURCE: *Capital*, 23 February, 1929, p. 456.

duction like the Bengal mills, its cost of production per unit was also lower which gave them a competitive advantage abroad. But probably more important was the fact that Calcutta lacked salesmanship which was so vital in overseas competition. Thus the German mills were at all times prepared to allow buyers options ranging from 25 to 60 inches and even more, without the addition of any premium, and would sell any of these sizes in lots of 5 bales. But the situation was quite different with the Calcutta mills. It was virtually impossible to secure any options more than 40-8 oz. option 7½ and 36 inches or 40-10½ oz. option 10 oz. and on very rare occasions when it was possible to secure large options a premium of Re. 1 to Rs. 2 was charged. Further, if the quantities were anything below 50,000 yards, an additional premium was enforced.[60] Another great disadvantage of Calcutta mills was the lack of diversity in their products. Excepting a very small quantity of twist and yard, rope and twine, and canvas; the vast majority of their products were either sackings or hessian cloth. It paid very little attention to commercial research or to new uses to which jute could be put to. The Minority Report of the Finlow Committee condemned the jute industry of Bengal for its "distinct lack of variety" and "the absence of enterprise" for restricting its manufacture to the production of practically two varieties of goods and reminded it of the significant fact that the continent of Europe "are not only earning profits for themselves by devising new and more costly uses of jute as a blending material for silk or wool, but also stimulating demand for jute and consequently helping the maintenance of its price."[61] One wonders whether the export duty was not also to a certain extent responsible for the increasing growth of overseas competition against the jute mill industry. This will be clear if we look at certain anomalies in con-

[60]Earnrst A. Feldmann, "The Indian Jute Mill Industry: How can the Hessian Industry be Improved?", *Capital*, 20 March, 1930, p. 674.

[61]*Report of the Bengal Jute Enquiry Committee*, Vol. I, Minority Report (Alipore, 1934), p. 79. A similar report on the Bengal jute industry (Fawcus Committee) in 1939 also urged the manufacturers to divert their financial resources to specially selected lines of manufacture. This, the report thought would be "an aspect of constructive rationalization". It felt that it was the only way in which they could permanently increase the demand for jute goods, and through them the demand for jute. *Report of the Bengal Jute Enquiry Committee*, Vol. I (Alipore, 1939), p. 20.

TABLE 6.8

EXPORT OF JUTE MANUFACTURES FROM INDIA (ALL SORTS), 1900-01 TO 1938-39

Year	*Bags* No. (*million*)	*Cloths* *Yards* (*million*)	*Total value* *Rs.* (*lakhs*)
1900-01	203	365	786
1901-02	230	419	871
1902-03	225	493	902
1903-04	206	552	947
1904-05	201	576	994
1905-06	233	659	12,45
1906-07	258	696	15,72
1907-08	293	790	18,30
1908-09	301	770	15,74
1909-10	364	940	17,10
1910-11	361	955	16,99
1911-12	290	871	16,01
1912-13	312	1,022	22,87
1913-14	369	1,061	28,27
1914-15	398	1,057	25,82
1915-16	794	1,192	37,97
1916-17	805	1,230	41,65
1917-18	758	1,197	42,84
1918-19	583	1,103	52,65
1919-20	343	1,275	50,02
1920-21	534	1,353	52,99
1921-22	387	1,121	29,99
1922-23	344	1,254	40,49
1923-24	414	1,349	42,28
1924-25	425	1,456	51,76
1925-26	425	1,461	58,83
1926-27	449	1,503	53,18
1927-28	463	1,553	53,56
1928-29	498	1,568	56,90
1929-30	522	1,651	51,93
1930-31	434	1,271	31,89
1931-32	389	1,021	21,92
1932-33	415	1,012	21,71
1933-34	402	1,053	21,37
1934-35	423	1,063	21,47
1935-36	459	1,218	23,49
1936-37	621	1,710	29,10
1937-38	612	1,643	29,08
1938-39	598	1,550	26,26

SOURCE: *Review of the Trade of India in 1900-01* (Calcutta, 1901), p. 27 and and subsequent annual issues till 1938-39.

nection with these duties. In the first place the export duty was highest on goods in which the Calcutta mills met with the severest competition, namely hessians. Thus hessians bore an export duty of Rs. 32 per ton against Rs. 25-3 per ton on raw jute. It was no wonder that the ratio of jute exported to that of the jute manufactured in India tended to increase in the post-war period. Secondly, cuttings had to pay an export duty of Rs. 7 per ton only which encouraged overseas competitors to build up an industry in the manufacture of heavy sacking in which cuttings were largely used. Moreover, it was claimed that a good quantity of raw jute also left the country under the description of cuttings.[62]

The jute industry had also come under increasing competition from substitutes during this period. The basic reason for this was that jute had lost, for the time being at any rate, its principal recommendation, namely, its comparative cheapness. Thus paper sacks which "cost little" came to be increasingly used all over the world.[63] It was estimated that the loss caused to the jute industry in Bengal on account of the changeover to paper in the United Kingdom and South Africa alone exceeded 20 million cement bags per annum.[64] Chile, which also imported substantial number of cement bags from Calcutta had practically changed over to paper bags made in the country and the few jute bags still used in this trade were supplied by the local factory.[65] In 1926 when burlap prices for a few months approached cotton prices, consumers in America began to use cotton sacks for packing fertilizers instead of burlap sacks and once U.S. consumers became accustomed to the use of cotton sacks, they continued to use them even when the price was a little higher. Thus prior to 1926, virtually all new fertilizer sacks, for instance, were made of burlap. By 1937, no less than 12 per cent of the fertilizers were packed in cotton sacks, and 6 per cent in paper sacks, and remaining 82 per cent were packed in burlap sacks.[66] In addition to price and choice of a particular vari-

[62]*Capital*, September 13, 1984, p. 471.

[63]IJMA: *Special Report on Markets for Jute* (Calcutta, 1947), p. 26. For the cost of different types of bags used for packing fertilizers in the United States in 1938, see, B.C. Kundu and others, *Jute in India* (Calcutta, 1959), Table 49, p. 280.

[64]*Report of the Bengal Jute Enquiry Committee* (Fawcus Committee), Vol. II (Alipore, 1939), p. 176. Replies to the questionnaire, by the Sectretary, British India Association.

ety, the desire of certain countries to utilize their internal resources whenever possible to the elimination of jute and jute fabrics also led to substitution. Thus with a view to encouraging flax and hemp cultivation in Poland, the management of the Polish Salt Monopoly bought 3,700,000 linen sacks from October 1932 to January 1934 to replace the jute hitherto used for bagging salt at the mines and in the warehouses.[67] The Polish Government also brought some kind of pressure in 1934 on the sugar manufactures which led to an order for 700,000 linen sacks instcad of jute sacks used hitherto.[68] In addition to these, the development of mechanical contrivances for bulk handling also contributed in undermining the demand for jute. Argentine which had so long used hessian sacks for packing and containing grain for transport had initiated a programme for erecting 600 grain elevators throughout the Argentine in 1931 and in 1937 the legislature of the Argentine had passed legislation authorising the provision of state funds for the erection of grain elevators to eliminate the use of jute bags as far as possible in the grain trade.[69] In Australia also, the bulk handling of grain and the extension of the silo system, sponsored by government of the various provinces deprived Indian mills of an outlet for their goods.[70]

The rise of competitive substitutes, however, did not take the IJMA by surprise. On the contrary, it had long been expecting such an event which led it in 1917 to call jute a conditional monopoly, the condition being price.[71] What surprises a casual observer, however, is the fact that in spite of such long warnings the jute industry failed to take any effective measure by way of quality control, price and research in allied fields. It was only in 1933 that a subcommittee of the IJMA for the first time seriously examined the question of substitutes and came to the conclusion that unless effective measures were taken at an early date to retain the trade which the industry then held, and to regain some of the markets which had been lost to substitutes, and to explore other avenues for new

[65]Economic and Overseas Department Collections, IOR. L/E/9/404.
[66]IJMA: *Special Report on Market for Jute*, p. 25.
[67]Economic and Overseas Department Conclusions, IOR. L/E/9/405.
[68]Ibid.
[69]*Capital*, 11 June, 1931, p. 1075; and *Ibid.*, 12 August, 1937, p. 217.
[70]*Report of the Bengal Jute Enquiry Committee* (Fawcus Committee), Vol. II, p. 99. Replies of the Bengal Chamber of Commerce to the questionnaire.
[71]*The Statesman*, 3 March, 1920, p. 17.

business, the jute industry in Bengal was faced with the prospect of a gradual but steady decrease in the use of the fabrics which it produced.[72] But it took another four years before another research larboratory of the IJMA was opened in September, 1937. In the same year the Government of India also established a committee—the Indian Central Jute Committee—to deal with the various aspects of the industry.

The gambling operations of the jute futures market (Fatka market or Bhitar bazaar) again emerged to the forefront during this period. Although in Bombay similar operations had been checked by the passing of the Bombay Cotton Standards Act, nothing like this had been done by the Government of Bengal to establish a properly organized jute futures market. Representations in this regard to the Government was futile and the trade was told to settle their own dispute.[73] The result was the continuation of speculative transactions both in raw jute and in jute manufactures (futures market in jute manufactures came into being after the war) to the detriment of legitimate trade. It caused buyers overseas to pay higher prices for jute manufactures and probably also drove away many overseas buyers from the Calcutta market.[74] Nor did it benefit the ryots (as was claimed by the East India Jute Association) by way of circulating information as regards trade movements through a daily quotation which had very little relation to actual dealings in the markets but were more the results of the whims of certain speculators.[75]

Another important issue of the period was the realtionship between the mills and the ryots. In normal years mills in India and abroad consumed more or less all the jute produced in Bengal. But the depression by lessening the world demand for jute manufactures, considerably lessened the demand for jute. This, coupled with the fact that mills had already substantial stocks of raw and manufactured jute in hand, slackened the demand further. The cumulative result was severe overproduction of the raw material which the

[72]*Capital*, 8 June, 1833, pp. 961-62.

[73]"*Capital*" *Indian Industries and Transport Supplement* (December, 1934), p. 13. Although negotiations were undertaken which resulted in the change of the East India Association's Articles and the formation of a Board of Control, differences of opinion remained throughout. See, *Capital*, 19 May, 1938, p. 747.

[74]*Report of the Bengal Jute Euquiry Committee*, Vol. I, Majority Report (Alipore, 1934), p. 28.

[75]*Capital*, 28 September, 1939, p. 475.

mills failed to consume, and consequently prices of raw jute came down very low, much sharper than the prices of jute manufactures. But since the price of other commodities of daily use did not proportionally fall, distress among the ryots became severe. Although the government carried out propaganda by circulating leaflets (and by other means) among the cultivators in the jute tracts of Bengal explaining the causes of the slump and urging them to reduce the area under jute cultivation, the propaganda seemed to have had little effect. The primary reason for this was the fact that jute was the only money crop of the ryots with which he paid the rent of the landlord, bought seeds, clothes, bullocks and other necessities of life. He could not possibly, therefore, reduce his acreage under jute cultivation without bringing further distress upon himself.

The situation, however, seemed to have improved slightly since 1935-36. But this was not so much due to Government's Voluntary Restriction Scheme followed since 1935 under the direction of Rural Development Commissioner but due mainly to increased world consumption of raw materials and falling stocks.[76] Yet by 1939, the price level of jute failed to come up to the expectations even when manufacturing industry had recovered under the strong demands for sandbags by the British Government. Having failed to effect a solution, the government in August 1939 promulgated an Ordinance fixing the minimum price of jute at Rs. 36 per bale, and from next year the government instituted a system of licensing of jute acreage under the Regulation of Jute Area Act, 1940.

Conclusion

The establishment of jute manufacturing industry in Bengal was one of the significant contributions of British enterprise in India. The men coming as they did from far-flung regions not only pioneered the industry but also developed and organized the industry efficiently and opened out a vast market for it products which not

[76]Actual world consumption of raw jute had increased from 89 lakh bales in 1933-34 to 93 lakh bales in 1934-35 and in 1935-36, 113 lakh bales in 1936-37 and 111 lakh bales in 1937-38. See, *Report of the Bengal Jute Enquiry Committee* (Fawcus Committee), Vol. II, p. 139. At the same time world stocks of jute had been decreasing as follows:
1935-36 by 19 lakh bales
1936-37 by 12 lakh bales
1937-38 by 11 lakh bales
See, *The Statesman* (weekly overseas edition), 9 March, 1939, p. 13.

TABLE 6.9

INDEX NUMBER OF WHOLESALE PRICES OF RAW JUTE, JUTE MANUFACTURES AND THE ANNUAL AVERAGE INDEX OF WHOLESALE PRICES OF ALL COMMODITIES, 1914, 1921-1939

Year	*Jute, raw*	*Jute, manufactures*	*Annual average index of wholesale prices (all commodities)*
1914 (end of July)	100	100	—
1921 (annual average)	83	104	179
1922	110	144	176
1923	90	138	172
1924	102	159	173
1925	154	177	159
1926	120	147	148
1927	93	146	148
1928	100	150	145
1929	95	122	141
1930	63	88	116
1931	49	76	96
1932	45	75	91
1933	41	77	87
1934	39	77	89
1935	50	74	91
1936	50	64	91
1937	56	67	102
1938	49	62	95
1939	80	102	108

SOURCE: *Statistical Abstract for British India with statistics, where, available, relating to certain Indian States from 1930-31 to 1939-40* (seventy-second number) (London 1943), pp. 475-77.

only provided jobs for hundreds of thousands of their employees but also benefitted millions of agriculturists in the jute products district of Bengal. In their effort they were highly successful due to certain locational advantages, the most important of these being the close proximity of jute growing districts of Eastern Bengal and Assam and a relatively cheap labour before.

Once Calcutta was able to capture the American market towards the end of the last century, the development of this industry was rapid and phenomenal and continued to be so till the beginning of the First World War. The war demands and consequent profits of the period gave a further momentum to the industry and mills proliferated with resultant overproduction and glut in the market. The problem was accentuated further due to the shrinkage of world demand in the 1930's as a result of depression and the aspirasions of certain countries to be self-sufficient in this respect. Laek of diversity in Calcutta's Production and poor salesmanship also positively contributed to a fall in demand. Thirties also brought other problems, the most important of which was the growth of substitutes in the wake of paper bags and cotton sacks; and the use of mechanical contrivances for bulk handling. The only possible solution to these problems seemed to lie in the rationalization of the industry and in co-operation between the IJMA and the Indian section of the industry.

7 The Handloom Cotton Weaving Industry in Bengal

Before the days of the Industrial Revolution, Bengal was not only self-sufficient in the cotton fabrics which she consumed but also exported her products to overseas markets in Asia, America and Europe. This supremacy in the production of handloom fabrics was due to two factors—the possession of highly specialized technical skills and lower costs of production per unit.[1] However, the fortunes of this once-flourishing-industry in Bengal underwent a dramatic change in the nineteenth century with the advent of power-loom. In the year 1747, for example, the cloths exported from Dacca on account of the Company and individuals, amounted to twenty-eight lakhs and a half; in 1792 the exports were estimated at twenty-five lakhs; in 1797 at not more than fourteen lakhs and in 1800 at eighteen lakhs.[2] The average amount of cloths exported by the East India Company during the decade ending around 1830 did not amount to more than six lakhs annually.[3] Likewise, the exports of piece-goods from Lakhipore which amounted to over sixteen-lakhs of rupees in 1795-96[4] gradually fell and ultimately disappeared altogether. The Government purchases of Santipur muslin, during the first twenty-eight years of the nineteenth century averaged, from £ 120,000 to £ 150,000.[5]

[1]K.N. Chaudhuri, 'The Structure of Indian Textile Industry in the Seventeenth and Eighteenth Centuries', *Indian Economic and Social History Review*, Vol. XI, Nos. 2-3, June-September, 1974.

[2]*Antiquities of Dacca*, No. 4 (London, 1830), p. 20. The British Library copy of the work which I have seen does not contain any date of publication, though the catalogue indicates it to be 1830 with a note of interrogation.

[3]*Ibid.*

[4]IOR. P/174/13, Bengal Commercial Reports, 1795-1802. See, "Abstract Statement of Piece-goods, exported from the Calcutta Custom House, from the 1st of June 1795 to the 31st of May 1796."

[5]W.W. Hunter, *A Statistical Account of Bengal*, Vol. II, Districts of Nadiya and Jessor (London, 1875), p. 95.

Not only had there been a decline in the export trade in cotton piece-goods but the Industrial Revolution also dislocated the home market of Bengal textile workers. Within a few years since 1821-22 when cotton yarn and twist was first imported into Bengal, it replaced the hand-spun threads universally and the importation of mass produced cotton piece-goods in increasing quantities began to displace indigenous handloom weavers, causing widespread unemployment and distress in the rural areas.[6]

> Since the introduction of European machine-made textiles into this country, it may be said that the indigenous industry has practically died out and the professional position of the weavers as a class has become very unsatisfactory... great majority of weavers have... given up their hereditary occupation and now have taken to cultivation and other remunerative pursuits... Those who still work at the loom are in more or less indigent circumstances, and are not able to depend upon weaving as the sole means of subsistence.[7]

[6]The value of importations of foreign cotton twist and yarn as well as piece-goods into Bengal could be seen from the following figures (in rupees):

Year	*cotton twist and yarn*	*piece-goods*
1820-21	Nil	34,52,851
1821-22	4,930	57,96,801
1822-23	Nil	73,41,493
1823-24	11,834	42,15,548
1824-25	1,24,811	56,05,746
1825-26	1,49,867	44,16,401
1226-27	8,24,362	49,08,972
1827-28	18,84,844	56,14,047
1828-29	34,82,730	80,92,809
1829-30	15,63,770	54,29,540

IOR. P/174/41, Bengal Commercial Reports, 1829-30. See, No. 8, "General Comparative Abstract Annual Statement of Imports and Exports from 1820/21 to 1829-30." The English thread, independent of its cheapness, was preferred by the natives on account of its uniform size and the facility of obtaining any quantity of a particular quality that might be required. "To procure country thread of a certain quality is a task attended with considerable labour and expenses; it can only be done by visiting the different marts in the district, and it is estimated that two-thirds of the time occupied in preparing the fine muslins, are spent in searching for thread suited for the manufacture." James Taylor, *A Sketch of the Topography and Statistics of Dacca* (Calcutta, 1840), p. 171.

[7]N.N. Banerjei, 'The Cotton Fabrics of Bengal', *Journal of Indian Art and Industry*, Vol. VIII (London, 1900), pp. 68-69.

The decline which set in at the introduction of machine made textiles continued throughout the nineteenth century.[8] The main reason was due to the relative cheapness of power-loom cloths in comparison with handloom products. The poorer classes naturally preferred to buy the cheapest cloths as they had no idea of economy in the first place, and if they had they could not afford the outlay necessary to buy a more costly, though longer lasting article. As regards the local specialities, the demand for those was due to their superiority but their cost, even when unfigured (in the case of Dacca muslins) was quite prohibitive and out of all proportion to that of machine-made muslins which fell not far short of them in appearance to the casual eye. Moreover, native tastes had in addition been attracted by the brilliant colouring and superior finish of the power-loom fabrics. Another, though a comparatively minor, cause which contributed to the decline of the indigenous handicraft was the disappearance of the regal courts scattered over the country, which generally maintained a considerable number of weavers. The slow, laborious and wasteful methods followed, and the ancient appliances employed, in the manufacture of cotton fabrics by the handloom weavers had also not been without their effect.[9] The general apathy of the British Government towards industrialization is also sometimes blamed for its decay.[10]

In spite of its decline, however, the handloom industry did not die entirely. Although in the medium and finer qualities the handloom weaver was beaten decisively, weavers continued to have an edge in the manufacture of cloths of coarser counts. As the Tariff

[8]Ramesh Dutt, *The Economic History of India*, Vol. II (New York, 1970), pp. 344-45; Vera Anstey, *The Economic Development of India* (London, 1952), pp. 207-09; D.R. Gadgil, *The Industrial Evolution of India in Recent Times* (Bombay, 1942), pp. 180.81; Toru Matsui, 'On the Nineteenth Century Indian Economic History—A Review of A "Reinterpretation", *Indian Economic and Social History Review*, Vol. V (1968), pp. 20-21; Bipan Chandra, 'Reinterpretation of Nineteenth Century Indian Economic History', *Indian Economic and Social History Review*, Vol. V (1968), pp. 52-59.

[9]IOR: Vol. 7407, India Commerce and Industry Proceedings (Industries), November 1906, No. 1, p. 3.

[10]An extreme opinion is that of William Digby who says that the British Government "deliberately strangled Indian manufactured exports and thereby gave English merchantile enterprise an opportunity to obtain a footing which, once obtained, has led to the whole country being covered with the product of English looms." William Digby, *'Prosperous' British India* (London, 1901), p. 261,

Board said, "the manufacturing charges in this class of cloth bear a relatively small proportion to the total cost and hence the scope for economies resulting from large scale production by machinery is limited."[11] On the other hand, a handloom weaver had not to find interest for his capital; not to protect his property by insurance; not to find power for driving his machinery; not to provide for repairs and renewals of same; nor obtain so many articles of stores both to keep the machinery going and to prepare the yarn. "It appears therefore that handloom production in India is not uneonomical and cannot be dismissed as an industry which will necessarily succumb to the mill industry."[12] Moreover, to a large section of the population, *vilayati* goods were, curiously enough, in discredit. They suspected mixture, false sizing and deficiencies, and from which they were comparatively secure in the handloom article.[13] Besides, the coarse cloths turned out by the handloom were more durable and strong and hence preferred by the common people to machine-made cloths.[14] But probably the more important reason for its survival was that the people of Bengal still retained a preferential taste for hand-woven products, particulary for their clothing on ceremonial and festive occasions, as distinct from clothing worn in their homes and in domestic seclusion. The adaptability of the handloom industry was continually utilized to vary particular details of its products in order to keep them distinct from the mass-production articles of the weaving mills or imported piece-goods.[15] Thus with a power-loom only one uniform texture in a piece of cloth was possible, while the hand weaver varied both the reed and the pick in the same piece at will, and made it look fuller at sides and ends. Then there were silk and even gold threads woven with the cotton and he had the advantage of making solid borders, or head lines of such valuable material, making as little waste as possible. It was in this way that the handloom products

[11]*Report of the Indian Tariff Board regarding the grant of protection to the Cotton Textile Industry* (Calcutta, 1932), p. 171.

[12]*Ibid.*

[13]Sir E.C. Buck, *Report on Practical and Technical Education* (Calcutta, 1901), Appendix VI, p. xvii. See Letter of B.J. Padshah to Sir Buck.

[14]T.N. Mukharji, *Art-Manufactures of India* (Calcutta, 1888), p. 193.

[15]IOR: Vol. 11960, BRP (Industries), October 1932, Nos. 7-8, p. 11. See, also D.H. Buchanan, *The Development of Capitalistic Enterprise in India* (New York, 1934), p. 76.

sought to escape from the continual encroachment and competition arising from the products of Indian mills.

PART I

Size and Composition of the Working Force

Before we proceed further to examine the state of the handloom cotton weaving industry in the twentieth century, we would like to examine the size and composition of the workforce engaged in this industry. This will give us an idea of the extent of the industry in this province and its role in the economy of Bengal. An examination of the size and composition would also allow us to compare the relative performance of the industry in various years and would enable us to gauge the trend and movement of the workforce.

The data used have been collected from the decennial census reports of the Government of India on details of occupations. However, it is not possible to say how far the data contained in the census reports are reliable as no detailed or systematic collection of similar data are available from any other official or non-official body. But it is probable that some degree of care had been taken by the Government of India, especially after 1901 to standardize the system of classification of weavers as a result of the discovery that the last three enumerations had varied greatly because the numbers of certain castes the names of which were synonymous with the craft of weaving had been numbered as weavers whether they were actually following their hereditary occupations or not.[16] For our purpose also we had to make certain adjustments, territorial or otherwise to make the data meaningful. Thus in our analysis, only those districts are taken into consideration which remained an integral part of Bengal throughout and others are omitted which later on formed parts of the provinces of Bihar and Orissa. Again, to standardize the data, we had no alternative but to give the combined figures of handloom weavers, spinners and sizers, as only combined data are available for the years 1911 and 1931.

From the data which we have processed in detail, some tables have been constructed in the following pages. Table 7.1 shows the average number of weavers, spinners and sizers (henceforth referred to as 'weavers' unless otherwise mentioned) in each district for the

[16]IOR: Vol. 7407, India Commerce and Industry Proceedings (Industries), November 1906, No. 1, p 3.

period 1901 to 1931 and also the percentage of weavers to the total weaving population of Bengal and the ratio of weavers per 100,000 persons. From the table it could be seen that handloom cotton weaving was practised in all the districts of Bengal although in some it was more extensive than others. Thus the eight districts, of Dacca, Midnapore, Chittagong, Faridpur, Tippera, Pabna, Mymensingh and Jessore together accounted for more than 50 per cent of the weaving population of the province. Among other important districts were Bankura, Backhergunj, Noakhali and Hooghly. In other words, if we look carefully we find that all these districts either belonged to Eastern or Western Bengal. The districts in the north like Darjeeling, Jalpaiguri, Dinajpur, Malda, Rangpur, Rajshahi contributed very little to the weaving population of the province.

It is extremely difficult to account for such regional variations in the distribution of the weaving population of the province. One of the probable reasons for not following the profession of weaving extensively in the northern districts of Bengal could be their inability to produce good varieties of cloth at a reasonable price. For example, F.W. Strong, the compiler of the District Gazetteer of Dinajpur mentions in 1912 that there was little demand for the cloth produced by the weavers in that district as their products were coarse and compared "very unfavourably in appearance and and evenness of texture with the imported Manchester cloth."[17] The same case was probably valid as regards Bogra and Rangpur. In Rajshahi it was possibly a question of greater specialization in silk spinning and weaving (perhaps also because it was more rewarding). O'Malley mentions that in 1916 silk spinning and weaving supported 3,000 people in Rajshahi of whom half were workers.[18] In the case of the two hilly districts of Jalpaiguri and Darjeeling workers were actively involved in agricultural pursuits, i.e., in tea gardens. In this regard they were also perhaps helped by the absence of functional castes which gave them greater occupational mobility than the people of the districts in the plains. On the other hand, the explanation of higher concentration of weaving population in most Eastern and Western Bengal districts could be attributed to their specialized manufactures. G.N. Gupta in his

[17]Eastern Bengal District Gazetteers, *Dinajpur* (Allahabad, 1912), p. 81,
[18]Bengal District Gazetteers, *Rajshahi* (Calcutta, 1916), p. 103.

TABLE 7.1
AVERAGE WEAVING POPULATION AND THEIR CONCENTRATION IN EACH DISTRICT, 1901-1931

District	*Average weaving population in each district*	*Percentage of Bengal's total*	*Average number of weavers per 100,000 persons in the district*
	1	*2*	*3*
Dacca	17,473	8.96	587
Midnapore	15,214	7.80	549
Chittagong	14,095	7.22	899
Faridpur	13,620	6.98	620
Tippera	12,914	6.62	499
Pabna	10,823	5.55	760
Mymensingh	10,377	5.32	225
Jessore	10,347	5.30	597
Bankura	9,275	4.75	846
Backhergung	9,202	4.72	360
Noakhali	9,099	4.66	647
Hooghly	8,218	4.21	759
Nadia	7,090	3.63	449
Burdwan	5,351	2.74	352
Murshidabad	5,258	2.69	400
24 Parganas	5,140	2.63	215
Khulna	5,119	2.62	357
Birbhum	4,799	2.46	526
Malda	4,731	2.42	474
Chittagong Hill Tracts	4,396	2.25	2,645
Howrah	3,653	1.87	376
Dinajpur	2,260	1.16	134
Bogra	2,040	1.04	199
Jalpaiguri	1,935	0.99	214
Rajshahi	1,380	0.71	97
Calcutta	518	0.27	50
Rangpur	507	0.26	21
Darjeeling	271	0.14	97
	195,105		

SOURCES and NOTES: The table has been constructed with the help of the *Census of India*, 1901, Vol. VIA, Bengal, Part II (Calcutta, 1902), pp. 388-89 *Ibid.*, *1911*, Vol. V, Bengal, Part II, Tables (Calcutta, 1913), p. 233; *Ibid.*, *1921*, Vol. V, Bengal, Part II, Tables (Calcutta, 1923), p. 228; *Ibid. 1931*, report on the industries and resources of Eastern Bengal and Assam observed that:[19]

> . . .the industry seems to have progressed most in Noakhali, Comilla, Pabna and Faridpur. All these districts, besides producing the usual *saris* and *dhuties*, turned out a very large quantity of checks and chintzes, both thick and thin, and suitable for the making of coats, shirts, *panjavis* and other wearing apparel mostly in vogue now.

Such specialized goods in addition to coarser materials were also woven in a number of other districts as we shall see later. A secondary explanation lay in the fact that these districts were historically textile producing ones. It was possibly because of this that the East India Company had established their factories in those places in the first place i.e., Santipur, Dacca, Haripur, Kishorgunj, Bajitpur, Jagdia, Charpara, etc. Even as late as 1880, George Birdwood found one-tenth of the population of Tippera employed in cotton weaving.[20]

There was also much unevenness in the distribution of sexes in this profession. In none of the censuses, the proportion of females to males was over 25 per cent. Taking the average of the period, we find that out of 195,105 weavers, 79.10 per cent were males and 29.90 per cent were female workers. This uneven distribution between the sexes was probably due to certain changes in the industrial practices. In the first place, spinning which was almost the sole preserve of female workers became defunct in the nineteenth cen-

Vol. V, Bengal and Sikkim, Part II, Tables (Calcutta, 1932), pp. 90-91; and *Ibid., 1941*, Vol. IV, Bengal, Tables (Simla, 1942), pp. 6-10. The data for the years 1911, 1921, & 1931 represent that of handloom cotton weavers, spinners and sizers for the British territory of Bengal. The data for the year 1901 represent that of handloom cotton weavers only as separate data for the spinners and sizers are not available. To standardize the data, we have also excluded the administrative divisions of Patna, Bagalpore (excepting Mala), Orissa and Chota-Nagpur for the year 1901 as these formed parts of other provinces and had been shown accordingly in the censuses of 1911 and afterwards. It is to be noted that the data for the district of Chittagong Hill Tracts seems to be very unreliable.

[19]G.N. Gupta, *A survey of the Industries*, p. 10.

[20]George C.M. Birdwood, *The Industrial Arts of India*, Vol. II (London, 1880), p. 83.

TABLE 7.2

PROPORTION OF MALE AND FEMALE WEAVING POPULATION IN EACH DISTRICT, 1901-1931

District	*Average number of males*	*Percentage of males to total weaving pop.*	*Average no. of females*	*Percentage of females to total weaving population*
	1	*2*	*3*	*4*
Burdwan	4,514	84.36	837	15.64
Birbhum	4,220	87.93	579	12.07
Bankura	7,762	83.69	1,513	16.31
Midnapore	11,727	77.08	3,417	22.92
Hooghly	7,443	90.57	775	9.43
Howrah	3,214	87.96	440	12.04
24 Parganas	4,377	85.14	764	14.86
Calcutta	464	89.58	54	10.42
Nadia	5,998	84.60	1,092	15.40
Murshidabad	4,268	81.17	990	18.83
Jessore	9,327	90.14	1,020	9.86
Khulna	4.739	92.58	380	7.42
Rajshahi	990	71.74	390	28.26
Dinajpur	1,922	85.04	338	14.96
Jalpaiguri	1,702	88.00	232	12.00
Darjeeling	172	63.47	99	36.53
Rangpur	452	89.33	54	10.67
Bogra	1,030	54.49	1,010	49.51
Pabna	10,166	93.93	657	6.07
Malda	2,891	61.11	1,840	38.89
Dacca	14,080	80.58	3,393	19.42
Mymensingh	8,061	77.68	2,310	22.32
Faridpur	11,595	85.13	2,026	14.87
Backhergunj	7,285	79.16	1,918	20.84
Tippera	10,938	84.70	1,976	15.30
Noakhali	6,687	73.50	2,412	26.50
Chittagong	5,974	42.38	8,121	57.62
Hill Tracts	2,338	53.20	2,057	46.80

SOURCES : As in Table 7.1

tury. Together with this, it was possible that (like South India[21]) men had also taken the place of women sizers as a result of the introduction of long warps. However, when we turn to individual districts in Bengal, we find certain variations to the general picture of the province. Percentagewise the proportion of female workers was higher in the districts of Chittagong Hill Tracts, Darjeeling, Bogra, Malda than the rest of the districts. The explanation to this may lie in the socio-economic pattern of the tribal people who constituted a fairly large segment of the population of the first three districts noted above. Bogra and Malda seem to be an exception to the general rule.

Another notable feature among a section of the weaving population of the province was their involvement in subsidiary occupations, i.e., agriculture. But the number of weaving population following subsidiary occupation was by no means so large as was the general notion of the period.[22] According to the 1901 census, only 12.79 per cent of the weavers were partially agriculturists. The figure further declined to 10.80 in 1911 and in 1931 it stood at 10.56 per cent.[23] This decline meant that weaving was becoming more and more a specialized occupation of particular classes of workers as a result of advances in the technique of the industry. That this was generally so could be verified from the fact that the districts which had a higher proportion of looms with fly-shuttles had a lower percentage of weaving population in agriculture.

Having looked into the size and composition of the handloom cotton weaving industry from various aspects, one is apt to question oneself whether the number of weaving population had actually increased or decreased for the period 1901 to 1931. The answer to this question could be found by looking into the census figures of various years. The weaving population of Bengal in 1901

[21]See, K.S. Venkataraman, *The Handloom Industry in South India* (Madras, 1940), p. 54.

[22]For contemporary opinion, see Bengal District Gazetteers; *Burdwan* (Calcutta, 1910), p. 123; *Hooghly* (Calcutta, 1912), p. 182; *Malda* (Calcutta, 1918), p. 65; and Eastern Bengal District Gazetteers, *Dinajpur* (Allahabad, 1912), p. 81.

[23]See, *Census of India*, 1901, Vol. VI A, Bengal, Part II, pp. 388-89; *Ibid.*, 1911, Vol V, Bengal, Part II, Tables, p. 233; *Ibid.*, 1931, Vol. V, Bengal and Sikkim, Part II, Tables, pp. 90-91. Percentages have been calculated.

TABLE 7.3

AVERAGE NUMBER OF WEAVERS FOLLOWING SUBSIDIARY OCCUPATIONS, 1901-1931

District	*Number of male weavers*	*Number of female weavers*	*Total*	*Percentage of (3) to total weaving pop. of the dt.*
	1	*2*	*3*	*4*
Burdwan	625	27	652	12.18
Birbhum	845	5	850	17.71
Bankura	771	29	800	8.63
Midnapore	2,800	141	2,941	19.33
Hooghly	554	15	569	6.92
Howrah	127	21	148	4.05
24 Parganas	278	7	285	5.54
Calcutta	4	Nil	4	0.77
Nadia	348	7	355	5.00
Murshidabad	601	5	606	11.53
Jessore	783	11	793	7.66
Khulna	706	3	709	13.85
Rajshahi	234	7	240	17.39
Dinajpur	208	6	213	9.42
Jalpaiguri	231	1	232	11.99
Darjeeling	4	Nil	4	1.48
Rangpur	63	3	66	13.02
Bogra	324	10	334	16.37
Pabna	1,024	17	1,041	9.62
Malda	365	4	369	7.80
Dacca	1,504	62	1,566	8.96
Mymensingh	1,016	82	1,098	10.58
Faridpur	1,216	33	1,249	9.17
Backhergunj	613	47	730	7.93
Tippera	2,568	58	2,626	20.33
Noakhali	1,614	75	1,689	18.56
Chittagong	560	106	670	4.75
Hill Tracts	1	Nil	1	0.02

SOURCES: As in Table 7.1

was 200,703; whereas in 1931 this figure came down to 186,798 or in other words even without taking into consideration the figures for cotton spinners and sizers for the year 1901 (1901 figures represented only actual weavers unlike other years) there had been a net decrease of 13,905 weavers or 6.93 per cent over the 1901 census figures.[24] If allowance is made for the rising population during the period under review, the fall appears to be all the more dramatic. In 1901, there were 476 weavers per 100,000 persons whereas in 1931 it was down to 373.[25] A closer examination of the figures reveals that the fall in the weaving population was entirely due to large-scale desertion from the industry by male weavers. In 1901, the total number of male weavers had been 170,971 and in 1931 it totalled only 149,814 or a net decrease of 21,157.[26] On the other hand there was an actual increase of female weavers from 29,732 in 1901 to 36,984 in 1931.[27] This large-scale desertion of male weavers from their hereditary occupation (more so being so conservative in character) was perhaps an indication of the amount of economic distress prevailing among this section of the population. The increasing number of womenfolk practicing weaving strengthens the suggestion that their help was also enlisted to supplement the family income.

PART II

Handloom Production and Products

The next question that needs to be answered is whether the handloom production of cloth had increased or decreased or remained stationary during the period of our study. The answer to this question is much harder than one might realise for the simple reason that there was no census of production for handloom cotton weaving industry in Bengal. The alternative that remains is, therefore, to estimate the handloom production of cloth from the consumption of yarn. This could be found from the net imports of

[24]See, *Census of India*, 1901, Vol. VI A, Bengal, Part II, pp. 388-89; and *Ibid.*, *1931*, Vol. V, Bengal and Sikkim, Part II, Tables, pp. 90-91. For methods of calculation, see, sources and notes of Table 7.1.

[25]*Ibid*; and *Census of India*, *1941*, Vol IV, Bengal, Tables, pp. 6-10.

[26]*Census of India*, 1901, Vol. VIA, Bengal, Part II, pp. 388-89; and *Ibid.*, *1931*, Vol. V, Bengal and Sikkim, Part II, Tables, pp. 90-91.

[27]*Ibid.*

cotton twist and yarn into Bengal by all routes and deducting exports and re-exports. We have also to take into consideration the net balances of cotton mill yarn left after having produced woven goods. It may be pointed out that the same method of calculation had earlier been used by the IIC; by the Special Tariff Board on Cotton Textile Industry, 1936; and also by the Fact-finding Committee (Handloom and Mills), 1942 in estimating the all-India production of handloom cloth.[28]

The principal routes of imports and exports of cotton twist and yarn were by sea, coastwise or by rail and river. The net imports (after deducting exports and re-exports) have been collected and compiled from various sources as could be seen in Table 7.4. We have also worked out the production and consumption of yarn by the Bengal cotton mills for our period. However, it must be pointed out that our table of handloom production (Table 7.4) suffers from some deficiencies of statistics. In the first place, we have been unable to get inland trade statistics relating to rail and river from 1921-22 to 1932-33 due to the stoppage in the publication of such data "for reasons of economy".[29] Hence there is a gap of twelve years from 1921-22 to 1932-33 which cannot be filled up in any other way. Likewise, we did not take into account the yarn produced by hand spinning. This is because no statistics of the yarn supplied by spinners in Bengal is available. But then no allowance has also been made for cotton yarn used for rope and twine and used in other domestic purposes. We did not also take into account land frontier exports and imports but even then the calculation would be sufficiently near the mark to indicate the quantity of cotton cloth produced by handloom weavers.

From the total amount of yarn that was internally available in Bengal, we have attempted an estimate of the total handloom production of cloth (Table 7.4). Column (1) of the Table represents the total amount of yarn that was internally available each year.

[28]*Report of the IIC* (PP XVII of 1919), p. 436; *Report of the Special Tariff Board on the Enquiry regarding the level of duties necessary to afford adequate protection to the Indian Cotton Textile Industry against imports from the United Kingdom of Cotton piecegoods and yarn, artificial silk fabrics and mixture fabrics of cotton and artificial silk* (Delhi, 1936), 102; *Report of the Fact-finding Committee* (Handloom and Mills) (Delhi, 1942), Chapter III, pp. 45-57.

[29]*Accounts relating to the Inland (Rail and River-borne) Trade of India for April, 1933* (Delhi, 1933), p. 1.

TABLE 7.4

CONSUMPTION OF YARN AND PRODUCTION OF CLOTH IN HANDLOOMS AND COTTON TEXTILE INDUSTRY, 1900-01 to 1920-21; and 1933-34 to 1938-39

	1	2	3	4	5	6	7
	Consumption of yarn in handloom industry (in '000 lbs)	*Handloom production of cloth in '000 yds 1 lb. of yarn= 4 yds. of cloth*	*Percentage of (2) to total internal production of cloth*	*Consumption of yarn in cotton mills ('000 lbs.)*	*Cotton mill production of cloth ('000 yds.) 1 lb. of yarn=4.78 yds. of cloth*	*Percentage of mill made cloth to total internal production*	*Total internal production of cloth in Bengal (in '000 yds.)*
1900-01	43,096	172,384	99.21	286	1,367	0.79	173,751
1901-02	49,730	198,920	99.16	351	1,678	0.84	200,598
1902-03	53,026	212,104	99.17	370	1,769	0.83	213,873
1903-04	46,537	186,148	98.44	617	2,949	1.56	189,097
1904-05	48,385	193,540	98.44	643	3,074	1.56	196,614
1905-06	65,263	261,052	98.94	587	2,806	1.06	263,858
1906-07	52,463	209,852	97.39	1,175	5,617	2.61	215,469
1907-08	45,064	180,256	95.62	1,727	8,255	4.38	188,511
1908-09	47,539	190,156	93.96	2,555	12,213	6.04	202,369
1909-10	39,692	158,768	92.82	2,568	12,275	7.18	171,043
1910-11	45,640	182,560	93.85	2,504	11,969	6.15	194,529
1911-12	43,048	172,192	93 82	2,371	11,333	6.18	183,525

TABLE 7.4 Continued

	1	2	3	4	5	6	7
1912-13	33,964	135,856	88.82	3,579	17,108	11.18	152,964
1913-14	30,684	122,736	89.19	3,113	14,880	10.81	137,616
9114-15	31,193	124,772	91.52	2,418	11,558	8.48	136,330
1915-16	35,675	142,700	92.58	2,393	11,439	7.42	154,139
1916-17	31,812	127,248	87.71	3,729	17,825	12.29	145,073
1917-18	32,849	131,396	86.02	4,467	21,352	13.98	152,748
1918-19	30,062	120,248	84.30	4,685	22,394	15.70	142,642
1919-20	18,262	73,048	74.58	5,208	24,894	25.42	97,942
1920-21	39,540	158,160	87.96	4,530	21,653	12.04	179,813
1933-34	60,545	242,180	70.59	21,109	100,901	29.41	343,081
1934-35	48,220	192,880	58.27	28,900	138,142	41.73	331,022
1935-36	58,728	234,912	62.80	29,108	139,136	37.20	374,048
1936-37	53,161	212,644	58.75	31,238	149,318	41.25	361,962
1937-38	57,265	229,060	59.29	32,906	157,291	40.71	386,351
1938-39	62,147	248,588	57.07	39,114	186,965	42.93	435,553

SOURCES : See Appendix III.

This figure when multiplied by four (on the assumption that one pound of yarn gives a yield of four yards of cloth)[30] gives the total amount of handloom production of the province and which could be seen in column (2). An analysis of the production figures show that the output varied greatly from year to year. One of the primary reasons was the changing structure of political boundaries till 1911-12. Till 1904-05 the production figures represent that of Bengal (including Eastern Bengal) and Bihar and Orissa; the figure of 1905-06 being not reliable as trade statistics had not been even, i.e., sea-borne trade of Eastern Bengal and Assam being included with Bengal's figures; the figures of 1906-07 to 1911-12 do not include the handloom production of Eastern Bengal as it had been constituted into a separate province with Assam in 1905; and from 1912-13 the figures do not include that of Bihar and Orissa for similar reasons. Therefore, standard data for the Bengal province could be found from 1912 onwards after territorial adjustments.

Although changes in the political boundaries were responsible to some extent in the variation of production figures for the first decade of the twentieth century, it was not the only one. It cannot explain, for example, the great increase in the handloom production for the period 1905-06 to 1911-12, the period which incidentally coincided with the partition of Bengal. The explanation lies partly therefore in the Swadeshi movement of the period, the object of which was the production and manufacture of articles which were of general use among the people and the creation of a market for those articles in the country by the exclusion of foreign manufactures.[31] The partition scheme "gave a fresh impetus to the Swadeshi movement—an impetus which has given rise to tremendous upheaval, the like of which has not been witnessed in this country within the memory of the oldest man living"—observed the *Bengal Review*[32] while another contemporary reported "a growing desire of the people to patronise indigenous goods" on the eve of partition.[33]

[30]*Report of the Indian Tariff Board* (*Cotton Textile Industry Enquiry*), *1927*, *Vol. I*, *Report* (Calcutta, 1927), Appendix IV, pp. 238-39; *Report of the Special Tariff Board on Cotton Textile Industry*, *1936*, p. 101; and also IOR : Vol. 11960, BRP (Industries), October 1932, Nos. 7-8, p. 8. The width of the cloths were assumed to be of 44".

[31]*Industrial India*, Vol. II, No. 8. 9, August and September 1905, p. 210.

[32]*The Bengal Review*, Vol. I, No. 10, October 1905, p. 248.

[33]*Industrial India*, Vol. I, No. 4, April 1904, p. 56.

Government reports and research also confirm the impact of this movement in stimulating production and creating a demand.[34]

However, with the outbreak of the war in 1914, the demand for handloom products diminished greatly and continued to be so till about 1920. This was mainly due to three principal reasons—the continuous rise in the price of cotton goods in Lancashire; the rise in the price of Indian cotton; and the economic condition of India. The last one, so far as Bengal was concerned, had been accompanied by a large fall in the prices of jute and rice which made it very difficult for the cultivators and poorer classes generally to pay the abnormally high price demanded for cloth. In this regard Hon'ble A.K. Fazl-ul-Huq pointed out:[35]

> . . .in former years a cultivator could purchase at least two pairs of *dhotis* by selling one maund of rice and at least three pairs by selling one maund of jute. Roughly speaking, under the present conditions he has to sell about two maunds of rice or jute in order to be able to buy one pair of *dhoties*—I am told that even two maunds would not be sufficient. Roughly speaking, the expenses of a cultivator have gone up four times and have put an unnecessary heavy burden on his otherwise slender resources.

It is quite probable that with the return of normalcy in the 1920's and the intensification of the swadeshi movement, the demand for handloom products picked up again. "As a result, however, of the intensive and extensive swadeshi feeling in the country, particularly since 1930", wrote the Secretary, Indian Chamber of Commerce, "the production of cloth on the handlooms has increased greatly".[36] The economic problems of the 1930's which led to a fall in the general purchasing power of the people must have also diverted the demand for cloth from high priced goods and thereby exerting influence in the same direction as that of Swadeshi movement.[37]

The increased demand of handloom production in the twentieth century (excepting inter-war period) was supplied, however, with-

[34]J.C. Cumming, *Review of the Industrial Position and Prospects, Part II of Special Report*, p. 7; Sumit Sarkar, *The Swadeshi Movement in Bengal, 1903-1908* (New Delhi, 1973), pp. 121-22.

[35]IOR: Vol. 10298, BFP (Commerce), September 1918, No. 21, p. 19.

[36]IOR: Vol. 11960, BRP (Industries), October 1932, Nos. 7-8, 15.

[37]*Report regarding the grant of protection to the Cotton Textile Industry* (Calcutta, 1932), p. 174.

out any addition to the total number of weavers. On the contrary, as we saw earlier, there was rather a decline in the number of professional workers. How are we then to explain this increased output per unit of labour? The answer to this question lies in the technological changes brought about at this time in the methods of production, the most important of which was the gradual replacement of the old throw shuttle looms with fly-shuttle looms. Fundamentally of course there was not much difference between these two types of looms excepting in one motion, viz, picking. In the Indian handloom, the picking motion was performed by the weaver who threw the shuttle with one hand from one side of the loom and held it with the other when it reached the other side of the loom. The chief disadvantage of this loom was that if the width of the cloth woven was greater than the stretch of a man's arms, two operations were necessary, one at each end of the loom. Moreover the weaver had to change his hand constantly to hold the lay in beating up the weft. On the other hand, in the fly-shuttle loom, two boxes were placed, one at each end of the lay, for the reception of the shuttle instead of the weaver's hands which had to be held out in the ordinary handloom. In each of these boxes a spindle extending the whole length of the box was fitted and each carried a shuttle driver or picker, as it was technically termed. Between these, a cord was extended and attached to each, and affixed to this cord in the centre of its length, was the peg or handle by means of which the shuttle was jerked from one box to the other through the open shed.[38] From this description it is clear that in the fly-shuttle loom, the necessity of employing two weavers when weaving a wide cloth was obviated by the addition of the shuttle-boxes, and the weaver had not to change hands, as he could now hold the lay with one hand and throw the shuttle by pulling the cord with the other, and these were no doubt great advantages. J.G. Cumming who made a survey of the Bengal industries in 1908 checked the weaving in many places and found that the fly-shuttle loom averaged sixty-five picks against twenty-two per minute in the country loom.[39] P.C. Mitter

[38] *Industrial India*, Vol. II, 8,9, August and September 1905, pp, 189-90.

[39] J.G. Cumming, *Review of Industrial position*, p. 8. This was the effective speed and must not be confused with the working speed which was much higher. For an arithmetical clarification, see Rao Bhadur B. Patel, 'Hand-loom Weaving in India', *Report of the Second Indian Industrial Conference held at Calcutta, December 1906* (Calcutta 1907), p. 209.

speaking in the Bengal Legislative Council claimed that a weaver could weave 10 to 12 yards of cloth per day by using the fly-shuttle loom against five yards with ordinary looms.[40] The Government of Bengal also believed that the fly-shuttle looms doubled the output of the worker at once.[41] Moreover, the cloths turned out by these looms had also been claimed to be "excellently strong and durable, better in this respect than the imported cloth".[42] As regards the price, the pit fly-shuttle looms cost from Rs. 20 to Rs. 30 including two rollers and the Serampore fly-shuttle looms cost from Rs. 40 to Rs. 60. The output of the two was the same—about a yard per hour with medium counts of yarn.[43]

In spite of its acknowledged advantages, till the end of the nineteenth century the fly-shuttle loom (which was invented by John Key in 1733) remained confined to Serampore, a Danish Settlement on the river Hooghly and by adopting this, and a few simple improvements in the preparing processes of weaving the Serampore weavers "had raised themselves into a comparatively flourishing and independent position, a striking contrast to that of their fellow-workers in other less advanced districts"—observed Havell.[44] To spread the use of fly-shuttle loom in other parts of the country early in this century he took up the matter and was able through lectures, letters and advertisements to create an interest among the public on the subject. The Swadeshi movement which soon followed gave further encouragement to the movement and by 1908 it was claimed that 10,000 new looms were working in the province.[45] The Government of Bengal also seemed to have favoured the idea which led to the appointment of N.N. Pillai as its Weaving Expert. The officer made extensive tours of the weaving centres in the province to demonstrate and supply improved apparatus and to instruct

[40]*BLCP*, July 3, 1918, Vol. L, p. 726

[41]DOIB: *Annual Administration Report*, 1926, p. 14.

[42]IOR: Vol. 7861, BGP (Education), December 1908, No. 153, p. 1415.

[43]The pit fly-shuttle loom was generally used by country weavers in which case pits were dug underneath the loom to accommodate the weavers feet operating the treadle levers. In the case of the Serampore fly-shuttle looms, although the operation was similar to the pit-loom it was mounted on a frame and as such no pits were required to be dug. These looms could also be moved, if necessary, from place to place without any difficulty. A. Guha, *The Installation of Small Weaving Factories* (Calcutta, 1924), pp. 5-6.

[44]E.B. Havell, *Essays on Indian Art, Industry and Education* (Madras, 1910), p. 58.

[45]J.G. Cumming, *Review of the Indurstrial position*, p. 8.

the people on improved methods of weaving.[46] An industrial census taken in 1921 showed nearly 30 per cent of the looms fitted with fly-shuttles (see Table 7.5). With the establishment of the Industries Department the drive to introduce fly-shuttle looms was carried out all the more vigorously. In their propaganda for the dissemination of the use of fly-shuttle looms and other improved devices like and dobbies jacquard machines, the Peripatetic and District Weaving Schools were of invaluable aid. Up to March 1935, the Government District Weaving Schools (numbering nine) had introduced 2,381 improved weaving appliances including sleys and the Peripatetic Weaivng Schools (numbering twenty-five) had introduced no less than 10,157 sleys and other improved appliances.[47] The Government of Bengal also agreed from around 1928 to supply cost effective weaving appliances to the weavers at cost price and bear the packing and transport charges of such appliances.[48] As a result of such activities of the Industries Department and due to intercommunication among the people themselves; the use of fly-shuttle looms and other improved weaving appliances had greatly increased in Bengal. In 1942, according to the Fact-finding Committee, 67 per cent of the handlooms of Bengal were of this improved variety.[49] In addition to the introduction of Key's fly-shuttle looms, other improved varieties of looms also came to be in use. Mention may be made of the Salvation Army loom and the Hattersley automatic loom but their number was insignificant.[50]

[46]Prior to 1912, the officer worked as weaving master in the province of Eastern Bengal andAssam (*Report of the Agricultural Department, Bengal, for the year ending 30th June, 1912*, p. 1). From 1912 to 1919, he worked under the charge of the Director of Agriculture when his services was transferred to the administrative control of the Director of Industries from the 1st of December 1919. *RAB*, 1920-21, p. 64.

[47]IOR: Vol. 12075, BRP (Industries), June 1936, Nos. 67, p. 41.

[48]IOR: Vol. 11865, BRP (Industries), October 1930, Nos. 17-18, p. 11., See, "Rules for the Supply of Weaving Appliances to the Handloom Weavers of Bengal".

[49]*Report of the Fact-finding Committee (Handloom and Mills)*, (Delhi, 1942), p. 32.

[50]These semi-automatic and automatic looms were used by former students of the Serampore Weaving Institute at their factories and also by unemployed *bhadrologs* and students. See, *IIC*, Vol. II (PP XVIII of 1911), p. 214; *Star of India*, February 12, 1936, p. 3. Wider dissemination of such looms was impossible in view of their prohibitive price. The price of the Salvation Army loom, for example, was Rs. 110 and that of Hattersley automatic loom about Rs. 600. See, A. Guha, *The Installation of Small Weaving Factories*, p. 6.

TABLE 7.5

PROPORTION OF LOOMS WITH FLY-SHUTTLES, 1921

District	*Number of looms*			*Handlooms per million of the population*	*Handlooms per sq. mile*	*Proportion of looms with fly-shuttle per cent*
	With fly-shuttles	*Without*	*Total*			
Burdwan	2,011	1,931	3,942	2,739	146	51
Birbhum	1,645	4,199	5,844	6,895	333	28
Bankura	2,428	5,746	8,174	8,014	311	30
Midnapore	4,314	10,962	15,276	5,728	277	28
Hooghly	3,877	2,111	5,988	5,544	507	65
Howrah	598	510	1,099	1,102	207	54
24-Parganas	967	5	972	370	20	99
Calcutta	—	—	—	—	—	—
Nadia	2,762	2,199	4,925	3,311	177	55
Murshidabad	1,656	5,705	7,361	5,830	347	22
Jessore	5,818	1,114	6,932	4,025	239	84
Khulna	3,619	143	3,762	2,589	80	96
Rajshahi	118	379	497	334	18	24
Dinajpur	88	3,841	3,929	2,303	160	3
Jalpaiguri	14	2,531	2,545	2,718	87	—

TABLE 7.5 Continued

Darjeeling	—	464	464	1,641	40	—
Rangpur	3	401	404	161	12	1
Bogra	274	1,591	1,865	1,779	137	15
Pabna	2,929	5,693	8,622	5,204	466	34
Malda	1,025	903	1,928	1,956	102	53
Cooch Behar	—	2,083	2,083	3,516	158	—
Dacca	6,375	5,423	11,798	3,774	432	54
Mymensingh	958	10,671	11,629	2,404	185	8
Faridpur	6,004	1,958	7,962	3,539	136	75
Bakargunj	3,900	3,029	6,929	2,641	198	56
Tippera	986	11,446	12,432	4,532	486	7
Noakhali	826	8,205	9,031	6,132	596	9
Chittagong	6	6,812	6,818	4,231	273	—
Chittagong Hill Tracts	—	29,190	29,190	168,492	568	—
Tripura State	12	31,473	31,485	10,342	765	—
Total	53,168	160,718	213,886	272,846	7,463	951

SOURCE : *Census of India, 1921*, Volume V, Bengal, Part I, Report (Calcutta, 1923), pp. 400-401.

After having analysed the production figures of handloom goods, we now proposed to look into the types of fabrics that the weavers generally manufactured in Bengal. Broadly speaking, the fabrics were of two kinds—coarser goods made from lower counts of yarn for the consumption of the poorer classes and fine and superfine goods. The relative volume of production of these two classes of goods and their money value is however difficult to estimate in view of the unorganized nature of the industry. According to the Tariff Board on Cotton Textile Industry (1932), the bulk of the handloom products consisted of cloth of counts 20s and below.[51] Another estimate made by the Industries Department of Bengal also claimed that over 80 per cent of the Indian yarn used by the handloom weavers were of counts in between 12s and 32s and the remaining 20 per eent were of 40s counts and upwards.[52] "Such development", observed the Bengal Industrial Survey Committee "reflect the present general standard of living of the people of the province, majority of whom are engaged in the precarious occupation of under-developed agriculture."[53]

The various products turned out by the weavers were ordinary saris, special saris, special dhuties, ordinary dhuties, lungis, mosquito curtains, gamchas or towels, chadars. etc. According to the provincial government figures supplied to the Fact-finding Committee, 40 per cent of these products were saris, 40 per cent lungis, 9 per cent chadars, 6 per cent gamchas and 5 per cent dhuties.[54] But such figures are open to question as other varieties of products like table-cloths, mosquito-nets, pardahs, cloth for coats and shirts, cotton petticoats, etc., have been left out of account in the estimate.

Although ordinary cotton stuffs were woven in all the districts, the finer varieties of products were woven only in some of the centres of Dacca, Nadia, Mymensingh, Tippera, Hooghly, Howrah, Pabna, Birbhum, Burdwan, Midnapore and Noakhali. The most famous of the finer varieties were the muslins of Dacca. Although Dacca no longer manufactured the exquisite plain muslins like *sangati* (meaning presentation), *sharbati* (sweet as

[51]*Report of the Indian Tariff Board regarding the grant of protection to the Cotton Textile Industry* (Calcutta, 1932), p. 17.

[52]IOR: Vol. 11960, BRP (Industries), October 1932, Nos. 7-8 p. 12.

[53]Report of the *BISC* (Alipore, 1948), p. 43.

[54]*Report of the Fact-finding Committee*, p. 120.

sarbat), *abrawan* (running water), or *shabnam* (evening dew); it still manufactured figured muslins called *jamdani* saris. The speciality of these saris was that these were hand-embroidered with needles of bamboo or tamarind wood and with the help generally of a pattern on paper which was pinned beneath. These had ornamental borders of gold and silver thread, with large bold corner pieces. Collin reported in 1890 that there were only some five hundred families who made these saris in Dacca out of English thread while Gupta in 1908 found that its manufacture had spread even in the interior of Dacca to such villages as Demra, Sidhigunj, Katchpur, Dhamrai, etc., where caste weavers combined their occupation with that of agriculture and were undercutting their products compared to Dacca town weavers.[55] In 1912, the following fine cloths were being manufactured in Dacca.

(1) Mulmul prepared from British yarn, size 20 yards by 1 yard, cost from Rs. 5 to Rs. 60, exported to Upper India and Nepal for wearing apparel.

(2) Saris with borders embroidered in gold thread, size 5 to 6 yards long by 44″ to 50″ wide, price from Rs. 5 to Rs. 40. The best saris were only prepared to order costing from Rs. 50 to Rs. 150.

(3) Ordinary saris with coloured thread borders of the same size selling from Rs. 2 to Rs. 15 a piece.

(4) Dhuties with coloured and white borders 5 to 6 yards long by 44″ to 50″ were generally sold for Rs. 1-8 to Rs. 12. A superior kind adorned with gold borders and gollabottom fetched from Rs. 5 to Rs. 10.

(5) Urnis of different sizes 5 to 7 cubits long by 1½ to 3½ cubits wide were sold for from annas 8 to Rs. 16 a piece.

(6) Handkerchiefs 18 to 24 inches square were prepared and sold per dozen Rs. 3 to Rs. 8.[56]

Next to Dacca, Santipur in Nadia was perhaps the most famous place for the manufacture of fine cotton goods. Its fine muslin was known as Santipur cloth, and was admired for its thin textures, and embroidered and flowered work. Banerjei, in his monograph on the cotton fabrics of Bengal, published in 1898, estimated the

[55] Collin, *Report on the Existing Arts and Industries in Bengal*, p. 11; and Gupta, *Survey of Industries*, p. 12.

[56] Eastern Bengal District Gazetteers, *Dacca* (Allahabad, 1912), p. 113.

outturn of the cotton cloths of Santipur then about 3¼ lakhs of rupees per annum, but its value had somewhat fallen by 1909.[57] Likewise, production of fine cloths for which Kishorgunj and Bajitpur also the other Bajitpur in Tangail were renowned, had fallen. Around 1917, some 40 families in Bajitpur manufactured muslin and the products sold in Dacca.[58] In the Brahmanbaria subdivision, good cotton cloth suitable for dhuties, chadars and saris were made. The weavers of Sarail, Brahmanbaria, and Kalikacha made also dhuties and chadars of a finer quality which sold for Rs. 16 to Rs. 20 a pair.[59] Finer varieties of cloth in Hooghly were made at Serampore, Haripal, Dhaniakhali and Kalme, as well as in French Chandernagore. The cloths made in the first and last towns were specially known as Farasdanga.[60] In Howrah, finer cloths were woven in thana Dumjor, but in very small quantities.[61] Pabna fabrics had also a high reputation on account of their fine texture, and it was claimed that they challanged comparison with the products of Dacca and other historical seats of the weaving industry. Fine cloths were made at Sadullapur, Nishchintapur, and Amirpur in the Sadar subdivision and at Delua. Gachhapur, and Chotadhul in the Serajgunj subdivision. The chadars and cloths made at Delua were of specially fine quality and in good demand among the upper classes. The annual outturn of cloth in the Pabna district was reported to be 7,500,000 yards a year.[62] In Birbhum, finer cloths such as twills, table cloths, pardahs, bed sheets, and cloth for coats and shirts, were manufactured at Bolpur, Dubrajpur, Karidha, Tantipara and Alunda.[63] Fine cloths were also made in a number of centres in Burdwan district like Purbasthali, Kalna, Manteswar, Bahadurpur, Baje, Itta and their products were usually sent to Howrah. The district outturn of cotton cloth during 1908-09 was estimated at 2,585,400 yards, valued at Rs. 2,81,378.[64] In Faridpur, bed-sheets

[57]Bengal District Gazetteers, *Nadia* (Calcutta, 1910), p. 93.
[58]*Ibid.*, *Mymensingh* (Calcutta, 1917), p. 77.
[59]Eastern Bengal and Assam District Gazetteers, *Tippera* (Allahabad, 1910), p. 56.
[60]Bengal District Gazetteers, *Hooghly* (Calcutta, 1912), p. 183.
[61]Bengal District Gazetteers, *Howrah* (Calcutta, 1909), p. 98.
[62]*Ibid.*, *Pabna* (Calcutta, 1923), pp. 62-63.
[63]*Ibid.*, *Birbhum* (Calcutta, 1980), p. 76.
[64]*Ibid.*, *Burdwan* (Calcutta, 1910), pp. 122-23.

of fine quality, and checked and striped fabrics suitable for coats and shirts, were made in large quantities at Rajbari, the headquarters of the Goalundo subdivision, the yarn being obtained from the *hat* held at Kumarkhali in the Nadia district.[65] At Chandrakhona and Radhanagar in the Midnapore district, good quality dhuties, saris, and urnas were manufactured and exported in considerable quantities every week to the Howrah mart.[66] Lungis of superior quality in fast colours were being made in Noakhali and competed successfully with those imported from Holland and Burma. A species of coloured sari, known as *jam sari*, was made in the district and was much in demand. The mosquito nets of Chaumuhani, white and coloured, had also a great reputation.[67]

Mixed fabrics or *baftas* were woven in a number of places. In these cloths the warp was usually tussar and the woof cotton. In Hooghly, mixed fabrics known as *rangina* were made at Bali, Diwanganj, Undayrajpur and some other villages in the Arambag subdivision. According to variations of size and colour, these fabrics were divided into different classes, e.g., *swagaji* (red and white stripe on an orange ground), *muskha* (with black and orange stripes), *selai-khata* (black stripes on orange ground), *phularu* (red flowers on yellow or while ground), *jarda* or *sujasdi* (red or white stripes on a yellow ground), and *shshi* (in red and blue checks).[68] Most of these products were made for export to the Punjab and the United Provinces. In Bhagalpore, superior quality *bafta* chadars were made which cost Rs. 3-8 to Rs. 15 against Rs. 0-10 to Rs. 15 in the case of cotton chadars. But the product was extremely durable and could last at least five to six years.[69] Dacca used to manufacture a kind of *baftas* known as *azizi* from bleached cotton and Assamese silk. But Dacca was more famous for its *kasida* cloth which was a coloured cotton muslin embroidered with untwisted *muga* silk thread (when the cloth was woven, a pattern was stamped on it which was embroidered). These were usually

[65]Bengal District-Gazetteers, *Faridpur* (Calcutta, 1925), p. 77.
[66]*Ibid.*, *Midnapore* (Calcutta, 1911), p. 126.
[67]Eastern Bengal and Assam District Gazetteers, *Noakhali* (Allahabad, 1911), p. 71.
[68]Bengal District Gazetteers, *Hooghly* (Calcutta, 1912), p. 185.
[69]J.G. Cumming, *Review of Industrial position*, p. 12.

used as turbans by Muhammadan gentlemen in near Eastern countries. Prior to the First World War, a considerable quantity of these cloths were exported to North Africa and Constantinople but the industry was reported to be experiencing difficulty in disposing off their stocks for want of regular markets.[70] It may also be mentioned here that there were some fifty to sixty varieties of *kasida* cloth and the prices ranged from Rs. 50 to Rs. 80 per piece according to quality.

PART III

Cost Structure of Production

After having looked into the handloom production figures as well as fabrics produced, we propose to look at the cost structure of the industry. A study of the relative proportion of costs of production would enable us to form a better understanding of the problems of the industry which we propose to study in the next section. But it is not always easy to discover the relative costs of handloom products. The industry being unorganized and scattered, no census of production costs had ever been undertaken by the local government, not the least because it involved substantial expenditure which the provincial government was unable to incur due to financial difficulties. Government records of the period also throw no light on the subject. It was only in the 1930's when weaving operations became an important aspect of government's industrial poilcy that we come across occasional references to actual costs of production of particular types of cloths.

The two most important components of the cost of production were the cost of materials and that of labour charge. Cost of material involved the price of yarn, which again depended upon its fineness, the cost of other materials such as *jari* in the case of fine dhuties and saris and also the cost of dyeing and bleaching. On the other hand, the most important item in the labour cost was the cost of weaving; and other costs in this category included the cost of sizing, preparing the warp (including drawing and twisting), cost of winding the weft and the cost of finishing. The respective costs of materials and labour, however, differed widely from one class of goods to another as could be seen in Table 7.6. From the table, we

[70] *RAB*, 1920-21, p. 75; and DOIB : *Annual Administration Report*, 1921, p. 15.

TABLE 7.6

COST OF PRODUCTION OF HANDLOOM GOODS IN BENGAL, c. 1932

Class of goods	Dimentions	Counts of warp and weft	Cost of yarn	% of (4) to cost of manf.	Labour charges	% of (6) to cost of manf.	Cost of manufacture
1	2	3	4	5	6	7	8
	Yards		Rs. As. P.		Rs. As. P.		Rs. As. P.
Coloured saris	45×5	40×40	0-15-9	74.12	0-5-6	25.88	1- 3-5
Chadars	54″×3	20×10½	0-15-0	75.0	0-5-0	25.0	1- 4-0
Towels	22″×1	42×10½	0- 2-3	69.23	0-1-0	30.77	0- 3-3
Lungis	45″×2½	40×40	0- 9-0	75.0	0-3-0	25.0	0-12-0
Checked saries	45″×5	$\frac{42}{60} \times \frac{42}{60}$	1- 5-0	68.85	0-9-6	31.15	1-14-6
Dhuties Striped	44″×5	40×40	0-11-6	68.66	0-5-3	31.34	1- 0-9
Shirting	34″×24	$\frac{2}{42} \times 22$	4-12-0	76.0	1-8-0	24.0	6- 4-0
Dobby bordered dhuties	44″×5	40×40	0-12-0	41.38	1-1-0	58.62	1-13-0
Gamchas	27×1½	48×40	0- 4-0	80.0	0-1-0	20.0	0- 5-0
Mosquito nets	36×20	$\frac{2}{42} \times 40$	1- 2-0	45.0	1-6-0	55.0	2- 8-0

SOURCE : *Report of the Indian Tariff Board regarding the grant of protection to the Cotton Textile Industry* (Calcutta, 1932), Appendix IX, p. 236.

find that the cost of yarn was the single most important item in the cost of production. The cost of yarns in the case of gamchas, striped shirting, lungis, chadars, and that of coloured saris represented over 70 per cent of the cost of production. It may also be mentioned that these were the common items of mass consumption. In the case of fancy products like saris with golden *Jari* borders yarn costs, however, represented only 19 per cent of the total cost of production against 49 per cent being the cost of other materials, i.e., *jaris*. In relation to cost of materials, the percentage of labour costs, i.e., weaving (and other preparatory processes also usually done by the weaver) were small. In the case of ordinary common woven goods like chadars, coloured saris and lungis, it hovered around 25 per cent. However, weaving charges were higher in the case of fancy products like fine dhuties and fine saris.[71] This was in view of the fact that on yarn of fine counts he expends a very much larger amount of labour per Ib. of material used than on coarse yarn.[72] Thus when the time factor is taken into consideration, it is probable that the average weaving charges in Bengal were more or less the same for most products. The average weaving charges when translated into money income was, however, far from satisfactory in view of the fact that most weavers were dependent on *mahajans* for the materials of his products. Thus Gupta found the weavers of the Dacca town of whom more than 90 per cent were indebted to *mahajans* earning not more than 2 to 3 annas a day, while those who worked with their own capital admitted earning on the average from Rs. 15 to Rs. 20 a month.[73]

PART IV

Problems of Weavers and Government attempts to solve them

While the preceding section showed the relative percentages of the cost of production of handloom goods, in this section we will discuss the problems connected with the production and distribution of handloom cloths in Bengal vis-a-vis the attempts made by the government to ameliorate the economic condition of those engaged in the industry. Among the problems (other than that of improve-

[71]IOR: Vol. 11960, BRP (Industries), October 1932, Nos. 7-8, p. 19.

[72]*Report of the IIC* (PP XVII of 1919), p. 435.

[73]G.N. Gupta, *A Survey of the Industries and Resources of Eastern Bengal and Assam for 1907-08* (Shillong, 1908), p. 14.

ments in the mechanical processes which has been discussed earlier were (*a*) the difficulty of supply of yarn at a cheap rate, (*b*) the dispersal of the finished products at the best possible price, (*c*) lack of finance, and (*d*) want of training of weavers in new designs and patterns, textures and finish. It was largely because of these problems that the handloom weavers in Bengal were to a very great extent at a disadvantageous position in relation to textile mills.

Supply of Yarn

The problem of getting a sufficient supply of cheap yarn was the most pressing of all, especially as we found earlier that yarn price constituted more than 70 per cent of the cost of manufacture in the case of ordinary handloom products of daily use. Unfortunately, the internal trade of this important raw material was in the hands of a chain of middlemen which necessarily increased the yarn price and placed the poor weavers in a disadvantageous position in relation to mills. Such a chain of middlemen included the big yarn dealers (mainly Marwaris) in Calcutta who procured yarn from mills upon forward contract or imported them from abroad; *paikars* who usually bought on wholesale from yarn merchants or dealers; the innumerable grades of middlemen called *farias*, who sold yarn in rural *hats* and bazaars or itinerated from village to village. Unfortunately, however, there are no statistical figures to show the margin of profits that each grade of middlemen earned on their transactions but it is believed that the differential between the mill price of yarns and the actual amount paid by the weavers must have been substantial. Not only were the prices high, but instances were not rare when unscrupulous yarn dealers resorted to unfair means, i.e., short reeling, false packing or even over declaration of weight. Hoarding was also a common occurrence among a section of yarn dealers and speculators which occasionally resulted in high and fluctuating price of yarns.

To eliminate the profits of the middlemen, the Government attempted to solve the problem of yarn supply through co-operative methods. It established a number of yarn banks or depots at convenient places, i.e., at Nadia, Serampore, Zorwargunj, Chapra, Begumgunj, Mankar and arrangements were also made for the supply of yarns to these banks at market rates with a number of Calcutta merchants.[74] Members of co-operative societies could buy their yarn

[74]DOIB: *Annual Administration Report*, 1922, p. 18.

from these places at a chaper rate than prevailing in the local bazaars. However, the number of such banks or depots seems to have been very limited. Members of co-operative societies affiliated to particular Industrial Unions could also procure yarns under "yarn-sale system". Under this system, the weavers through their societies purchased yarn from the Union at thirty-five day's sight, disposed of their finished products themselves, and paid the Union the actual price of the yarn plus one anna per rupee on the price.[75] But such a system of yarn supply could not work satisfactorily owing to the inability of the Unions to obtain yarns at wholesale rates through forward contract with mills. As a result the price of the yarn supplied to weavers was not always lower than the rate prevaling in the local bazaars.[76] In some cases, Industrial Unions (e.g., Industrial Union of Chaumohini) even had to purchase yarns from local markets for distribution amongst its member societies.[77] This inability to supply yarn at cheap rates greatly hampered the successful working of the Industrial Unions and disheartened most weavers who saw no benefit accruing to them from joining the co-operative movement.

Problem of Marketing

One of the probable reasons for the higher price of handloom products was the higher costs of marketing the individual items of handlooms as contrasted with the bulk transactions by which the mill-made fabrics were marketed and sold. Not only did the yarn prices go up as it passed from the big importing houses to the weaver through serveral middlemen, the same process was also repeated with regard to finished articles. If he had worked to order, he was fortunate; otherwise he had to take his goods to one of the nearest *hats* which were commonly held throughout rural Bengal at regular intervals usually once or twice a week or to daily bazaars. There he would sell his products either to retail customers or to *farias* who would usually buy for cash. The *farias* in their turn sold their goods to *paikars* or *beparis* who had their establishments in the principal

[75]*Annual Report on the Working of Co-operative Societies in the Presidency of Bengal*, 1924-25, p. 20.

[76]J.P. Niyogi, *The Co-operative Movement in Bengal* (London, 1940), p. 240.

[77]*Annual Report on the Working of Co-operative Societies in the Presidency of Bengal*, 1927-28, p. 28.

centres of trade. After collecting large quantities of commodities, the *paikars* disposed them off in bulks to the bigger *mahajans* at a convenient time when prices were good. Sometimes shopkeepers would also send their agents to make purchases at these *hats*. In some towns, weavers themselves hawked about their goods from house to house or from shop to shop. In marketing their products, handloom weavers had relatively little difficulty during the months from October to January and June and July when new paddy enabled the agriculturists to buy their yearly requirements of cloth. But for the remaining six months, the weaver was virtually at the mercy of *mahajans* (who were aften also yarn dealers and money-lenders) as he had no holding capacity and was unable to pay cash for more yarns. Under the circumstances, he had no alternative but to accept one of the following courses if he wished to keep his loom working:

(*a*) He deposited his finished cloth with the yarn dealer against the price of new yarn taken, in the hope that the market would improve and enable him to get his full price. This was, of course a very temporary expedient;

(*b*) He could sell the cloth outright to the dealer at a discount on the usual sale price;

(*c*) If the yarn dealer was unwilling to buy the cloth, the weaver was compelled to sell his products to any private customer at any price he could get. In some cases, when sales were slack, he could get no more than the value of the yarn in the cloth.

To tackle the problem, Government encouraged co-operative methods of sale through Industrial Unions and also granted loans and subsidies to different organizations and associations devoted to the cause of marketing the products of cottage industries, i.e., Bengal Home Industries Association, Goods Companions, etc.[78] The Industrial Unions (which were seven in number in 1934) supplied yarn to their respective affiliated societies which worked on *bani* (wages) system and when cloths were woven took them for sale. It was up to the Unions to find markets for the disposal of finished products. In doing so, however, the Unions continually faced difficulties as a result of which many Unions suffered financial losses, i.e.,

[78]The work of the different private organizations and associations which carried out the task of marketing the products of the cottage industries has already been dealt with in Chapter II, Part II.

the Bankura Industrial Union which worked with 77 affiliated societies had to sell its goods at less than the cost price in order to compete in the market.[79] The principal reasons for the failure of the Co-operative Unions to solve the marketing problem was due, firstly, to the high price charged for mill yarns; and secondly, to the heavy overhead charges of the Co-operative Industrial Unions as a result of which the minimum market price of cotton fabrics of the handloom industry was found to be much higher than the prices at which the mill products of similar quality and attractiveness were sold. To relieve the Industrial Unions in disposing of their finished goods, the Unions were federated into a provincial organization in 1929 called the Bengal Provincial Co-operative Industrial Society, Limited. But "for want of sufficient funds as its disposal" and because it worked mainly with borrowed capital for which it had to pay a high rate of interest, the provincial organization could not be of much help to the Industrial Unions and maintained only a Sale Depot in Calcutta in which finished goods were displayed.[80] Apart from Co-operative methods of marketing which had not been quite satisfactory for obvious reasons (and grants and subsidies to some organizations), no serious attempt was made by the provincial government to solve the problem. This was quite in contrast to the Punjab and the United Provinces where the provincial governments maintained emporiums for stocking and advertising the products of the cottage and small industries of those provinces and in charge of each of those emporiums there was an officer of gazetted rank who did the necessary marketing and publicity work and gave marketing advice to cottage industrialists.[81] However, as a result of a strong recommendation of the Director of Industries, Bengal (G.S. Dutt), the Government in 1933 decided to appoint a Marketing and Publicity officer under the Unemplyment Relief Scheme for facilitating the marketing of the products of the cottage and small industries in Bengal with effect from 1934-35.[82] But it is unlikely that any significant change had been brought by the mere appointment of a marketing and publicity officer only when the problem needed to be tackled in big way.

[79] *Annual Report on the Working of Co-operative Societies in the Presidency of Bengal*, 1931-32, pp. 14-15.

[80] *Bulletins of Indian Industries and Labour*, *No. 52* (Proceedings of the Sixth Industries Conference) (Delhi, 1934), pp. 44-45.

[81] IOR: Vol. 11988, BRP (Industries), October 1933, Nos. 1-2, p. 3.

[82] IOR: Vol. 11988, BRP (Industries), October 1933, No 3, p. 6.

Problem of Finance

Handloom weavers needed capital for a variety of reasons. Firstly, he needed block capital to purchase his appliances like looms, preparatory machinery and accessories. This itself, however, was not sufficient; he also needed money to purchase raw materials like yarns to work upon. Together with these, he required reserve capital as finished goods often remained unsold for want of markets, especially during slack seasons when he had to purchase yarn to keep himself employed. Secondly, he had also to maintain his family which often consisted of four to five members on the average. Since handloom weavers lived at subsistence level, he had virtually no reserve capital to fall back upon and had ordinarily to rcsort to money-lenders or yarn dealers or cloth merchants who were often one and the same person. Once the handloom weaver got indebted to the *mahajan* it was very difficult if not impossible for him to get out. The *mahajans* on their part also rather encouraged them in this as a certain amount of indebtedness on the part of the weaver was a considerable safeguard during the months when he was likely to become a defaulter.[83] In such a contractual relationship, the *mahajan* being the dominant partner determined the terms and conditions in his own favour, leaving only a bare subsistence to the actual worker and appropriated to himself all the commercial advantages of the processes of buying and selling. Any attempt to organize the handloom industry by capitalists was strenously opposed by *mahajans*, and their control over the weavers was sufficient to ensure its defeat.

The Government in its turn also did next-to-nothing to improve the financial position of the weavers so that they could free themselves from the clutches of the middlemen. It is true that the Bengal Agricultural Debtor's Act, 1935 was passed but the cottage industrialists did not come within the Act and hence could not claim relief from their indebtedness. The All-Bengal Jamiatul Momineen (Central organization for Bengal weavers) was very bitter at the apathy and neglect of the state and complained that the weavers of Bengal had not profited by the Co-operative movement, either for credit or for production and marketing and

[83]A.E. Brown, 'The Economic Conditions of the Cotton Weavers of the Bankura District', *Bengal Economic Journal*, Vol. I, No. 3 (Calcutta, January 1917), p. 312.

hence they had to depend on the *mahajans* in consequence of which they were compelled to sell their finished goods at a rate less than the market price.[84] It called upon the Government to protect and subsidize the actual and real weavers with money grant and regulate prices of yarn. The state, however, granted loans to the ex-students of Government Weaving Institutes in order to enable them to follow the profession independently. These loans were granted against efficient security bearing an interest of 6½ per cent per annum repayable in 24 equal instalments.[85] But the amount of such annual grants was ridiculous both in terms of total amount sanctioned and in terms of average loans granted (see Table 7.7). Apart from such small loans, no other financial support was forthcoming from the Government or from other known sources.

TABLE 7.7

LOANS SANCTIONED TO PASSED STUDENTS OF GOVERNMENT WEAVING INSTITUTES, 1929-30 to 1938-39

Year	*No. of students receiving loan*	*Total amount sanctioned*
1929-30	60	4,949
1930-31	48	3,910
1931-32	71	3,950
1932-33	73	3,975
1933-34	57	3,995
1934-35	57	3,775
1935-36	53	3,680
1936-37	49	3,940
1937-38	46	3,588
1938-39	18	1,800

SOURCES: DOIB: *Annual Administration Report*, 1929-30 (Calcutta, 1930), p. 38 and subsequent annual issues till 1938-39. Loans advanced to ex-students of government weaving institutes from 1921-22 to 1928-29 amounted to Rs 22,885. Particular of loans granted, if any, prior to 1920-21 could not be traced by the Industries Department. See, BSR: Bundle No. 7, PAI (Industries), B Proceedings, File No 1L/20 of 1936.

[84] *Star of India*, 24, July 1939, p. 7.
[85] DOIB : *Annual Administration Report*, 1936-37, p. 37.

Want of Training

Although due to intensive propaganda work carried out by the demonstration parties and various schools like Peripatetic Weaving Schools and District Weaving Schools, improved Serampore fly-shuttle looms had been introduced widely in Bengal; yet there had been little change in respect of new designs and patterns, texture and finish of the handloom products. This was basically due to ignorance and lack of proper training facilities in this respect. It was only after 1934 when the Government of India decided to assist the handloom industry for a period of five years that this aspect of the industry was looked into. By November 1935, skilled staff consisting of one weaving expert and a number of weaving supervisors had been allotted to all important weaving areas under the operation of Industrial Unions.[86] The duties allotted to the experts and supervisors of the Industrial Unions were to train up the weavers in producing fabrics of improved and new designs, texture and finish as also to supply them with dyed yarns and to advise them in the reduction of the cost of production.[87] A designer was also attached to the Bengal Provincial Co-operative Industrial Society, Limited, to supply new designs to the Industrial Unions.[88] The Designer, it was claimed at the Ninth Industries Conference had supplied 120 new designs to the different Industrial Unions and weaving organizations out of which 80 had been successfully adopted by the weavers and depicted on fabrics.[89] In addition to providing experts, money was also sanctioned from the Government of India fund for the purchase of dobbies, jacquard machines, dyeing appliances and other improved machinery like sizing machine and calendering machine which definitely enabled weavers of co-operative societies to weave fabrics of new designs and fashions and gave them a better finish.[90] But unfortunately, the entire process of training up weavers in respect of developing the artistic value of their products remained arrested within a

[86] *RAB*, 1935-36, p. 126; and *Bulletins of Indian Industries and Labour, No. 59* (Proceedings of the Eighth Industries Conference) (Delhi, 1937), p. 26.

[87] *Bulletins of Indian Industries and Labour, No. 59*, p. 26.

[88] *Ibid.*

[89] *Ibid., No. 65* (Proceedings of the Ninth Industries Conference) (Delhi, 1938), p. 22.

[90] IOR : Vol. 12049, BRP (Industries), November 1935, Nos. 5-8, 20-25, pp. 5-11, 21-26.

narrow fraction of the weaving population, and no appropriate measures had been taken to tackle the problem at micro level. This was a serious flaw in government planning, especially when they themselves had realized that the future of the industry lay "in the direction of developing the artistic value of their products and a continuous living touch with the market. . .as to the requirements of the consumers in respect of textures, designs and other particulars".[91] The weavers on their part also showed a general reluctance to get themselves trained as new designs involved the use of improved appliances like dobbies and jacquard machines which they were too poor to purchase. Nor could they afford to attend the training centres for days together at the sacrifice of their daily earnings. Moreover, a certain quantity of raw materials was also wasted in the process of learning which the Unions were generally unable to supply.[92]

Conclusion

In the context of India's twentieth century industrial history, no topic was discussed more frequently and with such emotional surcharge than that of handloom cotton weaving industry. To nationalist politicians the question of its revival and regeneration became almost a symbol of India's economic and political freedom. Popular sentiment was roused and the public were instructed to encourage in every possible way the expansion for the sake of the ailing country.[93] The efforts of politicians to patronize handloom products did not go entirely in vain. After years of decay in the nineteenth century, the industry at last began to take off due to increased demand for handloom products on the part of the people and improvements in the mechanical processes of weaving appliances which enabled weavers to meet this increased demand. In spite of such increased output, it is doubtful whether the economic condition of the actual producers had improved in any appreciable manner. The industry remained, according to the Bengal Industrial Survey Committee:[94]

[91] *Bulletins of Indian Industries and Labour, No. 50* (Proceedings of the Fifth Industries Conference) (Delhi, 1933), p. 66.

[92] IOR : Vol. 12075, BRP (Industries), October 1936, Nos. 7-8, p. 18.

[93] *Industrial India*, Vol. IV, No. 7, July 1907, pp. 211-12.

[94] *BISC*, p. 45.

> . . .generally under the grip of the mahajans who in most of the cases act as creditors and suppliers of yarn to the weavers and also market the finished stuffs. The mahajans' interposition between the weaving community and the market is primarily due to the lack of any organization amongst the workers, whose principal difficulty is want of funds.

To improve weavers' economic condition no doubt the Government made attempts to reorganize the industry on co-operative lines but failed miserably due to inadequate resources at its command.

8 Perspectives

In the previous chapters, we have made a critical review of some aspects of the industrial growth and development of Bengal during the period 1900 to 1939. Here we intend to summarize in brief the trend and extent of industrial development during our period of study.

Since there are no agreed criterion by which such historical development can be measured and weighed, we have arbitarily decided to apply the following standards to evaluate the extent of industrial progress in this province, firstly, by the shifting distribution of labour as registered in the factories reports. An important limitation of this standard is that it does not take into consideration those factories which do not employ at least a certain number of labour-force. As a result, cottage industries which employ perhaps the greater number of industrial labour-force and the labour-force employed in the smaller organized factories of the province are excluded. Or, in other words, it records only the shifting distribution of labour in the larger industrial establishments minus colliery workers and also the tea garden labourers (includes, however, those who work in the tea factories). Secondly, we can measure industrialization by the consumption of power as indicated by the growth of electric power for industrial purposes. Here, the limitations are two-fold. Firstly, we do not have the separate statistics of electric power used for industrial purposes. The figures are that of units sold alike for domestic, industrial or public uses. Secondly, the statistics available for any continuous period of time are that of the Calcutta Electric Supply Corporation, Limited, which covered the major industrial belt around Calcutta. These two standards, although they suffer from obvious limitations, will probably give some indication of the industrial growth of Bengal. A third criterion which will be used is that of the variations in the aggregate paid-up capital of the important manufacturing industries of the province. This in our opinion is a much better guide than the previous two standards. One defect in the statistics is, however, that of absence of proper notes so as to show, for example, which companies have been classified under 'iron, steel and ship-building' and which under 'engineering companies'. But this will not alter the total investment figure as both are manufacturing companies and perhaps interchangable too.

Coming to the shifting distribution of industrial labour-force in Bengal, we find from Table 4.7 that their numbers had increased nearly three-fold from around 200,000 in 1901 to around 571,000 in 1939. During the same period, the number of factories at work had also increased nearly seven-fold from around 250 to around 1,750. But it should be borne in mind that this increase includes many factories which were working earlier but had not been brought under the Factories Acts like the tea factories (which came under the Act in 1922) and also many which were not detected earlier by the factory inspection staff.

The increase in the number of workforce and factories in Bengal was coupled with the growth of electric power used for industrial purposes. Thus in 1924, the consumption of electric power in and around Calcutta was round about 55 million units which increased to over 100 million units by 1928.[1] The growth was even more remarkable later—171 million units in 1930 which again more than doubled by the end of 1938 to over 365 million units.[2] Here again one should not forget that the growth of electric power was not entirely due to power consumed in new ventures. Some displacement of oil engines, gas engines and in some cases steam power had undoubtedly taken place in favour of electricity, but the general trend of the figures support the view expressed.[3]

Capital investment in various industries had also increased during the period under review. Thus the aggregate paid-up capital of the tea and other planting companies at work on 31 March, 1900-01 was Rs. 328 lakhs which increased to Rs. 1,236 lakhs in 1935-36.[4] Paid-up capital of jute mills and jute presses during the same period increased from Rs. 303 lakhs to Rs. 1,985 lakhs and

[1]DOIB: *Annual Administration Report*, 1928-29, see graph on page 40.

[2]*Annual Report on the Administration of the Indian Electricity Act, 1910 in Bengal for the year 1931* (Calcutta, 1932), p. 26; and *Ibid., 1939* (Alipore, 1940), p. 32.

[3]DOIB: *Annual Administration Report*, 1928-29, pp. 8-9.

[4]DOIB: *Bulletin No. 83, Report on the Growth of Joint Stock Companies in Bengal* (Alipore, 1939), p. 9.

that of mining and quarrying companies from Rs. 151 lakhs to Rs. 1,035 lakhs and cotton mills from Rs. 78 lakhs in 1900-01 to Rs. 380 lakhs in 1935-36.[5] A some-what less spectacular growth so far as aggregate paid-up capital of industries was concerned was marked in the chemical and pharmaceutical industries, engineering companies, iron, steel and ship-building companies, etc.[6]

All these criteria indicate that some progress had been made in the industrial development of the province. In fact by 1939, Bengal was industrially the most advanced province within British India. With 15.5 per cent of the population, she accounted for 28.7 per cent of the total number of industrial workers in 1939.[7] Of the joint stock companies at work in India at the close of the year 1935-36, 49.6 per cent were in Bengal with 44.2 per cent of the total paid-up capital of India employed in them.[8]

In the case of small and cottage industries as well, some progress was made. Thus the output of handloom cotton cloth had nearly doubled from 136 million yards in 1912-13 to nearly 249 million yards in 1938-39 (see Table 7.4). This great increase was made possible by the introduction of fly-shuttle looms and other improved accessories in place of primitive looms used by the indigenous handloom weavers of Bengal. In the field of tanning, the introduction of western processes of chrome tanning and an improved process of vegetable tanning also led to an increased output of leather. However, it is doubtful whether any marked progress was made in other small and cottage industries, such as pottery, cutlery, etc., in view of lack of sustained effort by the government in this line.

In spite of some advancement, industrial development could hardly be said to be adequate. It did not result in any marked change in the occupational distribution of the people of Bengal. Thus in 1911, only 7.4 per cent of the people were engaged in industry and in 1931 it was 8.80 per cent.[9] The large majority of the people remai-

[5]DOIB: *Bulletin No. 83, Report on the Growth of Joint Stock Companies*, pp. 9, 11-12.

[6]*Ibid.*, pp. 10-11.

[7]Bimal C. Ghose, *Industrial Location* (Oxford pamphlet on Indian affairs, No. 32) (Madras, 1945), pp. 15-16.

[8]DOIB: *Bulletin No. 83, Report on the Growth of Joint Stock Companies*, p. 16.

[9]*Census of India*, 1911, Vol. V, Bengal, Bihar and Sikkim, Part I, Report (Calcutta, 1913), p. 560; and *Census of India*, 1931. Vol. V, Bengal and Sikkim, Part I, Report (Calcutta, 1933), p. 261.

ned engaged in the agricultural pursuits with virtually no growth in that sector as well. Not unnaturally, economic progress, if at all was slow and halting. Moreover, the entire development was unrelated and patchy as exemplified by the regional distribution of industries within Bengal and the inadequate development of certain vital industries like chemical works, iron and steel, and engineering. "The lack of a strong metallurgical industry, and of subsidiary and auxiliary industries to cater to the needs of the established major industries, explains the weakness of Indian industrialization".[10]

Various reasons could be ascribed for this slow and unsteady growth of industries in Bengal. But probably the most important factor was the lack of state patronage in this direction. The laissez-faire policy followed in the nineteenth century was continued till the end of the First World War. In the midst of fierce foreign competition and the virtual absence of markets for manufactured goods within the country and outside (largely brought about by the Government of India's 'Stores Rules') industrial development with the exception of export-oriented industries and collieries was almost nil. It was only during the First World War when Indian industries got natural protection and in the subsequent period when discriminatory protection was afforded to certain industries and stores rules modified that industrial development went ahead but only to be interrupted in the 1930's by the world-wide depression. As for the Department of Industries, Bengal, it was ill-suited from the beginning to foster the development of industries due to lack of funds and concentrated thus on the small and cottage industries of Bengal where too it met with only a limited success due to the same reason.

In the absence of state patronage, capital funds flowed towards the more profitable and secure avenues of investment which included with the exception or few industries, trade and commerce, money-lending and investment in land. The few entrepreneurs who went to promote untried and new industrial ventures were thus from the beginning starved of adequate and cheap sources of capital supply. Banks would not also give long term loans nor would they accommodate generous working capital as their business was

[10]P.S. Lokanathan, *Industrialization* (Oxford pamphlets on Indian affairs, No. 10), p. 10. No date of publication is indicated but India Office catalogue mentions this to be 2nd Edition, Bombay, 1944.

geared towards export trade in agricultural commodities. The provincial government was too poor to be of any considerable help as could be seen from the amount of loan sanctioned under the Bengal State Aid to Industries Act, 1931 (see Table 4.8). In the absence of adequate and cheap sources of capital supply many nascent industries failed to take root in Bengal. It not only discouraged potential entrepreneurs from launching into new and untried ventures but also sapped the confidence of the investing public who so often found such projects coming to grief for want of fresh capital supply. Howevever, some reputable managing agents by virtue of their good-will were able to raise the required amounts but very often they chose to follow traditional lines of businesses in which profit was assured rather than embarking into new and hence risky undertakings.

Another contributary factor which considerably slowed down the rate of industrial progress was the lack of proper facilities for technical and commercial education as well as for acquiring practical business experience. In the absence of such training and experience little regard was paid to costs, transport and market facilities, and to the relation of demand to the existing supplies. Sometimes companies were floated with insufficient funds or with obsolete machinery. No wonder many industrial ventures failed which in its turn chilled the ardour of many, who might otherwise have ventured to establish new industrial enterprises.

There were also certain inherent limitations within the economy which restricted the fuller development of industries in Bengal. In the first place, although it had many valuable raw materials, it did not produce all that was needed to meet the demand for various sorts of industries. Thus Bengal did not produce sufficient raw cotton, the natural advantage of which lay with Bombay. Similarly, she did not produce enough sugar-cane and was at a disadvantage as regards its cost of production with the northern Indian provinces. Likewise, the province did not have sulphur for the manufacture of sulphuric acid, nitrate for the production of nitric acid or salt for the production of hydrochloric acid. Moreover, its colliery deposits were awkwardly located in one corner of the province which made power supply very costly for most regions of Bengal, especially in the Eastern Bengal. These together with an undeveloped transport system precluded the establishment of some important consumer good industries for which there was an internal demand. Furthermore, the over-all size of the internal market for various manufactured goods was itself extremely limited in view of the proverty of the people. The situation was made worse in the 1930's due to the fall in the purchasing power of the ryots as a result of world-wide depression.[11]

When all these shortcomings are taken into consideration, the reasons for the slowness of Bengal's industrialization becomes obvious. Only those industries which could counteract the above mentioned disadvantages succeeded in establishing themselves to the exclusion of others. Yet most of these difficulties were removable evils and could have been obviated by the adoption of a systematic planned action on the part of the state in co-operation with private enterprise. At least that was what the civilized governments in Japan, Germany and in most other European countries were doing at this period of time. But in India, the government played a diametrically opposite role—choosing not to co-operate but to confront in matters industrial whenever imperial interests clashed with India's. Under such circumstances, it is not to be wondered why Bengal should remain economically one of the world's poorest regions after about two centuries of British rule in that area.

[11]Social factors are also sometimes blamed for the retarded growth of industries. But it should be pointed out that social factors cannot be separated from political life. Since Indians were totally cut off from any effective participation in the process of political decision making, the whole conscious development of social aspirations remained emasculated.

Appendix I

GROWTH OF EXPENDITURE FOR THE DEPARTMENT OF INDUSTRIES, BENGAL, 1917-18 TO 1938-39

Year	*Direction*	*Ind. Dev.*	*Ind. Edc.*	*Sericulture*	*Total*
1917-18 (from 29 Oct; 1917	—	—	—	—	44,746
1918-19	—	—	—	—	87,787
1919-20	—	—	—	—	1,50,461
1920-21	—	—	—	—	2,70,415
1921-22	—	—	—	—	4,08,614*
1922-23	2,85,000	77,000	4,67,000	—	8,29,000
1923-24	2,57,000	81,000	4,09,000	—	7,41,000
1924-25	2,00,000	84,000	3,36,000	—	6,20,000
1925-26	1,90,000	79,000	4,63,000	—	7,32,000
1926-27	1,67,600	77,000	5,42,000	—	7,27,600
1927-28	1,87,000	77,000	4,83,000	—	8,06,000
1928-29	1,70,000	87,000	5,55,000	—	8,12,000
1929-30	1,74,000	95,000	5,02,000	—	7,71,000
1930-31	1,79,000	1,06,000	5,32,480	—	8,17,480
1931-32	1,62,800	86,200	5,03,900	—	7,52,900
1932-33	1,48,000	85,000	4,59,000	—	6,92,000
1933-34	1,48,000	1,89,000	4,02,000	—	7,30,000
1934-35	1,29,000	2,01,000	4,06,000	—	7,36,000
1935-36	1,37,000	2,23,000	4,72,800	1,60,000	9,93,100
1936-37	1,37,600	2,25,300	4,77,100	1,32,500	9,72,500
1937-38	1,29,600	2,50,600	5,62,200	2,05,600	11,48,000
1938-39	1,34,900	3,64,300	6,19,400	1,95,300	13,13,900

*Upto December.

SOURCES: Figures from 1917-18 to 1920-21 obtained from the *BLCP*, 4 July, 1921, Vol. III, p. 49; 1921-22 figures from IOR: Vol. 11155, BRP (Industries), April 1922, No. 4, p. 6; and the rest from *BISC*, Appendix XVIIA, p. 320. Breakdown figures are not available for the years 1917-18 to 1921-22 and Sericulture Section was not transferred to the Industries Department till 1935-36.

Appendix II

TABLE I
AVERAGE NUMBER OF PERSONS EMPLOYED IN THE JUTE MILL INDUSTRY, 1900-01 TO 1939

Year	*Men*	*Women*	*Children*	*Total*
1900-01	—	—	—	111,272[1]
1901-02	—	—	—	114,795
1902-03	—	—	—	118,904
1903-04	—	—	—	123,869
1904-05	88,301	21,793	21,792[2]	131,886
1905-06	96,978	23,218	23,233	143,429
1906-07	112,159	27,435	26,098	165,692
1907-08	126,190	30,009	29,708	185,907
1908-09	129,005	30,620	30,263	189,888
1909-10	135,012	32,417	34,829	202,258
1910-11	140,314	33,762	40,431	214,507
1912	145,389	31,329	23,007	199,725
1913	158,261	34,010	24,106	216,377
1914	167,858	36,800	25,969	230,627
1915	181,445	40,674	26,606	248,725
1916	191,036	42,145	27,606	260,787
1917	192,667	41,395	27,320	261,382
1918	199,977	43,278	27,709	270,964
1919	201,009	43,112	28,628	272,749
1920	207,255	44,545	28,521	280,321
1921	207,908	44,705	29,235	281,848
1922	239,660	49,257	28,267	317,184
1923	242,652	51,495	28,400	322,547
1924	252,107	54,801	27,823	334,731
1925	256,312	55,511	26,474	338,297
1926	253,935	52,827	20,785	327,547
1927	253,681	52,935	19,249	325,865
1928	260,342	53,678	17,879	331,899
1929	267,717	54,670	17,278	339,665
1930	264,417	52,114	11,646	328,177
1931	222,573	42,254	3,462	268,289
1932	212,505	40,294	1,515	254,314

1933	208,246	37,337	1,134	246,717
1934	213,894	36,932	915	251,741
1935	223,449	37,520	2,430[3]	263,399
1936	231,401	38,050	2,295	271,746
1937	246,775	37,564	3,404	287,743
1938	241,271	36,537	1,226	279,034
1939	241,976	37,534	1,719	281,229

[1]Till 1903-04 figures represent that of India.
[2]Includes 'young persons' till 1910-11.
[3]Figures till 1939 include that of 'adolescents'.

SOURCES: *Statistical Abstract relating to British India from 1900-01 to 1909-10* (45th Number) (London, 1911), p. 263; *Statistics of British India for 1906-07 and preceding years, Part I, Industrial* (Calcutta, 1908), p. 42, and its succeeding annual issues. The data from 1912 onwards obtained from *AFR*.

TABLE II

DAILY AVERAGE NUMBER OF PERSONS EMPLOYED IN THE TEA AND COAL INDUSTRIES OF BENGAL, 1900-1939

Year	*No. employed in the tea industry*	*No. employed in the coal industry*
	1	*2*
1900	176,469	58,081
1901	114,813	74,030
1902	106,714	83,290
1903	108,349	73,928
1904	38,246	75,749
1905	41,095	74,071
1906	39,422	82,885
1907	36,997	96,301
1908	36,868	112,219
1909	36,968	102,253
1910	37,837	98,268
1911	40,847	99,183
1912	124,412	36,828
1913	133,731	38,553
1914	130,438	38,879
1915	133,341	42,093
1916	132,514	43,040
1917	138,401	38,585
1918	132,808	46,149
1919	161,382	48,642
1920	151,008	43,782

1921	141,421	45,813
1922	136,503	44,893
1923	146,330	44,251
1924	158,394	43,621
1925	166,985	42,781
1926	170,966	43,506
1927	181,849	44,285
1928	185,399	43,855
1929	196,899	44,303
1930	190,313	46,592
1931	185,811	44,642
1932	182,943	43,423
1933	185,594	43,651
1934	194,757	44,619
1935	205,428	49,913
1936	203,398	51,061
1937	199,712	51,077
1938	202,609	59,364
1939	204,981	59,632

[1] The figure of tea industry for the year 1900 is obviously wrong as it puts the labour-force of Chittagong alone at 58,191 (permanent plus temporary). Correct statements appear in the later issues.

SOURCES: For column (1), see IOR, V/14/272, Production and Cultivation of Tea in India, Reports 1900-1020; Supplement to the *Indian Trade Journal* (relevant issues) from 1921 to 1929; and the annual publication, *Indian Tea Statistics* from 1930 to 1939. For column (2), see *AMR*, 1900 to 1939.

Appendix III

Sources and Notes on The Construction of Table 7.4

Column (1) has been obtained from the estimated balances of Indian cotton mill yarn available for consumption in handloom weaving in Bengal together with the estimated balances of foreign yarn available for consumption in handloom weaving in Bengal. Data for the overseas trade obtained from the *Annual Statement of the Sea-Borne Trade and Navigation of British India with British Empire and Foreign Countries in the year ending March 31, 1950 and the four preceding years*, Vol. I (Calcutta, 1906) and the subsequent relevant issues; figures of coasting trade from the *Annual Statement of the Trade and Navigation of British India with Foreign Countries and of the Coasting Trade in the year ending March 31, 1901, Vol. II, Coasting Trade and Trade of Each Port in Each Province* (Calcutta, 1901) and the subsequent annual issues (title varies) till 1921. Data for the years 1933-34 to 1938-39 from *Accounts relating to the Coasting Trade and Navigation of British India*, for *March, 1935* (Delhi, 1935); *Ibid.*, March, 1936, and *Ibid.*, March, 1939. Data for Rail and River-borne trade obtained from the *Accounts of the Trade carried by Rail and River in India in the official year 1903-04 and the four preceding years* (Calcutta, 1904) and the subsequent annual issues (title varies) till 1920-21. Data for the years 1933-34 to 1938-39 from *Accounts relating to the Inland* (*Rail and River-borne*) *Trade of India for March 1935* (Delhi, 1935), *Ibid.*, March, 1937, and *Ibid.*, March, 1939. Balance mill production from *Statistics of British India* (*with statistics, where available, relating to certain native states*), *for 1911-12 and preceding years, Part I, Industrial* (Calcutta, 1913), p. 59; *Statistical Abstract for British India with statistics, where available, relating to certain Indian states from 1911-12 to 1920-21* (Fifty-sixth number) (London, 1924); and *Ibid., 1930-31 to 1939-40* (72nd number) (London, 1943), pp. 626-29. In compiling the data, such figures as 'maunds' and 'cwts' were converted into lbs. to standardise the data. Figures of re-exports were taken into account whenever it occured. For finding out the total balance of yarn of Bengal cotton mills we naturally deducted the yarn consumed in producing cloths. The calculation was done on the basis of 100 Ibs. of yarn=112 Ibs. of cloth as used by the *IIC*. See, *Report of the IIC* (PP XVII of 1919), p. 395. Column (4) from *Statistics of British India (with statistics, where available, relating to certain native states) for 1911-12 and preceding years, Part I, Industrial* (Calcutta, 1913), p. 59; *Statistical Abstract of British India with statistics, where available, relating to certain Indian states from 1911-12 to 1920-21* (fifty-sixty number) (London, 1924), and *Ibid., 1930-31 to 1939-40* (72nd number) (London, 1943), pp. 626-29.

Bibliography

Primary Sources

A. *Official Proceedings*

(*i*) *India Commerce and Industry Proceedings*:

Vol.	*Year*	*Vol.*	*Year*
7407	1906	10221	1917
9023	1912	10431	1918
9780	1915		

(*ii*) *Bengal Financial Proceedings*:

Vol.	*Year*	*Vol.*	*Year*
9370	1914	11422	1924
9635	1915	11632	1927
9882	1916	11866	1930
10298	1918	11938	1931
10503	1919	11961	1932
10749	1920	12019	1934
10971	1921	12077	1936

(*iii*) *Bengal General Proceedings*:

Vol.	*Year*	*Vol.*	*Year*
5851	1900	7861	1908
6087	1901	8139	1909
6791	1904	8416	1910
7036	1905	9139	1913

(*iv*) *Bengal Revenue Proceedings*:

Vol.	*Year*	*Vol.*	*Year*
7574	1907	11865	1930
8136	1909	11960	1932
11155	1922	11988	1933
11293	1923	12018	1934
11630	1927	12049	1935
11784	1929	12075	1936

B. *Economic and Overseas Department Collections*:

File Nos. L/E/9/404, L/E/9/405, L/E/9/939, L/E/9/994, L/E/9/999/, L/E/9/1004, L/E/9/1027, L/E/9/1030, L/E/9/1144, L/E/9/1294, L/E/9/1296.

C. *Collections of Provincial Government Records transferred to London*:

File Nos. R/3/2/69, R/3/2/70, R/3/2/71

D. *Private Papers*:

Sir Charles Wood Collection, MSS. Eur. F. 78, File No. 59/8B.
Meston Collection, MSS, Eur. F. 136, File Nos. 30 & 32.
Curzon Collection, MSS. Eur. F. 111, No. 514.

E. *Other India Office Records*:

L/E/7/855, L/E/7/938, L/F/9/20, L/F/9/22, V/14/76, V/14/272 F. 5. VII. 1904.

F. *Bangladesh Secretariat Records*:

Proceedings of the Department of Agriculture and Industries (Industries Branch):

(*i*) 'A' Proceedings of the year 1940.

(*ii*) 'B' Proceedings: Bundle No. 1, File No. 4L/4 of 1934.
Bundle No. 1, File No. 1W/3 of 1936.
Bundle No. 6, File No. 8E/8 37 & 8E/6 of 1937-38.
Bundle No. 7, File No. 1L/20 of 1936.

G. *Official Reports and Publications*: U.K.

(*i*) *Parliamentary Papers*:

Report of the Indian Famine Commission, PP LII of 1880.

Report on the Conditions of India, PP LIII of 1880.

Report of the Indian Factory Labour Commission, Vol. I, Report and Appendices, PP 74 of 1908.

Report from the Joint Select Committee on the Government of India Bill, Vol. I, Report and Proceedings, PP IV of 1919.

Report of the Indian Industrial Commission, 1916-18, PP XVII of 1919; *Minutes of Evidence* Vol. II, PP XVIII of 1919.

Report of the Committee appointed by the Secretary of State for India to enquire into the administration and working of Indian Railways Report, PP X of 1921.

Report of the Indian Fiscal Commission, 1921-22, PP II of 1922, Second Session; *Minutes of Evidence*, Vol. I (Calcutta, 1923). This is not a PP.

Report of the Royal Commission on Labour in India, PP XI of 1930-31; *Minutes of Evidence*, Vol. V, Part I (London, 1931). This is not included in PP.

(*ii*) *Other UK Publications*:

Report on the Work of the India Store Department, London (London, annual).

Statistical Abstract relating to British India from 1900-01 to 1909-10 (Forty-fifth number) (London, 1911).

Statistical Abstract for British India with statistics, where available, relating to certain Indian States from 1911-12 to 1920-21 (Fifty-sixth number) (London, 1924). *from 1921-22 to 1930-31* (Sixty-fifth number) (London, 1933). *from 1930-31 to 1939-40* (Seventy-second no.) (London, 1943).

H. *Official Reports and Publications of the Government of India*:

Accounts of the Trade carried by Rail and River in India (Calcutta, annual); afterwards *Inland Trade (Rail and River-borne) of India* (Calcutta, annual), afterwards *Accounts relating to the Inland (Rail and River-borne) Trade of India* (Delhi, monthly).

Administration Report of the Indian Stores Department (Delhi, annual).

Annual Statement of the Sea-Borne Trade and Navigation of British India with British Empire and Foreign Countries, Vol. I (Calcutta, annual).

Annual Statement of the Trade and Navigation of British India with Foreign Countries and of Coasting Trade (Calcutta, annual); afterwards *Annual Statement of the Coasting Trade and Navigation of British India* (Calcutta, annual); afterwards *Accounts relating to the Coasting Trade and Navigation of British India* (Delhi, monthly).

Bulletins of Indian Industries and Labour:

No. 50, Proceedings of the Fifth Industries Conference (Delhi, 1933).

No. 52, Proceedings of the Sixth Industries Conference (Delhi, 1934).

No. 57, State Action in Respect of Industries, 1928-35 (Delhi, 1936).

No. 59, Proceedings of the Eighth Industries Conference (Delhi, 1937).

No. 65, Proceedings of the Ninth Industries Conference (Delhi, 1938).

Bulletins of Indian Industrial Research:

No. 8, Development of the Heavy Chemical Industries in India (Delhi, 1937).

Census of India, 1901, Vol. VIA, the Lower Provinces of Bengal and their Feudatories, Part II, the Imperial Tables (Calcutta, 1902).

Census of India, 1911, Vol. V, Bengal, Bihar and Orissa and Sikkim, Part I, Report (Calcutta, 1913).

Vol. V, Bengal, Part II, Tables (Calcutta, 1913).

Census of India, 1921, Vol. V, Bengal, Part I, Report (Calcutta, 1923).

Vol. V, Bengal, Part II, Tables (Calcutta, 1923).

Census of India, 1931, Vol. V, Bengal and Sikkim, Part I, Report (Calcutta, 1933).

Vol. V, Bengal and Sikkim, Part II (Calcutta, 1933).

Census of India, 1941, Vol. IV, Bengal, Tables (Simla, 1942).

Indian Central Banking Enquiry Committee, Vol. I, Report, and Vols. II & III, Evidence (Calcutta, 1931).

Indian Central Jute Committee: *Report on the Marketing of Jute and Jute Products, Second Report* (Calcutta, 1941).

Indian Coal Statistics (annual)

Indian Tea Statistics, 1930-1939.

Index Numbers of Indian Prices, 1861-1931 (Delhi, 1933).

Large Industrial Establishments in India, 1937 (Delhi, 1939).

Report of the External Capital Committee (Simla, 1925).

Report of the Fact-finding Committee (Handloom and Mills) (Delhi, 1942).

Report of the Financial Relations Committee (Delhi, 1920).

Report of the Inspection of Mines in India (Calcutta, annual); from 1901 onwards, *Report of the Chief Inspector of Mines in India*, (Calcutta, annual).

Report of the Stores, Printing and Stationery Sub-Committee of the Retrenchment Advisory Committee, September, 1932 (Simla, 1932).

Review of the Trade of India (Calcutta, annual).

Statistical Tables relating to Banks in India, 1938 (Delhi, 1941).
Statistics for British India for 1906-07 and preceding years, Part I, Industrial (Calcutta, 1908); and the succeeding annual issues till 1910-11.
Statistics of British India for 1909-10 and preceding years, Part II, Commercial (Calcutta, 1911).
Statistics of British India (with statistics, where available, relating to certain native states) for 1911-12 and preceding years, Part I, Industrial (Calcutta, 1913).

(ii) *Tariff Board Reports and Minutes of Evidence*:
Evidence recorded during enquiry into the Steel Industry, Vol. II (Calcutta, 1924).
Report of the Indian Tariff Board (Cotton Textile Industry Enquiry), 1927, Vol. I, Report (Calcutta, 1927).
Report of the Indian Tariff Board regarding the grant of protection to the Cotton Textile Industry (Calcutta, 1932).
Report of the Special Tariff Board on the Enquiry regarding the level of duties necessary to afford adequate protection to the Indian Cotton Textile Industry against imports from the United Kingdom of cotton piece-goods and yarn, artificial silk fabrics and mixture fabrics of cotton and artificial silk (Delhi, 1936).
Report of the Indian Tariff Board on the Sugar Industry (Delhi, 1938); and *Evidence*, Vol. II (Delhi, 1938).
Report of the Indian Tariff Board on the continuation of protection to the Iron and Steel Industry (Bombay, 1947).

(iii) *Other Government of India Publications listed under individual authors*:
Adarkar, B.P. *Report on Labour Conditions in the Rice Mills* (Delhi, 1946).
Buck, Sir E.C. *Report on Practical and Technical Education* (Calcutta, 1901).
Clow, A.G. *The State and Industry* (Calcutta, 1928).
Datta, K.L. *Report on the Enquiry into the Rise of Prices in India*, Vol. I & III (Calcutta, 1914).

I. *Official Reports and Publications of the Government of Bengal*:
Annual Report on the Working of Co-operative Societies in the Presidency of Bengal.
Annual Report on the Administration of the Indian Electricity Act, 1910, in Bengal.
Annual Report on the Working of the Indian Factories Act in the province of Bengal; afterwards *Annual Report on the Working of the Indian Factories Act, Bengal, Bihar and Orissa and Assam;* afterwards *Annual Report on the Working of the Indian Factories Act in Bengal and Assam;* afterwards *Annual Report on the Administration of the Indian Factories Act in Bengal* (Calcutta, annual till 1932, and Alipore from 1933 onwards).
Annual Administration Report of the Department of Industries, Bengal (Calcutta, annual till 1932-33 and Alipore from 1933-34 onwards).
Annual Report on the Working of the Jalpaiguri Labour Act, 1912.
Annual Report of the Board of Industries, Bengal, for the year 1936-37 (Alipore, 1938).
Bengal Commercial Reports, 1795-1802; and *1829-30.*
Bengal Legislative Council Proceedings.
Bengal Legislative Assembly Proceedings.

Bulletins of the Department of Industries, Bengal

No. 3, Handbook of Tanning (Calcutta, 1922).

No. 33, Rice Milling Industry (Calcutta, 1928).

No. 75, Cotton Mill Industry in Bengal (Alipore, 1937).

No. 83, Report on the Growth of Joint Stock Companies in Bengal (Alipore, 1939).

No. 86, Report on the Survey of Leather Industries in Bengal (Alipore, 1941).

No. 95, Report on the Cutlery Industry in Bengal (Alipore, 1941).

Eight Quinquennial Review on the Progress of Education in Bengal for the years 1927-1932 (Calcutta 1933).

Progress of Education in Bengal, 1917-18 to 1921-22., Sixth Quinquennial Review (Calcutta, 1923).

Quinquennial Report of the Ahsanullah School of Engineering, Dacca for the years 1922-23 to 1926-27 (Calcutta, 1927).

Report of the Agricultural Department, Bengal, for the year ending 30th June, 1912 (Calcutta, 1912).

Report of the Bengal Provincial Banking Enquiry Committee, 1929-30, Vol. I, Report (Calcutta, 1930); *Evidence*, Vol. II (Calcutta, 1930).

Report of the Bengal Jute Enquiry Committee (Finlow Committee), Vol. I (Alipore, 1934).

Report of the Bengal Jute Enquiry Committee (Fawcus Committee) (Alipore, 1939); *Evidence*, Vol. II (Alipore, 1939).

Report of the Land Revenue Commission, Bengal, Vol. I (Alipore, 1940).

Report of the Maritime Trade of Bengal, 1910-11 (Calcutta, 1911).

Report on Public Instruction in Bengal, 1932-33 (Alipore, 1934). Also *1938-39* (Alipore, 1940).

(*ii*) *Other Government of Bengal Publications listed under individual authors*:

Collin, E.W. *Report on the Existing Arts and Industries in Bengal* (Calcutta, 1890).

Cumming, J.G. *Technical and Industrial Instruction in Bengal, 1888-1908* (Part I of Special Report) (Calcutta, 1908).

Review of the Industrial Position and Prospects in Bengal in 1908 with special reference to the Industrial Survey of 1890 (Part II of Special Report) (Calcutta, 1908).

Foley, B. *Report on Labour in Bengal* (Calcutta, 1906).

Gupta, G.N. *A Survey of the Industries and Resources of Eastern Bengal and Assam for 1907-08* (Shillong, 1908).

Swan, J.A.L. *Report on the Industrial Development of Bengal* (Calcutta, 1915).

Watson, E.R. *A Monograph on Iron and Steel Work in the Province of Bengal* (Calcutta, 1907).

J. *Official Publication of the Government of West Bengal*:

Report of the Bengal Industrial Survey Committee (Alipore, 1948).

K. *District Gazetteers*:

Darjeeling (Calcutta, 1907).

Howrah (Calcutta, 1909).
Burdwan (Calcutta, 1910).
Nadia (Calcutta, 1910).
Tippera (Allahabad, 1910).
Birbhum (Calcutta, 1910).
Jalpaiguri (Allahabad, 1911).
Midnapore (Calcutta, 1911).
Noakhali (Allahabad, 1911).
Dinajpur (Allahabad, 1912).
Hooghly (Calcutta, 1912).
Dacca (Allahabad, 1912).
Rajshahi (Calcutta, 1916).
Mymensingh (Calcutta, 1917).
Malda (Calcutta, 1918).
Pabna (Calcutta, 1923).
Faridpur (Calcutta, 1925).

L. *Unofficial or Semi-official Reports and Publications*:

Anglo-Indian Home Industries conducted by the Anglo-Indian District Committee (Calcutta, 1917).

Indian Jute Mills Association: *Special Report on Markets for Jute* (Calcutta, 1947).

Investor's India Year-Book (Calcutta, annual).

Report of the First Industrial Conference held at Poona, August, 1891 (Poona, 1891).

Report of the Second Indian Industrial Conference held at Calcutta, December 1906 (Calcutta, 1907).

Report of the Third Indian Industrial Conference held at Surat, December 1907 (Madras, 1908).

Report of the International Tea Committee, 1st July, 1933, to 31st March, 1934 (London, n.d.).

Sugar Technologists' Association (*of India*) *Cawnpur, Year-Book* 1938-40, (Cawnpur, n.b.).

Thackers Indian Directory (Calcutta, annual).

M. *Newspapers and Journals*:

Artha Vijnana
The Bengalee
Bengal Economic Journal
Bengal Past and Present
The Bengal Review
Capital (Calcutta, Weekly)
The Englishman
The Indian Agriculturist (Calcutta, montly).
The Indian Economic and Social History Review
The Indian Planters' Gazette and Sporting News
The Indian Railway Gazette
The Indian Trade Journal

Industrial India
Journal of Indian Art and Industry
Journal of Indian Industries and Labour
Star of India
The Statesman and Friend of India (weekly edition); afterwards *The Friend of India and Statesman* (weekly edition); afterwards *The Statesman* (weekly overseas edition).
The Times

N. *Acts*

The Indian Factories Act, 1911 (XII of 1911).
The Imperial Bank of India Act, 1920 (XLVII of 1920).
The Indian Factories (Amendment) Act, 1922 (II of 1922).
The Bengal State Act to Industries Act, 1931 (Bengal Act III of 1931).
The Imperial Bank of India (Amendment) Act, 1934 III of 1934).
The Factories Act (XXV of 1934).

Secondary Sources

(*i*) *Books and Articles*:

Anstey, Vera. *The Economic Development of India* (London, 1952).
Antiquities of Dacca, No. 4 (London, 1830?).
Bagchi, A.K. *Private Investment in India* (Cambridge, 1972).
Balakrishna, R. *Industrial Development of Mysore* (Bangalore City, India, 1940).
Banerjei, N.N. 'The Cotton Fabrics of Bengal', *Journal of Indian Art and Industry*, Vol. VIII (London, 1900), PP. 65-72.
Basu, S.K. *Industrial Finance in India* (Calcutta, 1939).
Birdwood, G.C.M. *The Industrial Arts of India*, Vol. VII (London, 1880).
Broughton, G.M. *Labour in Indian Industries* (Bombay, 1924).
Brown, A.E. 'The Economic Conditions of the Cotton Weavers of the Bankura District', *Bengal Economic Journal*, Vol. I, No. 3 (Calcutta, January, 1917), PP. 306-12.
Buchanan, D.H. *The Development of Capitalistic Enterprise in India* (New York, 1934).
Chandra, B. *The Rise and Growth of Economic Nationalism in India*, (New Delhi, 1966).
Reinterpretation of Nineteenth Century Indian Economic History', *Indian Economic and Social History Review*, Vol. V (1968), pp. 35-75.
Chatterton, A. *Industrial Evolution in India* (Madras, 1912?)
Indian Industries', *Capital*, February 13, 1929, PP. 327-28.
Chaudhuri, K.N. 'The Structure of Indian Textile Industry in the Seventeenth and Eighteenth Centuries',*Indian Economic and Social History Review*, Vol. XI, Nos. 2-3, June-September, 1974, PP. 127-82.
Clapham, J.H. *The Economic Development of France and Germany, 1815-1914* (Cambridge, 1945).
Collected Works of John Stuart Mill, Vol. III (University of Toronto Press, 1965).
Cunningham, W. *The Case against Free Trade* (London, 1911).

Deole, C.S. *The State in relation to Indian Industries* (Bombay, 1916).

Digby, W. *'Prosperous' British India* (London, 1901).

Dutt, R. *The Economic History of India*, Vol. II (New York, 1970).

Feldmann, E.A. 'The Indian Jute Mill Industry: How can the Hessain Industry be improved?', *Capital*, March 20, 1930, PP. 674-75.

Gadgil, D.R. *The Industrial Evolution of India in Recent Times* (Bombay, 1942).

Ghose, B.C. *Industrial Location* (Oxford pamphlet on Indian affairs, No. 32) (Madras, 1945).

Ghosh, H.H. *The Advancement of Indian Industry* (Calcutta, 1910).

Gille, B. 'Banking and Industrialisation in Europe 1730-1914', in Carlo M. Cipolla (edited) *The Industrial Revolution, 1700-1914* (Harvester Press/Barnes Noble, 1976), PP. 255-300.

Griffiths, P. *The History of the Indian Tea Industry* (London, 1967).

Guha, A. *The Installation of Small Weaving Factories* (Calcutta, 1924).

Haberler, G. *The Theory of International Trade, with its Application to Commercial Policy* (William Hodge and Company, Ltd. Eighth Impression, 1961).

Havell, E.B. *Essays on Indian Art, Industry and Education* (Madras, 1910).

Hunter, W.W. *A Statistical Account of Bengal*, Vol. II, Districts of Nadiya and Jessor (London, 1875).

Khaitan, D. 'Survey of Indian Sugar Industry', Supplement to '*Capital*', December 14, 1939, PP. 17-18.

Kundu, B.C. & Others. *Jute in India* (Calcutta, 1959).

Lees, M.N. *The Land and Labour of India. A Review* (London, 1867).

Lokanathan, P.S. *Industrialization* (Oxford pamphlet on Indian affairs No. 10) '2nd edition, Bombay, 1944).

Lovett, Pat *The Mirror of Investment, 1927* (Calcutta, 1927).

Mann, H.H. 'The Early History of the Tea Industry in North-East India', *Bengal Economic Journal*, Vol. II, No. 1 (January, 1918), PP. 44-59.

Matsui, T. 'On the Nineteenth Century Indian Economic History—A Review of a "Reinterpretation", *Indian Economic and Social History Review*, Vol. V (1968), PP. 17-33.

McPherson, K. *The Muslim Microcosm: Calcutta, 1918 to 1935* (Wiesbadem, 1974).

Mukerji, K. 'Trends in real wages in Jute Textile Industry from 1900 to 1951', *Artha Vijnana*, Vol. 2, No. 1, March 1960, PP. 57-69.

Mukharji, T.N. *Art-Manufactures of India* (Calcutta, 1888).

Niyogi, J.P. *The Co-operative Movement in Bengal* (London, 1940).

Patel, Rao Bahadur B. 'Hand-loom Weaving in India', *Report of the Second Indian Industrial Conference held at Calcutta, December 1906* (Calcutta, 1907), PP. 204-15.

Peterson, J.C.K. 'Industrial Development in Bengal', *The Englishman* (Annual Financial Review), March 4, 1918, PP. 11, 13.

Ranade, M.G. 'The Reorganization of real credit in India', *Report of the First Industrial Conference held at Poona, August 1891* (Poona, 1891), PP. 59-76.

Sarassas, P. *Money and Banking in Japan* (London, 1940).

Sarkar, S. *The Swadeshi Movement in Bengal, 1903-1908* (New Delhi, 1973).

Schiffer, H.F. *The Modern Japanese Banking System* (New York, 1962).

Sen, S.K. 'Government Purchase of Stores for India (1858-1914)', *Bengal Past and Present*, Vol. LXXX (1961), PP. 47-64.

Studies in Industrial Policy and Development of India, 1858-1914 (Calcutta, 1964).

Sinha, H. 'The Jute Mill Industry Today: jute futures in Calcutta', *Capital*, January 16, 1930, PP. 139-40.

Sinha, N.K. Indian Business Enterprise: Its Failure in Calcutta (1800-1848)', *Bengal Past and Present* (Diamond Jubilee Number, 1967), PP. 112-23.

Smith, A. *An Inquiry into the Nature and Causes of the Wealth of Nations*, Vol. I (London, 1904).

Taylor, J. *A Sketch of the Topography and Statistics of Dacca* (Calcutta, 1840).

Venkataraman, K.S. *The Hand-loom Industry in South India* (Madras, 1940).

Wright, A. (ed.) and Playne, S. (compiler). *Bengal and Assam, Bihar and Orissa* (London, 1917).

(*ii*) *Unpublished Secondary Works*:

Dewey, C. 'The Government of India's New Industrial Policy, 1905-25, a Study in Failure', a paper presented a at the Institute of Commonwealth Studies on 10 July, 1975.

Islam, M.M. Agricultural Development of Bengal: a quantitative study, 1920-1946 (Unpublished Ph. D. thesis, London University, 1972).

O. *Selected List of Works Consulted but not Cited*:

Das, N. *Industrial Enterprise in India* (London, 1938).

Huque, M. Azizul. *The Man Behind the Plough* (Calcutta, 1939).

Jack, J.C. *The Economic Life of a Bengal District* (Oxford, 1916).

Lewis, W.A. *The Theory of Economic Growth* (London, 1955).

Lockwood, W.W. *The Economic Development of Japan* (Princeton, 1954).

Mazumdar, D. 'Labour Supply in Early Industrialization: The case of the Bombay Textile Industry', *The Economic History Review*, August 1973, pp. 477-96.

Mehta, S.D. *The Cotton Mills of India 1854-1954* (Bombay, 1954).

Morris, M.D. *The Emergence of an Industrial Labour Force in India* (University of California Press, Berkley, 1965).

'Private Industrial Investment on the Indian Subcontinent 1900-1939: Some Methodological Considerations', *Modern Asian Studies*, Vol. 8, Part 4 (October, 1974), pp. 535-555.

Myrdal, G. *Economic Theory and Underdeveloped Regions* (London, 1957).

Sharma, T.R. *Location of Industries in India* (Bombay, 1946).

Simmons, C.P. 'Indigenous Enterprise in the Indian Coal Mining Industry c. 1835-1939', *The Indian Economic and Social History Review*, Vol. XIII, No. 2, April-June, 1976, pp. 189-218.

Tyson, G. *The Bengal Chamber of Commerce and Industry* 1853-1953. *A Centenary Survey*, (Calcutta, 1953).

Wallace, D.R. *The Romance of Jute* (London, 1928).

Index